THE Cyclothymia WORKBOOK

Learn How to Manage Your Mood Swings
& Lead a Balanced Life

PRENTISS PRICE, PH.D.

New Harbinger Publications, Inc.

Distributed in Canada by Raincoast Books.

Copyright © 2004 by Prentiss Price
New Harbinger Publications, Inc.
5674 Shattuck Avenue
Oakland, CA 94609

Cover design by Amy Shoup
Acquired by Melissa Kirk
Edited by Jessica Beebe

ISBN 1-57224-383-X Paperback

New Harbinger Publications' Web site address: www.newharbinger.com

06 05 04

10 9 8 7 6 5 4 3 2 1

First printing

To my parents, Albert and Sandra Price, who have always supported me in everything I've ever done.

To Andrea, my sister, my best friend.

And, to Nate, thanks for your support during the writing of this book.

Contents

Introduction

While there have been numerous books published about mental health issues such as bipolar disorder and clinical depression, this is the first self-help workbook devoted to addressing a lesser-known form of bipolar disorder called *cyclothymic disorder,* or *cyclothymia* (pronounced sigh-klo-THIGH-me-uh). Although cyclothymia is a mild version of bipolar disorder (or "manic depression"), it is nevertheless a serious condition that can cause you devastating mood swings, bring chaos into your relationships, and sabotage your work and life aspirations. The purpose of this workbook is to help you educate yourself about this condition and learn how to manage your symptoms so you can minimize the negative impact they have on your life.

Each year, millions of American adults struggle with cyclothymia. Many do not even know they have the illness; the public is generally unaware of this condition. This is unfortunate, since unchecked cyclothymia can lead to full-blown bipolar disorder in 15 to 50 percent of those with it (American Psychiatric Association 2000). The earlier cyclothymia is detected and managed, the less it may interfere with your life in the long run. Getting an accurate diagnosis can be difficult, and several treatment options are available, so the better informed you become, the better you will be able to make good decisions about how you want to manage your symptoms.

A ROAD MAP FOR THE WORKBOOK

I recommend that you proceed through this workbook in the order it is laid out for you. Each chapter builds upon material previously addressed. You will be guided through self-exploration exercises and worksheets that will help you gain a broader understanding of the various ways cyclothymia affects your life. Your efforts will lay the groundwork for building effective strategies for managing your mood swings and leading a balanced life.

In part 1 of this workbook, "All about Cyclothymia," I provide a comprehensive overview of the nature of cyclothymic disorder. In chapter 1, I begin by discussing the concept of mood disorders, bring attention to what we do not yet know about cyclothymia, and give a brief history of our understanding of this illness. I also offer short personal stories as examples of how some people experience cyclothymia. We'll follow these people throughout the workbook to help illustrate concepts being addressed. Chapter 2 discusses suspected causes of cyclothymia, with particular attention paid to the influence of heredity and stress. You will construct your own *genogram,* or "family tree," to look at hereditary influences. In chapter 3, I outline the difficulties with properly diagnosing cyclothymia and differentiating this condition from other mood disorders. You will learn what you can expect from the diagnostic process if you seek an evaluation from a medical or mental health professional. I also provide diagnostic criteria with detailed explanations of symptoms in terms that are easy to understand so you can see how your symptoms compare. Chapter 4 reveals how cyclothymia can affect your life, as well as your family and friends. Cyclothymia can interfere with many aspects of life, including parenting, work, personal goals and achievements, and overall satisfaction in life. I identify complicating issues of mood disorders such as alcohol and drug use and suicide. Chapter 5 details what we know to be effective treatments for cyclothymia, including medications and counseling approaches. I also provide tips on how to get good professional help.

In part 2, "Managing Cyclothymia," I offer research-based strategies for coping with and preventing cyclothymic symptoms. From identifying patterns in your mood swings and social relationships using charts provided in chapter 6 to immersing yourself in cognitive-behavioral strategies in chapter 7, this section provides the next step in honing your tools to make them work for you. I offer practical tips for managing the highs and lows of mood swings in chapter 8. Chapter 9 addresses how to handle difficulties in relationships and the workplace, how to help others understand your illness, and how to develop a support network. The workbook culminates in chapter 10 as you put everything together and learn how to set appropriate, reachable goals for managing cyclothymia. I also offer thoughts about the challenges that lie ahead for you and encouragement for facing them.

I'd also like to let you know that I maintain the Web site www.CyclothymiaWorkbook.com to provide updates to this workbook, blank copies of charts found in this workbook, and extensive resources for those who struggle with cyclothymia. I hope you'll stop by for a visit.

Since this is a workbook, I hope you will write in the margins, make notes to yourself, pose questions, work out ideas, and respond to the exercises. It is my sincere hope that you will find this workbook helpful and that you will be able to use it well in your life.

Warmest regards,
Prentiss Price, Ph.D.

PART I

All about Cyclothymia

CHAPTER 1

What Is Cyclothymic Disorder?

Almost everyone has heard of depression or clinical depression as a serious mental health condition. Many people have also heard of bipolar disorder, otherwise known as manic depression. However, few people have ever heard of cyclothymic disorder or cyclothymia. In fact, the majority of those who are familiar with this condition either work in the mental health field or struggle with the condition themselves. If you have been diagnosed with cyclothymia, or you are wondering whether you might have it, you may have discovered that there is little information readily available about this illness.

CYCLOTHYMIC MOOD SWINGS

Cyclothymia is characterized by mood swings between the lows of depression and the highs of *hypomania,* or feeling euphoric, energized, and driven. The mood swings are not extreme enough, nor do they last long enough, to qualify for a diagnosis of bipolar disorder. If you have cyclothymia, you may already know that a mood of one extreme or the other can last as long as several hours, or days. Commonly, though, cycling from one mood to the next happens rather suddenly and irregularly, with periods of "normal" or even mood being rare. Those who know the person with cyclothymia often notice the behavior and mood changes, and they may say things like, "Joe is just going through one of his blue periods again" or "Sarah has been in her workaholic mode for a while now" or "Steve has been more irritable than usual lately."

Cyclothymia tends to be a chronic condition, with symptoms of depression and hypomania lasting an entire lifetime. The American Psychiatric Association (2000) estimates that cyclothymia affects 0.4 to 1 percent of the population, which translates to between 1.2 million and nearly 3 million Americans. This condition often begins early in life, usually in adolescence or early adulthood, and it affects men and women almost equally. As with other mood disorders, there appears to be some hereditary influence. It is common for those with cyclothymia to have *first-degree relatives* (parents, children, or siblings) who have struggled with cyclothymia, major depressive disorder, or bipolar disorder.

Depression and Hypomania

So, what do I mean when I speak of swings between symptoms of depression and hypomania? Table 1.1 is a brief list of symptoms. I will go into more detail when I talk about the diagnostic process in chapter 3.

Table 1.1 Symptoms of Depression and Hypomania	
Symptoms of Depression	Symptoms of Hypomania
Down, sad, or depressed mood; tearfulness	Elevated, overly gregarious, or irritable mood
Low energy or motivation; accomplishing tasks is an effort	Increased self-esteem, grandiosity
Sleeping too much or too little; difficulty falling asleep or staying asleep	Reduced need for sleep, feeling rested with only a few hours of sleep
Problems with concentrating, thinking, or making decisions	Increased talkativeness, feeling pressure to keep talking
Changes in appetite; marked weight loss or gain	Racing thoughts, continuous stream of ideas that may be fragmentary
Feeling slowed down or agitated	Being easily distracted
Loss of interest or pleasure in activities that were once enjoyable	Increase in activity that is goal-directed
Feelings of worthlessness or guilt	Being overly involved in pleasurable activities that are potentially risky or could have painful consequences
Feelings of hopelessness	
Thoughts of death or suicide	

Adapted with permission from *The Diagnostic and Statistical Manual of Mental Disorders, Text Revision,* Copyright 2000. American Psychiatric Association.

People with cyclothymia often experience feelings of irritability, annoyance, or frustration in addition to the symptoms listed above. They may be quick-tempered, react hastily, and display occasional outbursts of anger, even over small things. Friends or family may regard the person with cyclothymia as moody, unreliable, or unpredictable.

In fact, it is quite common for people with cyclothymia to have significant problems in their relationships with partners, family, and friends. They may get into arguments at the drop of a hat. Conflicts may seem to come out of nowhere. They can be difficult to get along with consistently. Their proneness to reactivity can lead to an avalanche of emotions and extreme behaviors capable of seriously damaging, if not destroying, important relationships. These and other difficulties can plunge the person with cyclothymia into periods of sullen introspection, shame, guilt, and social embarrassment over their actions.

When engaging in the gregarious and outgoing behaviors associated with hypomania, those with cyclothymia may come across as very charming. They seem warm and inviting. People are often drawn to this kind of energy and self-confidence. It is not unusual for people with cyclothymia to have had numerous, yet brief, intense romantic relationships, perhaps with partners who are unsuitable for them. For some, marriages or committed relationships may be forever damaged by extramarital affairs or brief sexual liaisons. The risk-taking behaviors of hypomania can manifest in poor judgment and actions that have serious consequences.

The workplace does not go unaffected. Those with cyclothymia may have a history of variable work performance, sometimes struggling to keep the same job for a length of time. They can be argumentative, easily frustrated, inconsistent, and difficult to get along with. For some, hypomania can enhance productivity, but for others, it can create disorganization and unfocused energy that leads to a drop in work performance. The lows of depression can also affect functioning at work and lead to problems with motivation, concentration, energy, and self-image.

Helen's and Marcus's stories illustrate some of the difficulties that may arise in the lives of those with cyclothymia. We will follow their stories throughout the entire workbook.

■ Helen

Helen, a thirty-four-year-old mother of two, remembers her mood swings beginning when she was a freshman in college. She recalls, "My roommates thought I was pretty moody and snappy. I didn't really see it at the time. One day my best friend took me aside and told me she felt as if she had to walk on eggshells around me. Sometimes I would go out and party with my friends for days. I felt good. I was the life of the party. Other times I really didn't want to go out at all. I would get the blues for a week or so and really keep to myself."

■ Marcus

Marcus, age twenty-eight, is single and a talented computer programmer. He has had difficulties at work, however, having been fired from three companies in the span of six years. According to Marcus, "Some people just don't do things efficiently. They get on my case when I try to tell them how they can do things better." Marcus acknowledges that while he has been able to churn out a number of impressive computer programs in short periods of time, he has also missed some important deadlines. He chalks these up to "not feeling motivated" and "having a hard time focusing on work."

MOOD DISORDERS

A brief overview of how mental health professionals think about psychiatric disorders may put cyclothymia into a context that helps you understand it better. Mental health professionals use the *Diagnostic and Statistical Manual of Mental Disorders* (American Psychiatric Association 2000), or "DSM," to help diagnose mental illnesses or disorders. There are hundreds of mental disorders listed in the DSM. These disorders have been grouped into more than a dozen categories based upon similarities among them. Some of those categories include anxiety disorders, eating disorders, sleep disorders, and personality disorders. Of course, there is also a category of *mood disorders*. The mood disorders are divided into two groups: unipolar and bipolar disorders.

Unipolar Mood Disorders

The aptly named *unipolar* disorders refer to one pole of mood, namely depression. The unipolar disorders include *major depressive disorder* (also known as clinical depression) and *dysthymic disorder* or *dysthymia*, which is a chronic, low-grade depression that lasts for more than two years. People with dysthymia may seem to have mild depression as a part of their personality.

Bipolar Mood Disorders

The *bipolar* disorders refer to two poles of mood, namely the lows of depression and the highs of *mania* or hypomania. There are three types of bipolar disorders. *Bipolar I disorder* is characterized by a history of one or more manic episodes, usually along with depressive episodes. *Bipolar II disorder* is characterized by a history of one or more depressive episodes and at least one hypomanic episode. An *episode* is a cluster of symptoms experienced at about the same time.

Bipolar I and bipolar II disorders are often serious, debilitating, and sometimes life-threatening illnesses. It is not unusual for people who have either of these conditions to occasionally need intensive psychiatric care, including inpatient hospitalization. In the manic phase of bipolar I disorder, people may experience *psychotic* symptoms such as hearing voices, seeing things that are not there, or losing touch with reality. Many people with these more severe bipolar illnesses need long-term psychiatric treatment that includes taking mood-stabilizing medication daily.

Cyclothymia: A Mild Form of Bipolar Disorder

The third type of bipolar disorder is cyclothymia. Cyclothymic disorder is to bipolar disorder what dysthymia is to unipolar disorder. It is a milder form of bipolar disorder that includes the changes in mood from feeling depressed to feeling hypomanic. It is not as debilitating as either bipolar I or bipolar II disorders, and those with cyclothymia do not experience psychotic symptoms or need hospitalization.

Although cyclothymia does present a number of difficulties, many people with cyclothymia have never sought an evaluation or treatment for their condition. Also, while the more severe bipolar disorders very often require medication to help stabilize moods, those with cyclothymia may not need medication to manage their symptoms, particularly if they have good coping skills, develop supportive relationships, and recognize their symptoms early. These are the things I will address in great detail throughout this workbook.

When I describe cyclothymia as a mild form of bipolar disorder, I generally mean that the highs and lows are not as severe as those experienced by people with bipolar I or II disorder. The depressive symptoms of cyclothymia are not severe enough to meet diagnostic criteria for a depressive episode, and the hypomanic symptoms are not severe enough to meet criteria for a manic episode.

Table 1.2 provides a general comparison between symptoms of mania and hypomania.

Table 1.2 Mania versus Hypomania	
Symptoms of Mania	**Symptoms of Hypomania**
Elevated, overly gregarious, or irritable mood lasting at least seven days, or any amount of time if hospitalization is required	Elevated, overly gregarious, or irritable mood lasting at least four days and different from normal mood
Symptoms are severe, cause significant impairment in usual functioning, and may require hospitalization to prevent harm to self or others, or there are psychotic symptoms	Symptoms are not severe enough to lead to significant impairment in usual functioning or to require hospitalization, and there are no psychotic symptoms
Three or more of the symptoms listed below (four if mood is irritable)	There is a marked change from normal functioning, which others are able to notice
	Three or more of the symptoms listed below (four if mood is irritable)

- Increased self-esteem, grandiosity

- Reduced need for sleep, feeling rested with only a few hours of sleep

- Increased talkativeness, feeling pressure to keep talking

- Racing thoughts, continuous stream of ideas that may be fragmentary

- Being easily distracted

- Increase in activity that is goal-directed (being overly focused on one goal or activity to the exclusion of other important or practical matters)

- Being overly involved in pleasurable activities that are potentially risky or could have painful consequences (like spending sprees, reckless driving, or promiscuous sex)

Adapted with permission from the *Diagnostic and Statistical Manual of Mental Disorders, Text Revision*, Copyright 2000. American Psychiatric Association.

Figure 1.1 illustrates the differences between cyclothymia, bipolar disorder, and major depressive disorder. On the left side, you see mood episodes listed. *Euthymic mood* is a clinical term for what you might think of as "normal" mood, or the absence of extremes in mood. Although both cyclothymia and bipolar disorder have mood swings between highs and lows, the bipolar mood swings are more extreme.

People with mood disorders may experience different rates of mood swings over time. Some people with bipolar disorder may not have a manic or depressive episode but once every year or so. Those with cyclothymia, however, have more frequent mood swings and do not have euthymic or normal mood for more than two months within a two-year period.

In chapter 6, you will have the opportunity to record your own mood swings so you can create a chart similar to figure 1.1. This will help you learn about your mood patterns, stressors, and triggers and decide when to use techniques to help manage your mood.

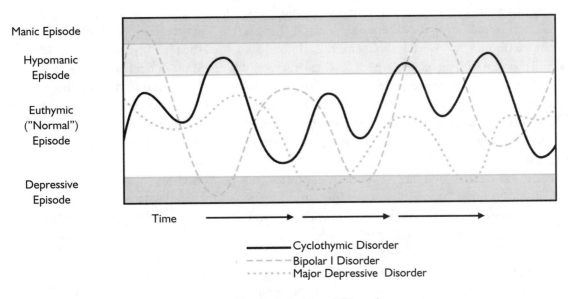

Figure 1.1 Mood Disorders

Below, Jerry and Maria describe how their mood swings affect their relationships and work. We will follow them, along with Helen and Marcus, throughout the rest of the workbook.

■ Jerry

Jerry is forty-seven years old, has four children, and has been married three times. Jerry admits that he has had a problem with his temper for most of his life and that it has hurt a number of important relationships. He says, "I just go off sometimes and yell too much. I always regret it later on. My first wife and I used to argue a lot, and I would get on her about stupid little things. My two oldest kids don't have much to do with me anymore. They said I can be unpredictable and moody." Jerry goes on to say, "I can be irritable one minute and then kind of down the next. My current wife is a good lady. She just puts up with me."

■ Maria

Maria is a twenty-year-old college student majoring in English literature. She does well in school and particularly enjoys writing short stories. Maria has noticed that she goes through phases in which she feels creative and her writing flows easily. Other times, however, she struggles with writer's block and gets down on herself and her abilities. Maria says, "When I write well, I have my muse with me. The words come with little effort. I can stay focused on my writing for long periods of time, and the hours seem to pass quickly. During those times, I feel like I can write a great novel." Maria's mother and maternal grandfather have bipolar disorder and have struggled for years with their symptoms. While she has seen her mother take on large projects in her career as a fine artist, working for days with little or no sleep, Maria doesn't believe she has ever been as "obsessed" as her mother about her work.

THE HISTORY OF CYCLOTHYMIC DISORDER

The concept of cyclothymia as a condition involving mood swings has been around since the early days of the science of psychiatry. In 1877, German psychiatrist Ewald Hecker introduced the word "cyclothymia" to describe a distinct disorder involving experiences of mood changes that today we would likely characterize as full-blown bipolar disorder. Conversely, his mentor, Karl Kahlbaum, used the term "cyclothymia" in 1882 to describe a mild problem with mood, or a type of "cyclical insanity." He noted the difference between this condition and a more severe form, which we may currently understand as bipolar I or II disorder. Kahlbaum concluded that cyclothymia had a good prognosis, being seen infrequently by physicians of the time. Hecker continued his work in understanding cyclothymia as he documented case descriptions of patients with this condition. Over time, he found that some of these patients developed more severe symptoms (Brieger and Marneros 1997).

In the late nineteenth and early twentieth centuries, the renowned psychiatrist Emil Kraepelin researched various forms of "manic-depressive insanity." His studies included what was seen as a milder form of this condition, referred to as the "cyclothymic temperament." Kraepelin believed that having a cyclothymic temperament predisposed a person to developing the cyclical phases of mania and *melancholia* or depression (Howland and Thase 1993). In his work, Kraepelin appeared to promote the concept of a continuum from the mild form of cyclothymia to the more severe bipolar disorders.

Ernst Kretschmer (1936) differentiated cyclothymic temperaments from more serious mood illnesses based upon the severity of symptoms and degree of problems they caused in patients' lives. He also preferred the term "cyclothyme" to describe a person predisposed to occasional hypomanic and depressive temperaments. According to Kretschmer, these temperaments could be found in people without a serious mood disorder, but they were also related to bipolar illness. Again, we see a prominent researcher advocated the concept of cyclothymia as a mild form of bipolar disorder.

Like Kretschmer, Kurt Schneider (1958) believed that the varieties of "manic-depressive insanity" were all related as various forms of a single, overarching disorder. Unlike Kretschmer, however, Schneider believed that cyclothymia was a problem of mood, not temperament, although he acknowledged the difficulties with making this distinction. He rejected the notion of a continuum from normality to severe mental disorder, instead using the term "cyclothymia" to capture all forms of bipolar disorder. His influence was so strong that for many years thereafter, the term "cyclothymia" remained a synonym for bipolar disorder.

The 1960s and '70s saw controversy over the shortcomings of diagnostic strategies for mood disorders. Mental health professionals agreed that mood disorders should be divided into unipolar and bipolar categories, but cyclothymia had not yet been included in the realm of mood disorders. While interest in research into the biological influences on the major mood disorders increased, interest in cyclothymia seemed to wane. This could explain why it remained under the diagnostic category of personality disorders for so long. In the 1970s, the concept of the "bipolar disorder spectrum" was revisited by Hagop Akiskal and his colleagues (Akiskal et al. 1977; Akiskal, Khani, and Scott-Strauss 1979), and cyclothymic disorder was moved to the mood disorders section of the *Diagnostic and Statistical Manual of Mental Disorders* (third edition) in 1980.

WHAT WE DON'T KNOW ABOUT CYCLOTHYMIA

Unfortunately, we really don't know as much as we need to know about cyclothymic disorder. While there has been much research about the prominent mood disorders of major depression and bipolar I and II disorders, there is still little research available on cyclothymia as a stand-alone illness. Studies of cyclothymia have often been subsumed under research designed to address issues about bipolar disorder, despite the general agreement that cyclothymia is a separate and distinct form of bipolar illness.

In reviewing research for this workbook, I found it necessary to incorporate information about the major bipolar disorders and major depressive disorder with studies about cyclothymia in order to fill holes in areas such as causes, treatment, and self-help topics and activities.

One of the most important things we know about cyclothymic disorder is that it can be a precursor to the development of bipolar disorder. Anywhere from 15 to 50 percent of those with cyclothymia will develop a full-blown bipolar disorder (American Psychiatric Association 2000). This fact alone leads to a very important question to which we don't yet know the answer: How can we prevent cyclothymia from developing into a more severe bipolar disorder?

CYCLOTHYMIA MAY ESCAPE DETECTION

We also know that even more than twenty years after cyclothymia received legitimacy as a mood disorder, it is not often seen or diagnosed by mental health professionals. There are several possible explanations for this. First, while symptoms of cyclothymia can cause major disruptions in a person's life, they are not so severe as to necessitate hospitalization. Cyclothymia does not lead to psychotic symptoms and infrequently causes people to harm themselves or others. If a person with cyclothymia does require hospitalization, this may indicate that a more severe form of bipolar disorder has developed.

Second, people with cyclothymia may not know that they have something that can be treated. They may simply attribute their mood states and behaviors, no matter how extreme, to their personality style or occasional "moodiness." Cyclothymia is not a mental health issue that is generally seen in the media, so few people are aware of it. Many people have never even heard of it.

Third, it is not unusual for people to avoid seeking mental health treatment because of social stigma. It is unfortunate that this still exists, but it does. Some people do not want to acknowledge that they have a difficulty with their mental health, and they can be apprehensive about seeking assistance for it.

Fourth, people with cyclothymia may have one or more close relatives who have struggled over the years with debilitating mental health issues. Bipolar disorder, major depression, alcoholism, and suicide are not uncommon problems in the families of those with cyclothymia. For some, seeking help for their problems may generate apprehension and fear about their own mental health. It may be that they don't believe their symptoms are severe enough, compared to their relatives', to warrant treatment, or they cannot bear to think that they may also struggle with similar difficulties.

Fifth, if people do come under the care of a medical or mental health professional, it is usually when they have been experiencing depressive rather than hypomanic symptoms. Initially, people with cyclothymia may be misdiagnosed as having major depressive disorder. It is common for people to enjoy some aspects of the hypomania, like feeling "up," productive, and self-confident. They may not realize that their irritability, reactivity, and extreme behaviors are related to an illness. Since cyclothymia tends to involve rapid shifts in mood, people are not necessarily depressed long enough to feel they need help. Even though they experience repeated problems with mild depression, people with cyclothymia know that if they just wait it out, their mood will change. They may not believe it is necessary to seek assistance when they are feeling better, even if it is temporary.

Summing Up

Up to this point, I have discussed the nature of cyclothymia and its relationship to other mood disorders. I've begun to paint a picture of how cyclothymia can affect people's lives, their families, and their work. I have also started to lay out how mental health professionals understand cyclothymia, and I will say more about diagnosis in chapter 3. Finally, we have begun to follow along in the lives of Helen, Marcus, Jerry, and Maria. Their stories will illustrate topics covered in this workbook, such as causes, diagnosis, treatments, self-help, and particularly how they have come to terms with this condition in their lives. In the next chapter, I will offer what we know about the causes of cyclothymia, which I hope will help you understand your symptoms in a larger context.

CHAPTER 2

What Causes Cyclothymia?

For several years, I have conducted Internet research to find out what information people want to know about clinical depression. Of the seventy-five informational topics people are asked to rate, the number one topic has consistently been "causes of depression." It's clear that this is a burning issue for many people. Interestingly, the number two topic of interest is "how to help yourself if you are depressed." It seems that people want to know what causes depression in the spirit of trying to figure out what to do about it.

It is human nature to want to know what causes something. We are curious, and we like to be able to solve our own problems. It seems that if we can figure out what causes a problem, it will naturally lead to answers about how to solve it. For many things this may be true, but for some things, such as mental illnesses, the issue can be a bit more complicated. Even if we could know what causes a particular mental illness, it does not necessarily mean that we will be able to remedy the problem. For instance, even if you could be 100 percent certain that you inherited a gene for cyclothymia from one of your parents, you still would not be able to fix the gene (at least not with our current scientific capabilities). Likewise, if you knew that one or more events in your life had something to do with the onset of your illness, you still could not go back and change what happened. Unfortunately, it is a bit misleading to say that understanding the cause of a mental illness will lead to its cure. The good news, however, is that you don't necessarily need to know what causes cyclothymia in order to treat it and experience improvement.

Researchers are also very interested in learning what causes certain illnesses, and they continuously follow promising leads they hope will unveil such mysteries. While their efforts have given us much valuable information, we still have no definitive list of causes for many illnesses, including cyclothymia. Despite the lack of conclusive research, you still may be quite eager to know what causes cyclothymia for you. Like a good researcher, you may even have some hypotheses or theories of your own. The current consensus among researchers who study the causes of mood disorders is that they are most likely caused by a combination of several factors. Some of these factors we have been able to identify through research, while other factors still elude us.

Researchers understand that there are relationships among factors, but they cannot make clear causal determinations. For instance, having a sibling, parent, or child with bipolar disorder does not mean you are destined to develop it. However, it does increase your likelihood of developing it. In other words, those with relatives who have bipolar disorder are more at risk than those without such relatives. You will notice that I use the terms "causes" and "risk factors" interchangeably. Risk factors are those conditions that are known to increase a person's chances of developing a disorder.

I hope that your interest in the causes of cyclothymia will lead not to frustration but to a better understanding of your condition overall. In learning about the causes of cyclothymia, you may come to understand that the development of your illness is something that you have no control over. It may also be useful as a path toward recognizing risk factors and early warning signs so that you can implement preventive strategies or seek help before symptoms become worse.

CAUSES OF THE DISORDER VERSUS CAUSES OF SYMPTOMS

One other important consideration is that there is a difference between what causes the development of cyclothymic disorder in a person and what causes symptoms to begin or recur. The causes of each may be different. For instance, a person who has numerous relatives with mood disorders can be reasonably certain that the development of cyclothymia is largely due to a genetic predisposition for the disorder. This same person may also realize that after experiencing initial symptoms of cyclothymia, subsequent episodes may be triggered by other causes such as environmental stressors (like problems in relationships, pressures at work), biological vulnerabilities (such as too much or too little of certain neurotransmitters in the brain), alcohol or drug abuse, noncompliance with prescribed medications, and so forth. In each case, the causes are different. However, both fundamental causes and maintaining causes are important to consider. I will try to clarify this difference as we proceed.

In this chapter, I will address what research has been able to tell us about what may cause cyclothymia and other bipolar disorders. The main areas of research that will be covered include genetics, biology, and stress.

THE ROLE OF GENETICS

Having a family history of mood disorders is probably the single most important risk factor when it comes to the development of cyclothymia. Research has shown that having a first-degree relative with a mood disorder increases your likelihood of developing one yourself. Research has been a bit mixed on whether cyclothymia is more prevalent in families with bipolar disorder than in those with major depressive disorder. However, the trend seems to favor cyclothymia occurring more frequently in families with bipolar disorders (Howland and Thase 1993).

Studies of family histories have shown that for those with bipolar disorder, about 8 percent of their first-degree relatives will also have the illness. Compare this to the 1 to 2 percent of the overall population who develop bipolar disorder. Of these same family histories, another 12 percent of relatives have major depressive disorder, compared with 5 percent in the general population (Gershon 1990). While we don't have these kinds of statistics for cyclothymia, it may be safe to assume that the rates are similar.

■ Maria

While Maria is aware that bipolar disorder and depression run in her family, she has rarely considered that she might have difficulties with her own mood. In fact, when the thought occasionally crosses her mind, Maria quickly whisks it away, saying to herself, "I could never be that bad." However, she has revealed to at least one close friend that it is frightening to her to think that she could ever develop the same problems as her mother. She says, "Over the years, my mother has gone from being hyper, to being full of irrational rage, then to the depths of despair for weeks at a time. She has attempted suicide twice and has been hospitalized a couple of times, too." Maria has recently learned that her maternal grandfather also had bipolar disorder, and her uncle has struggled many years with severe depression.

Twin and Adoption Studies

Researchers have been able to learn a great deal from studies conducted with twins. As you may know, there are two types of twins: identical and fraternal. Identical twins look alike, because they share the exact same set of genes. Fraternal twins do not necessarily look alike, because like nontwin siblings they share only 50 percent of the same genes. If cyclothymia and other mood disorders have a genetic component, we would expect that if one identical twin has the condition, then the other twin would have a very high likelihood of also developing the condition. If there were not a genetic component, then we would expect this concordance rate to be low. Similarly, if one fraternal twin has a mood disorder, then we might expect the likelihood for the other twin to develop the disorder to be higher than for someone who does not have a twin or sibling with a mood disorder.

Studies on twins and siblings who have been adopted and raised apart have allowed researchers to address how much influence the environment might have on the development of various disorders. For example, if twins raised in different homes with different experiences develop mood disorders at the same rate as twins raised together, then it would make sense that the environment has little influence on the occurrence of the disorder.

When it comes to bipolar disorder, research has given us very important information about the genetic basis of this illness. It turns out that when one identical twin develops this condition, 57 percent of the time, the other twin will also develop it. With fraternal twins, this rate is 14 percent. The illness occurs at the same rate whether twins are raised together or apart (Alda 1997). Compare these with the fact that bipolar disorder affects up to 3.7 percent of the general population (Hirschfeld, Calabrese, and Weissman 2002). As you can see, the rate of bipolar disorder in identical and fraternal twins is significantly higher than the rate in the general population, providing support for a genetic influence.

Research on bipolar disorder has demonstrated that there is a strong genetic component to the development of the illness. However, the illness does not occur in both identical twins 100 percent of the time (remember, they share the same genes); this tells us that there are more than just genetic factors involved in the occurrence of the illness. These findings support the theory that genetic vulnerabilities may predispose a person to develop a mood disorder such as cyclothymia. There may well be an important interaction between genetic and environmental factors (Rush 2003).

Your Genetic Factors

Now that you know the impact of genetic factors on the development of bipolar disorders, including cyclothymia, it's your turn to think about how this might apply to you. For a few moments, think about your immediate and more distant relatives. Have there been people in your family who have struggled with mood disorders such as depression or bipolar disorder? What about other mental health problems, such as schizophrenia, anxiety, eating disorders, or alcohol or drug abuse? Has anyone had problems keeping a job or maintaining a relationship? If you don't know much about your family history, you might ask others; perhaps some of your older relatives know the answers to these questions.

Sometimes, mental health problems in families have gone undiagnosed and untreated. Or, family members might put a different label on a mental health condition. Think about whether you are aware of anyone having had a "nervous breakdown" or a problem with "nerves." Perhaps you recall a family member who sometimes spent days or weeks sleeping or otherwise withdrawn. You might remember hearing about someone who would "go away" (to a psychiatric hospital) for a time or whose family members would "walk on eggshells" to avoid upsetting the person. If someone has died by suicide, this often signals that there was a psychiatric problem. These kinds of situations may indicate that people in your family have struggled with some degree of a mental health problem.

EXERCISE 2.1   FAMILY HISTORY

In the chart below, record what you know about your family history. You will use this information when you construct a diagram, or genogram, of your family tree.

Name of Relative	Age	Relationship to You	Nature of Problem	If Deceased, How Did He/She Die?
(example) John Doe	44	Father	Bipolar Disorder	Suicide

Again, if you have a number of blood relatives who have had bipolar disorder, major depression, or other related mental health issues such as alcohol or drug abuse, you may have evidence that your own struggles are related to genetic factors.

■ Helen

Helen knows very little about her family history. "We didn't have much contact over the years with grandparents or other relatives on either side of my family, since we lived so far away. My parents didn't talk much about them. It seemed that there had been some problems that my parents didn't want to discuss. If anyone had any mental illnesses, I wouldn't really know about it. No one would talk about that kind of thing in my family."

Constructing Your Genogram or Family Tree

As you consider how genetics may have influenced the development of your symptoms, it can be very helpful to see your family history in visual form. That's what a genogram, or family tree, can provide. A genogram is a diagram that illustrates aspects of your family history. Individuals are represented by shapes (males are squares, females are circles), and relationships, like those between siblings and spouses, are represented by horizontal lines. The youngest generation is at the bottom, their parents are just above them, and the grandparents are at the top.

Take a look at figure 2.1. In the middle, at the bottom, is Maria. As a female, she is represented by a circle. Maria has four siblings, arranged by age, oldest to youngest, from left to right. To the left of Maria is her older brother, represented by a square. To the left of him is their oldest sister. Maria also has two younger brothers.

Maria's father and mother are connected by a horizontal line, and their five children come down from that line. Maria's paternal grandparents are identified just above her father, and her maternal grandparents just above her mother. Maria's mother has three siblings: an older brother, and a younger brother and sister.

Those squares and circles marked with an X indicate that the person is deceased. Maria's only living grandparent is her paternal grandmother. The two angled marks through the horizontal line that connects her parents indicate that they are divorced. Maria's maternal grandfather and her aunt on her mother's side both are gray. This indicates that they committed suicide. If you look at the legend on the diagram, you'll see that A indicates the person has or had a substance abuse problem. H indicates the person has been hospitalized for a mental health problem. C represents cyclothymia, B represents bipolar disorder, and D represents depression.

To help you draw your own genogram, I have provided a template (exercise 2.2) with three generations and shapes displayed in light gray dotted lines. This drawing is just a guide to help you get started. You may need to modify this template by extending some horizontal lines to allow you to include more siblings or aunts and uncles. If you have children, simply draw a line down from yourself and use squares and circles to indicate your children. You will really only be interested in your blood relatives, since the goal of this exercise is to identify a genetic influence for your cyclothymia. Don't worry about leaving out your partner or spouse if you are creating your own genogram.

After you draw out the main symbols representing all of your family members, make sure you indicate those who have had mood disorders. If you know your family history well, this may be rather simple. If you don't know much about the mental health history of your family, ask relatives who may have this information. Remember, some mood disorders go undiagnosed. Sometimes, those who have had troubles with alcohol or drug abuse, suicide attempts, or hospitalizations for vague reasons have actually struggled with mood disorders.

When you create your genogram, you may also want to include people's names, dates of birth and death, whether they sought treatment, how severe their conditions are or were, and so forth. Put anything on your genogram that will help you understand your familial or genetic influences better.

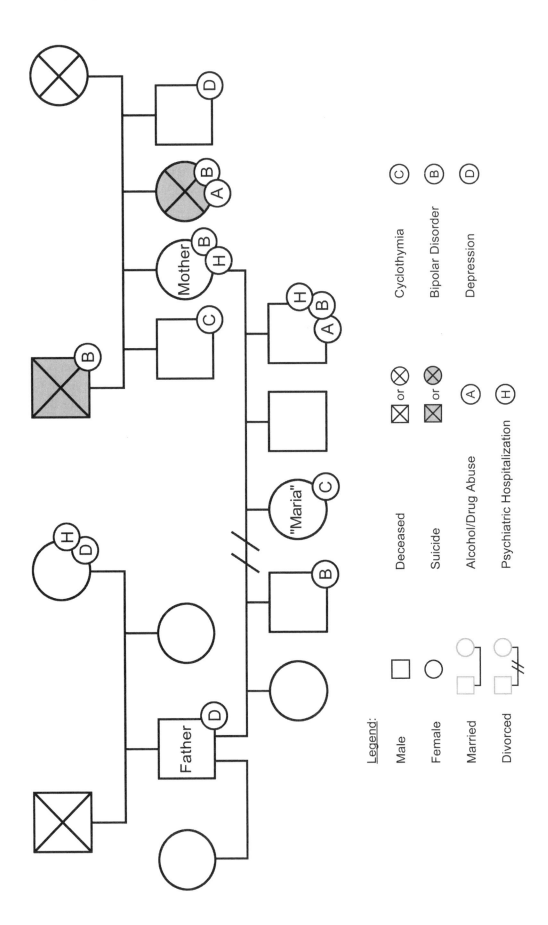

Figure 2.1 Maria's Genogram

EXERCISE 2.2 YOUR GENOGRAM

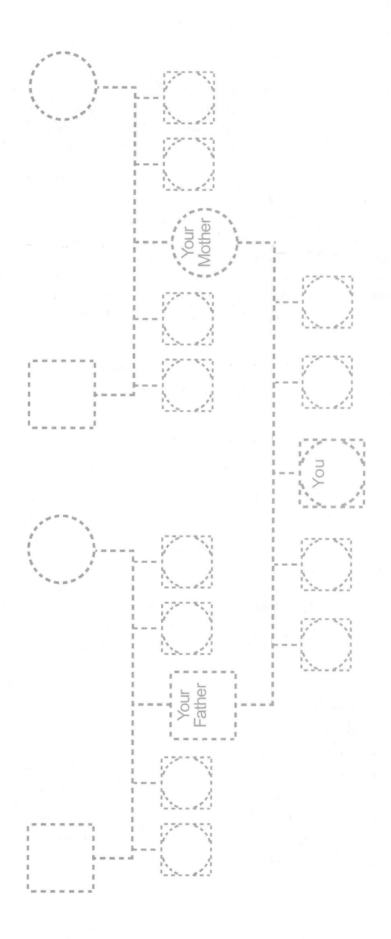

How to Interpret Your Genogram

After you have finished drawing your genogram and identifying who has had a mood disorder, you'll have a better view of how mood disorders have affected your family. Sometimes, when people draw out their genograms, they recognize interesting patterns or themes they have never noticed before. As you look at your genogram, see what you notice. Is there a pattern of unipolar or bipolar disorder? Do problems with mood affect women more than men, or vice versa? Have a number of people had trouble with alcohol and drug abuse? Do mood disorders appear to skip a generation? How many people have attempted or committed suicide? How do the patterns you notice affect you?

Another way to interpret your genogram is based upon what research has suggested about the prevalence of mood disorders within a family. We know that severe mood disorders affect about 7 percent of the population over a lifetime. For those who have a first-degree relative with unipolar disorder (such as depression), this risk jumps to about 20 percent, and for people with a close relative who has bipolar disorder, the risk is about 25 percent (Nurnberger and Gershon 1992). So, if you have a parent, sibling, or child with a mood disorder, your chance of developing one may be 20 to 25 percent—about three times greater than that of the general public. If you have a number of relatives with mental health difficulties, your risk could be even greater.

As we look at Maria's genogram, it is clear that she has a high number of relatives who have had significant problems with mood disorders. Because of this history, it appears that she has been at risk for developing a mood disorder.

What If No One in Your Family Has a Mood Disorder?

We know that a family history of a mood disorder increases a person's likelihood of developing cyclothymia, but it is only one risk factor. Not everyone who has cyclothymia has relatives who have also had a mood disorder. It is not unusual for those who have a mental health condition to have difficulty locating a family or genetic link to their own illness. Although I have emphasized genetic factors in the development of cyclothymia, it can definitely occur without an apparent genetic link.

Keep in mind that sometimes people don't have enough information about their family to know whether someone has had mental health problems. Also, it is not uncommon for a condition to skip a generation. Unless you have very good information about your family history, it may be easy to overlook relatives who have had a mood disorder. Again, it can be quite helpful to ask your older relatives if they can help you gather information about your family history.

THE ROLE OF BIOLOGY

Biological influences on cyclothymic disorder can include such things as brain structure, neurotransmitters, endocrine functioning, sleep disturbances, medical conditions, and effects of substances (like medicine, alcohol, or drugs). The little research that has been done on the biological nature of cyclothymia has suggested that there is a biological influence, although the exact relationships are unknown.

It may be useful to consider the concept of *biological vulnerabilities* in thinking about how cyclothymia develops or how symptoms may be triggered. Biological vulnerabilities are biological variables that, when brought together, make a person likely to develop cyclothymia. For instance, John Doe may have a genetic predisposition to develop cyclothymia, since a number of relatives have struggled with bipolar disorder. However, it takes an environmental stressor such as losing his job to cause sleep problems that in turn disrupt the neurotransmitters in his brain and trigger his first hypomanic episode.

The biological influences on depression and the major bipolar disorders have been studied more thoroughly than cyclothymia. Without getting too technical, I will briefly delve into what we have learned about the biology of other mood disorders and make some inferences about of the biological basis of cyclothymia.

Brain Structure

Research comparing the brain structures of people with bipolar disorder to those who do not have a mood disorder has shown some interesting results. Scientists have used *magnetic resonance imaging* (MRI) and *computerized axial tomography* (CAT) scans to measure the volume of the brain and various structures. Using these techniques, studies have shown differences in the brains of those with mood disorders and in those without psychiatric disorders. The MRI and CAT scans have shown that there are enlargements of parts of the brain known as the *cortical sulci* and *lateral ventricles* in those with mood disorders (Elkis et al. 1995). The cortical sulci are the gaps between the folds in the surface of the brain. The ventricles contain *cerebrospinal fluid*, which moves through and around the brain. Ventricles can become enlarged if there has been damage to the brain or if part of the brain has not developed properly. The ventricles of people with bipolar disorder are about 18 to 20 percent larger than those of people without bipolar disorder. These findings suggest that enlargement of the ventricles is somehow related to bipolar disorder.

Studies on brain tissue of those with bipolar disorder have also found a decrease in *glial cells* in the frontal lobe. Glial cells provide an important function for the neurons: they supply glucose, oxygen, and nutrients. They also protect neurons from harmful elements carried through the bloodstream, such as toxins and infectious agents. Torrey and Knable (2002) found that patients with a family background of bipolar disorder had a reduction in their glial cell density by 17 percent in the prefrontal cortex.

Neurotransmitters

Neurotransmitters are substances that function as the carriers of information between cells in the brain. There are currently about one hundred known neurotransmitters, and just a handful of them have been implicated in bipolar illnesses: *dopamine, serotonin, norepinephrine, acetylcholine,* GABA, and *glutamate*. A good deal of research time and money has gone into studying neurotransmitter functioning, although there is still much to learn. Thus far, we have learned that some substances that block dopamine, such as the antipsychotic medication Haldol (haloperidol), may reduce manic symptoms, while substances that increase dopamine, such as cocaine or L-dopa, may induce manic symptoms. People with major depressive disorder appear to have reductions in serotonin and GABA.

It is difficult to effectively study the influence of neurotransmitters on brain chemistry and brain cell functioning, since they can be measured only indirectly. Researchers must rely on methods that can be fraught with problems. For instance, they can measure bodily fluids, but these measurements are not always accurate. They can also measure enzymes that make up neurotransmitters, or the receptors in the brain cells to which they bind. None of these methods are ideal for determining the effects of neurotransmitters.

The Endocrine System

Much research on the endocrine system has been focused on the thyroid and adrenal glands. Diseases affecting these glands sometimes lead to symptoms of depression, elevations in mood, or hyperactivity. For instance, *hypothyroidism* (underactive thyroid) can cause depressive symptoms. Alternatively, *hyperthyroidism* (overactive thyroid) can lead to symptoms similar to mania or hypomania.

In one study of the adrenal glands, Depue and colleagues (1985) found problems in cortisol secretion and regulation of cortisol levels when participants with cyclothymia were subjected to stressful situations. *Cortisol* is a hormone found in the adrenal glands that helps with metabolism of certain substances. These results are similar to those found with other mood disorders.

Although problems in endocrine functioning seem promising in uncovering causes of bipolar illnesses, we have yet to find conclusive evidence for a cause-and-effect relationship.

Sleep Disturbances

Disturbances in sleep are a prominent feature of mood disorders. For some people with bipolar disorder, sleep deprivation can lead to manic episodes. This has lead researchers to study the effects of biological rhythms such as sleep patterns, circadian rhythms, biological clocks, and rhythms regulated by neurochemicals such as melatonin.

Researchers have learned that people with bipolar disorder may be sensitive to small changes in their sleep-wake cycles, or *circadian rhythms* (Frank, Swartz, and Kupfer 2000). This includes what time you go to bed, when you actually fall asleep, and when you wake up the next day. For the most part, we tend to have regular activities we do from day to day that help us maintain our circadian rhythms. For example, you might fix breakfast for the kids in the morning, go to a job for much of the day, walk the dog when you get home, engage in some activities in the evening, and go to bed at a somewhat regular time. If you travel across time zones, stay at work late to finish a project, or pull all-nighters to study for final exams, then your circadian rhythm may be disrupted. This could put you at risk for increased problems with mood.

If you think back on your own difficulties with mood swings, you might be able to recognize whether changes in sleep patterns or sleep deprivation played a role in your mood. Although I will address sleep patterns more thoroughly in chapter 8, please take a few moments to respond to the following questions.

As you move through this workbook over the next days or weeks, notice how your sleep patterns affect your mood. By the time you reach chapter 8, you will be well prepared to examine your sleep-wake cycle in more depth.

EXERCISE 2.3 SLEEP INVENTORY

Do you go to bed at a regular time each night and get up at a regular time each morning? If not, what is your current pattern of sleeping?

_____

_____

_____

Have there been periods of time in which you were able to go to sleep at a regular time each night and get up at a regular time each morning? If so, how did this affect your mood?

_____

_____

_____

How has too much or too little sleep affected your mood over time?

_____

_____

_____

Do you ever have problems with sleep? What gets in the way of your sleeping well?

_____

_____

_____

What things have you done in the past to help you sleep regularly and well?

_____

_____

_____

Medical Conditions

Other risk factors for cyclothymia or the cyclothymic symptoms of hypomania and depression include certain medical conditions. As mentioned earlier, problems with thyroid functioning (such as hyperthyroidism) have been connected with the manic symptoms of bipolar disorder (Rush 2003). Hypothyroidism, however, appears to be a risk factor for *rapid cycling,* or shifting rapidly between symptoms of mania/hypomania and depression (Ooman, Schipperijn, and Drexhage 1996).

Mania can be caused by infections such as influenza, mononucleosis, and the herpes simplex virus. Symptoms of depression and mania may also be caused by head injuries or brain disorders such as stroke, brain tumors, epilepsy, multiple sclerosis, and Huntington's disease.

■ Marcus

Growing up, Marcus remembers that his mother spent a lot of time in bed. "She seemed to really be down at times. Other times she was active and did a lot for me and my brother and sister. She recently told me her doctor put her on some medication about a year ago to help her with feeling depressed. She said it has been helpful." Family members have described Marcus's uncle, his mother's brother, as being manic-depressive. "Apparently he ran up all his credit cards, got some girl pregnant, and lost his license for traffic violations—all in one year!" Marcus admits that he has skirted trouble himself. "Sometimes I like to do a little cocaine with my friends. The cops nearly caught us once at a club. When I'm feeling good, I find that a little coke just helps to enhance the feeling."

Effects of Substances

People with bipolar disorder often use or abuse substances such as alcohol and drugs. I will address alcohol and drug use further in chapter 4. Unfortunately, substance use can cause complications in diagnosing and treating the problem, as well as exacerbate mania/hypomania and depression. Street drugs such as cocaine, amphetamines, methylphenidate, hallucinogens (like LSD), phencyclidine (PCP), inhalants, opiates, and marijuana can all induce or exacerbate symptoms of bipolar disorders. Mania or hypomania may also be caused by over-the-counter drugs or herbal medications. In fact, if a person experiences severe mania or depression for the first time, medication should always be considered as a possible cause, particularly if the person has never taken that medication before.

THE ROLE OF STRESS

Environmental stressors have consistently been found to have a negative impact on the course of bipolar disorder. Stressful events increase the rate of recurrence of bipolar episodes (Hunt, Bruce-Jones, and Silverstone 1992). They also increase the time it takes to recover from such episodes; in fact, when a person recovering from a bipolar episode experiences a significant life stressor, it may take three times as long for that person to recover than it would without the stressor (Johnson and Miller 1997).

There is some good and bad news about these facts. The bad news is that stress is all around you, and it can become worse when you least expect it. The good news is that you can have much more control over managing stress in your life than you can the genes you are born with or the biology of your brain. I will talk more about how to manage stress in chapter 8.

There are two general kinds of stress. *Eustress* is a good kind of stress. It may involve important changes in your life, but it is usually toward something that is desirable. For instance, if you are leaving a job you don't like to start a job you believe you will like, it can be very stressful to get used to new procedures, meet new people, and adjust to a new environment. Other types of eustress can include getting married, having children, graduating from school, and so forth. The other type of stress is *distress*. This is the bad type of stress. It involves changes that are not necessarily desirable, such as losing a job you do like, getting divorced, or the death of a loved one. Both types of stress can have a similar effect on your mood and could potentially exacerbate your cyclothymic symptoms.

■ Jerry

Jerry can't forget that his father was, in his words, "a raging alcoholic" all of his life, until he died of alcohol-related complications when he was sixty-three. Jerry recalls, "My father would go through drinking binges, yelling at us kids and breaking stuff. Sometimes he would just disappear for days. His own father was the same way." Jerry admits that in the past, when he was under great stress, he used alcohol to help calm himself down and get away from things. "My first marriage broke up because I was drinking too much. I was becoming like my father and grandfather. When I realized that, I started going to AA. I don't know if my father had a mood disorder. It would have been hard to tell with all of the drinking he was doing."

Social Support

Having a good social support system can be extremely important in helping you manage stress in your life. The extent to which a person with bipolar disorder has social support can have a significant impact on the course of his or her illness, as well as how long it takes to recover from a bipolar episode. For instance, having little social support may be related to an increase in both recovery time and depressive symptoms (Johnson et al. 1999). As you may know, maintaining a good social support system can be tricky for someone with cyclothymia. The effects of this illness often lead to problems in relationships, including conflicts, distrust, unpredictability, and estrangement. In chapter 9, I will address how to manage difficulties in relationships so that you can enhance your own support system.

In chapter 6, I will bring together the concepts of social support, daily routines, sleep cycles, and other factors that influence cyclothymic symptoms as I discuss principles of *interpersonal and social rhythm therapy.*

MORE RESEARCH IS NEEDED

As I mentioned in chapter 1, research on cyclothymia as a stand-alone disorder is quite slim. Over time, researchers have focused on studying major depressive disorder and bipolar I and II disorders. Several factors may explain the lack of studies on cyclothymic disorder. First, cyclothymic disorder is not as prevalent as other mood disorders or other psychiatric disorders in general. Psychiatric disorders that affect more people, or are more commonly diagnosed, tend to be more heavily researched.

Second, the effects of cyclothymia may not be as severe as other psychiatric conditions such as schizophrenia, substance abuse, eating disorders, major depression, and post-traumatic stress disorder. Some people consider these conditions to be more devastating than cyclothymic disorder, and therefore they have received more attention and funding for research.

EXERCISE 2.4 STRESS CHART

Now it's your turn to spend a few moments thinking about how stress has affected you and influenced your mood swings. I know it can be difficult to remember specific details of events that happened in the past, but do the best you can in filling in your information below. You will use some of this information again in chapter 8, when I discuss managing stress. In the first column, note the approximate date of some of the more difficult problems you have had with depressive or hypomanic symptoms. In the second column, describe the mood problems you experienced. In the third column, list the stressful events (eustress or distress) that happened at or near the time. And in the last column, try to remember what impact your mood and the stressful events had on other areas of your life. You may make additional copies of this chart if you need more space. This chart is also available online at www.CyclothymiaWorkbook.com.

Date	Mood Problems	Stressful Events	Outcome of Mood and Stress
May '03	irritable, angry depressed	laid off at work, fender bender	maxed out credit card, big fight with spouse

Third, cyclothymia can be difficult to research. When researchers study psychiatric disorders, they need participants who have pronounced conditions so that improvements in their problems or differences from other psychiatric conditions can be clearly detected. Think of it this way: Imagine that you have a really bad cold with lots of very unpleasant symptoms such as a sore throat, runny nose, headaches, fatigue, and fever. Because of your symptoms, there is no doubt that you indeed have a cold. If you take medicine to help relieve these symptoms, you will likely be able to detect even small improvements in how you feel. You will certainly be able to notice significant improvements. The worse you feel to begin with, the greater the potential for improvement. There is a similar concept in conducting psychiatric research. Experimenters prefer to have participants who have clear-cut symptoms of the disorder they are studying, with little or no overlap of other problems. They may also select people who have significant symptoms so that even slight improvements as a result of treatment can be detected, or, in the case of biology, differences in physiology will be noticeable. As you have learned, cyclothymic disorder is a milder form of bipolar disorder. It can also have symptoms that are similar to other disorders. Detecting treatment effects can be difficult.

Summing Up

In this chapter, I have shown how a variety of factors can influence the development of cyclothymic disorder. Although we know that genes play a very important role, they certainly don't account for everything. Researchers believe a combination of factors, including biology, stress, neurotransmitters, and sleep cycles, can make a person both susceptible to developing cyclothymia and vulnerable to the onset of mood episodes.

In the next chapter, we will look more closely at how cyclothymic disorder is diagnosed. You will learn the process by which medical and mental health professionals make diagnoses and learn how to tell if you are receiving a thorough evaluation of your problems. I will also provide some thoughts on the pros and cons of learning your diagnosis, as well as how to cope with it. In subsequent chapters, we will look at how cyclothymia affects you and what treatments are known to be effective.

CHAPTER 3

Do You Have Cyclothymia?

As I have mentioned, cyclothymia is not a commonly diagnosed illness. People who struggle with this condition often do not seek evaluation or treatment for a variety of reasons, some of which I addressed in chapter 1.

I hope this chapter will help demystify the diagnostic process. Perhaps if you know what to expect, not only will you feel more comfortable in getting a thorough evaluation, but you will also have valuable knowledge to help you make important decisions about managing your illness.

HOW IS CYCLOTHYMIA DIFFERENT FROM NORMAL MOODINESS?

Let's start by looking at differences between the normal moodiness that everyone experiences from time to time and mood states that qualify as a disorder. To paraphrase the *Diagnostic and Statistical Manual of Mental Disorders,* a mental disorder is a significant grouping or pattern of symptoms that is related to personal distress, difficulty in functioning, or an increased risk of pain, disability, death, or loss of freedom. Further, to qualify as a disorder, there must be "clinically significant distress or impairment in social, occupational, or other important areas of functioning as a result of the mood disturbance" (American Psychiatric Association 2000, 398). In other words, if it is not causing a problem in your life, it simply may not be a problem. Normal moodiness should not lead to such problems. In general, the differences between symptoms of cyclothymic disorder and normal moodiness have to do with the duration and severity of the moody feelings and behaviors, as well as the effect they have on a person's daily functioning.

Normal moodiness may not last longer than a few moments or hours, occasionally a few days. A person without a mood disorder may withdraw for a time, may be snappy or irritable in relationships, or may briefly feel uninterested in regular activities. Such feelings or behaviors generally do not last long. With cyclothymia, however, moody feelings and behaviors typically last longer. Similarly, those with cyclothymia tend to experience frequent swings in mood that can go from one extreme to the other very quickly. With normal moodiness, there generally are not rapid or extreme shifts in a person's mood.

For someone who does not have a mood disorder, moody feelings and behaviors are also not as severe as they are with cyclothymia. People with cyclothymia may react in ways that are out of proportion to the situation. They may express rage over small slights or otherwise respond with such intensity that important relationships suffer damage beyond repair. Because of rather quick swings in mood, they may express demonstrative behaviors in one moment and then plunge into a depressive melancholia the next. This is not often the case with someone who does not have a mood disorder. Instead, with normal moodiness, feelings and behaviors tend to be milder, and a person's reactions generally are not so severe that they negatively affect relationships or the workplace.

Normal moodiness also differs from cyclothymia in how feelings and behaviors influence daily functioning. With the depressive symptoms of cyclothymia, a person's ability to concentrate or make decisions may be impaired. It may require great effort to accomplish simple tasks. There may be problems with sleep, appetite, and self-esteem. Hypomanic symptoms can cause a person to feel too wired or energized, making it difficult to focus. Increased irritability can cause problems in relationships or work performance. These and other symptoms of cyclothymia can make it very difficult at times to sustain consistent day-to-day functioning. Normal moody behaviors and feelings do not tend to affect a person's daily functioning significantly.

What Is "Normal" When You Have Cyclothymia?

If you have cyclothymia, you might find yourself asking, "How can I tell the difference between my own 'normal' moodiness and symptoms of my disorder?" This can be a slightly tricky question to answer, as it won't always be easy to differentiate these. One way to think about it is to acknowledge that your "normal" moodiness will likely have some components of your cyclothymic symptoms. What is normal for you may not be normal for someone else, just as two people who do not have cyclothymia will have differing states that are normal for them. Another approach to answering this question will involve doing some self-exploration, which you are already accomplishing through the use of this workbook. Beginning in chapter 6, you will have opportunities to monitor your moods, behaviors, and perceptions. This will give you valuable information as you determine for yourself what is related to your disorder, what qualifies as normal moodiness, and what are appropriate reactions to challenging situations.

THE DIAGNOSTIC PROCESS

Now that I have discussed the differences between a disorder and normal mood states, it's time to look more closely at the disorder side of things. While you have had your own experiences with cyclothymic symptoms and know well how this condition has affected your life, it might be useful to gain some insight into how mental health professionals view your symptoms and decide upon a diagnosis. You recall that the DSM, or *Diagnostic and Statistical Manual of Mental Disorders* (American Psychiatric Association 2000), is the standard guide clinicians use to diagnose mental illnesses. It contains descriptions of several hundred mental disorders and lists criteria for diagnosing each one. The criteria for each disorder should not be used like a simple checklist by those who are not trained in diagnostic procedures. Sound clinical judgment by an experienced professional is crucial to making an accurate diagnosis. While your family physician is qualified to diagnose mental disorders, it may be helpful to receive an evaluation from a specialist such as a psychiatrist or psychologist. A psychologist or psychiatrist has been trained to know what questions to ask to assess diagnostic criteria and how to interpret your responses. The clinician must make judgments about the nature of your symptoms, their severity, the degree of impairment they cause, and whether they rise to the level of a disorder.

As you explain the difficulties you have experienced, your doctor will narrow down diagnostic possibilities, ruling disorders in or out based upon information you provide or responses you give to questions. Your doctor will initially be more interested in your inner experiences, your thought processes, your mood, and your behaviors than external events that seem to generate such experiences. It is quite common for people to report on situations, people, or events that appear to "cause" symptoms. While this can be an important part of treatment interventions, the diagnostic process has a slightly different focus.

■ Jerry

Jerry recalls that he has seen a handful of doctors and counselors over the years. He says, "It probably took about ten years to get a diagnosis of cyclothymia. My family doctor always said I was drinking too much because I was depressed. He put me on some antidepressants once, but I stopped taking them because they didn't seem to help. I finally saw a doctor who asked me a lot of questions about all kinds of things. She told me that my anger and irritability were mood problems just like the times when I feel depressed." Jerry acknowledges that he used alcohol to self-medicate when he felt stressed or angry or just wanted to escape for a while.

The Clinical Interview

When you go to your doctor's office for the first time, you will likely be asked to fill out some intake paperwork. On these forms, you may be asked to provide general information in a variety of areas such as gender, age, race, marital status, family information, treatment history, medical history, and alcohol or drug use. You will also be asked about symptoms that are distressing you and what you hope to gain from meeting with your doctor. Your doctor will review your intake paperwork to get an idea of areas that may be useful to ask about in more depth.

Your doctor will begin by gathering clinically relevant information to better understand the big picture of how your symptoms have developed and how they have affected your life. The clinical interview may last from one to several hours (or even take several sessions), depending on how much information needs to be gathered. Your doctor will ask you about your symptoms, how they have affected you, how severe they have been, how long they have lasted, and so forth. Background information on your personal and family history, work history, medical and psychiatric history, and your relationships and support system will be collected. During this interview, your doctor will also assess your overt behaviors, *affect* (mood and expression of feelings), cognitive functioning, how you present yourself, and how you interact. All these things will help your doctor better understand your concerns and determine an accurate diagnosis.

It is often very useful if your doctor can interview at least one other person in your life who knows you well. This can help provide another perspective on your symptoms and possibly add information to the big picture. Those who have cyclothymia often underreport hypomanic symptoms. You are likely to enjoy aspects of the hypomania, since it makes you feel "up," productive, and self-confident. You may not see it as a problem. It is common not to consider symptoms such as irritability, reactivity, and extreme behaviors to be related to an illness. Others close to you, however, may be able to offer insight into how these symptoms have contributed to your difficulties.

Medical Evaluation

Another very important part of the diagnostic process is to rule out medical causes of cyclothymic symptoms. As I mentioned in chapter 2, there are many conditions that can look a lot like depression (such as hypothyroidism or head injuries) and hypomania (such as hyperthyroidism, multiple sclerosis, or mononucleosis). Your doctor will likely advise you to get a thorough medical evaluation to look for physical causes. These assessments may include a complete physical examination, a blood chemical screening, a thyroid function test, urinalysis, neurological and psychological tests, MRI or CT scans, or other diagnostic tests.

■ Marcus

Although he had refused for years, Marcus finally gave in to his former girlfriend's insistence that he see his physician about his mood swings. His doctor gave him a full medical workup and referred him to a psychiatrist in the same office building. When he met with the psychiatrist, Marcus talked about his drug use, his problems at work and in relationships, his family history, and the "night and day" mood swings he's had since he was a teenager. Based on a full clinical interview and the results of the medical evaluation, his doctor determined that Marcus's occasional drug use was not the cause of his hypomanic symptoms. He had also never had a depressive episode. Instead, Marcus was diagnosed with cyclothymic disorder and cocaine abuse.

Diagnosis of Cyclothymia Can Be Difficult

An accurate diagnosis is not made hastily. It requires patience, skill, and experience on the part of the clinician. Bipolar disorders, more than many other disorders, can be tricky to diagnose because of the complexity involved. Your doctor must determine whether your current or past symptoms reflect a manic or hypomanic syndrome and whether a mood episode meets criteria for major depressive disorder. Other medical and mental disorders that can look like mania, hypomania, or depression must be ruled out.

Unfortunately, it occasionally happens that a clinician misses some diagnostic signs. Again, people with hypomanic symptoms may not report these as a problem. They may instead focus on difficulties with depressive symptoms, irritability, or anger. If a clinician does not probe thoroughly for the hypomanic symptoms and misses critical information, this could lead to a misdiagnosis. It is not uncommon for people with the mood swings of cyclothymia to initially be misdiagnosed as having major depressive disorder or other mental illnesses.

DIAGNOSTIC CRITERIA FOR CYCLOTHYMIC DISORDER

In this section, you will see diagnostic criteria for cyclothymic disorder summarized from the DSM. The information may look quite daunting at first glance. I have provided the criteria for cyclothymic disorder and then inserted criteria for hypomanic and depressive episodes where appropriate. I provide this criteria for you virtually as it appears in the DSM, not to overwhelm you with details but because I believe it is important that you have all the information you need and want as a consumer of mental health services. Please remember that if you suspect you have cyclothymia, it is important that you not jump to conclusions and instead seek a thorough evaluation by a trained, experienced mental health professional.

Keep in mind that while I provide the diagnostic criteria for a depressive episode, people who have cyclothymia have never met full criteria for a major depressive episode. Instead, they have met *some* of the criteria.

Table 3.1 Diagnostic Criteria for Cyclothymic Disorder

A. For at least two years (one year for children and adolescents), there have been numerous periods with hypomanic symptoms and numerous periods with depressive symptoms that do not meet criteria for a major depressive episode.

Criteria for Hypomanic Episode

1. A distinct period of persistently elevated, expansive, or irritable mood, lasting throughout at least four days, that is clearly different from the usual nondepressed mood.

2. During the period of mood disturbance, three or more of the following symptoms have persisted (four if the mood is only irritable) and have been present to a significant degree:

    - inflated self-esteem or grandiosity

    - decreased need for sleep (such as feeling rested after only a few hours of sleep)

    - more talkative than usual, or a pressure to keep talking

    - racing thoughts or *flight of ideas* (a continuous stream of thoughts, ideas, or images without an understandable pattern or focus)

    - distractibility, such as attention being easily drawn to unimportant or irrelevant things

    - increase in goal-directed activity (feels compelled to attain a goal, such as socially, occupationally, or sexually) or noticeable physical agitation (fidgeting, difficulty sitting still)

    - excessive involvement in pleasurable activities that have a high potential for painful consequences (such as spending sprees, sexual promiscuity, or risky driving)

3. The episode is associated with an unquestionable change in functioning that is uncharacteristic of the person when he or she does not have the symptoms.

4. The mood problems and change in functioning are noticeable to others.

5. The episode is not severe enough to cause marked impairment in social or occupational functioning or to require hospitalization, and there are no psychotic symptoms.

Criteria for Major Depressive Episode

Remember that those who have cyclothymia have never met full criteria for a major depressive episode. Instead, they have experienced *some* of the following symptoms.

1. During the same two-week period, for most of the day nearly every day, five or more of the following symptoms have been present and represent a change from previous functioning; at least one of the symptoms is either "depressed mood" or "loss of interest or pleasure."

   ■ Depressed mood by self-report (feeling "sad" or "empty") or by observation by others (such as appearing tearful). In children or adolescents, this can be irritable mood.

   ■ Significantly reduced interest or pleasure in all, or almost all, activities.

   ■ Significant weight loss or weight gain, or decrease or increase in appetite. In children, this can be a failure to make weight gains.

   ■ Sleeping too much or too little.

   ■ Noticeable physical agitation, or, alternatively, appearing slowed down.

   ■ Fatigue or loss of energy.

   ■ Feelings of worthlessness or excessive guilt.

   ■ Reduced ability to think, concentrate, or make decisions.

   ■ Recurrent thoughts of death or suicide; suicide attempt or plan for committing suicide.

2. The symptoms cause significant impairment in social, occupational, or daily functioning.

B. During the same two years (one year for children and adolescents), the person hasn't been symptom free for more than two months at a time.

C. During the same time period, there has not been a major depressive episode, manic episode, or *mixed episode* (having both major depressive and manic episodes at the same time, lasting for at least one week and causing significant impairment in daily functioning).

D. The symptoms are not better accounted for by another disorder.

E. The symptoms are not due to the effects of a substance (such as medication, drugs, alcohol, or toxins) or a medical condition (such as hyperthyroidism).

Reprinted with permission from the *Diagnostic and Statistical Manual of Mental Disorders, Text Revision*, Copyright 2000. American Psychiatric Association.

Symptom Checklists to Use with Your Doctor

The following worksheets will guide you in summarizing your symptoms in a way that will allow you to communicate with your doctor and work as a team toward arriving at a diagnosis. I have provided checklists of symptoms of depression, hypomania, and cyclothymia. Go through each of the checklists and mark the symptoms you have experienced according to the instructions. When you meet with your doctor, take these lists with you so that you can discuss them together in more depth. *Please remember that these lists are not intended to be used for self-diagnosis. Only a trained medical or mental health professional is qualified to make a diagnosis.*

EXERCISE 3.1 SYMPTOMS OF DEPRESSION

Symptoms of Depression

Has there been a two-week time period in which you have had either. . .

		Yes	No
A.	Depressed, down, or sad mood for most of the time, more days than not	_____	_____
	OR		
B.	Loss of interest or pleasure in activities that you once enjoyed	_____	_____

AND, *in that same two-week period, did you experience four of the following symptoms (three if you checked both A and B above) most of the day, nearly every day?*

		Yes	No
1.	Significant weight loss or weight gain, or a change in appetite	_____	_____
2.	Sleeping too much or too little	_____	_____
3.	Feeling slowed down (like slow motion), or physically agitated, restless	_____	_____
4.	Loss of energy, fatigue	_____	_____
5.	Feelings of worthlessness or guilt	_____	_____
6.	Difficulty with thinking, concentrating, or making decisions	_____	_____
7.	Recurring thoughts of death or suicide, or a suicide attempt or plan	_____	_____

If you checked five or more of the above symptoms (including either A or B or both), you may have experienced symptoms of a major depressive episode. Remember that those who have cyclothymia have never met full criteria for a major depressive episode.

This checklist is in no way intended to provide a diagnosis, and it should not be used as such. It is meant to be a guide to help you understand your symptoms. Only a trained medical or mental health professional is qualified to make a diagnosis.

Adapted with permission from the *Diagnostic and Statistical Manual of Mental Disorders, Text Revision.* Copyright 2000, American Psychiatric Association.

EXERCISE 3.2 SYMPTOMS OF HYPOMANIA

Symptoms of Hypomania

Has there been a period of at least four days in which you have experienced . . .

	Yes	No

A. Mood that is elevated, overly outgoing, or irritable _____ _____

    AND *three or more of the following symptoms (four if mood is irritable) have been present to a significant degree?*

    1. Inflated self-esteem or grandiosity _____ _____

    2. Decreased need for sleep _____ _____

    3. More talkative than usual, or feeling pressured to keep talking _____ _____

    4. Racing thoughts or a continuous stream of thoughts, ideas, or images _____ _____

    5. Easily distracted by unimportant things _____ _____

    6. Increase in goal-directed activity, feeling compelled to obtain a goal _____ _____

    7. Excessive involvement in pleasurable activities that have potential for painful consequences (such as spending sprees, risky behaviors) _____ _____

B. The symptoms are an obvious change in functioning and uncharacteristic of usual behaviors. _____ _____

C. The mood and change in functioning are noticeable to others. _____ _____

D. The episode is not severe enough to cause significant impairment in daily functioning or to require hospitalization. _____ _____

E. The symptoms are not caused by a substance (drug, alcohol, medication) or a medical condition. _____ _____

If you answered yes to A through E and three or more of symptoms 1 through 7, you may have experienced symptoms of hypomania.

This checklist is in no way intended to provide a diagnosis, and it should not be used as such. It is meant to be a guide to help you understand your symptoms. Only a trained medical or mental health professional is qualified to make a diagnosis.

Adapted with permission from the *Diagnostic and Statistical Manual of Mental Disorders, Text Revision.* Copyright 2000, American Psychiatric Association.

EXERCISE 3.3 SYMPTOMS OF CYCLOTHYMIA

Symptoms of Cyclothymia

For at least two years, have you experienced . . .

		Yes	No
A.	Numerous periods with depressive symptoms that do not meet full criteria for a major depressive episode (see the "Symptoms of Depression" Worksheet).	_____	_____
B.	Numerous periods with hypomanic symptoms (see the "Symptoms of Hypomania" Worksheet).	_____	_____
C.	You have not been without symptoms for more than two months at a time.	_____	_____
D.	The symptoms are not caused by a substance (drug, alcohol, medication), or a medical condition.	_____	_____
E.	The symptoms have caused significant problems in daily functioning.	_____	_____

If you answered yes to A through E, you may have experienced symptoms of cyclothymia.

This checklist is in no way intended to provide a diagnosis, and it should not be used as such. It is meant to be a guide to help you understand your symptoms. Only a trained medical or mental health professional is qualified to make a diagnosis.

Adapted with permission from the *Diagnostic and Statistical Manual of Mental Disorders, Text Revision.* Copyright 2000, American Psychiatric Association.

CYCLOTHYMIA VERSUS OTHER MENTAL DISORDERS

In making a diagnosis, your doctor's task is to determine whether your symptoms meet the criteria for a disorder, and if so, which one. Symptoms of cyclothymia overlap with those of a number of other disorders, including anxiety disorders, attention–deficit/hyperactivity disorder (ADHD), substance abuse, schizoaffective disorder, adjustment disorder, and personality disorders, as well as the other mood disorders. Your doctor will sort through all possible diagnoses, ruling out many very quickly in the process of gathering information during the clinical interview.

Early in the diagnostic process, it may be challenging to rule out some disorders or differentiate between disorders because the differences between them are subtle. For instance, to meet criteria for cyclothymia, a person will have had hypomanic symptoms or episodes but will *not* have met criteria for a major depressive episode. If the person has had major depression, then the correct diagnosis would be bipolar II disorder. Determining whether a person has had depressive symptoms but not met criteria for a major depressive episode takes delicate work on the part of the clinician. If you are the one being evaluated, you may find it challenging as well to remember the details of your past difficulties so that you can accurately report your symptoms to your doctor.

Another factor that complicates diagnosis is frequent use of drugs or alcohol. It presents the question "Which came first, the chicken or the egg?" Determining whether the person is having cyclothymic symptoms as a result of substance use or is using substances to "self-medicate" to try to alleviate the cyclothymic symptoms requires patience in collecting a thorough history.

Personality Disorders

Sometimes, people with cyclothymia are misdiagnosed as having a *personality disorder*. A personality disorder is a deeply rooted, enduring pattern of maladaptive behaviors, ways of relating to others, and perceptions of the world that are extreme to the point that they can cause significant impairments in day-to-day functioning. They often begin in childhood or adolescence and continue throughout adulthood. Because the symptoms of cyclothymia can lead to numerous interpersonal difficulties such as problems with work, marriage, and substance abuse, clinicians may initially see these problems as symptoms of a personality disorder. Cyclothymia is frequently mistaken for borderline personality disorder due to the rapid shifts in mood associated with each (Akiskal 1981). Those with cyclothymia may also be misdiagnosed as having narcissistic or histrionic personality disorders. Some of the effects of cyclothymia can lead to problems similar to those encountered with personality disorders, but what underlies the difficulties is a problem with mood, not a problem with an enduring character pattern.

■ Helen

When Helen was having problems in her marriage eight years ago, she went to see a counselor to help her decide what to do about her marriage and to get help with feeling depressed. Helen learned that her counselor diagnosed her as having both borderline personality disorder and major depressive disorder. She saw the counselor for about five sessions and found it only mildly helpful. It was a few years later that Helen decided to try counseling again. This time she saw a more experienced psychologist, who identified her symptoms as being predominantly related to difficulties with mood. Helen had been experiencing problems that initially appeared to be symptoms of borderline personality disorder, such as reactive mood, unstable relationships, and difficulty controlling anger. However, these symptoms had not been enduring patterns of problems in perceptions and relationships. After conducting a thorough clinical interview and obtaining detailed information about her mood swings, Helen's doctor correctly diagnosed her as having cyclothymic disorder.

Comorbidity of Disorders

You should know that it is possible to have more than one mental disorder at the same time. In fact, this is quite common. This is what mental health professionals refer to as *comorbidity*. It may be that a person has cyclothymia and borderline personality disorder at the same time. Neither diagnosis should be overlooked, just as neither diagnosis should be made prematurely. A person can also be diagnosed with more than one mood disorder. In fact, after the initial two years of cyclothymia, a person may meet criteria for an additional mood disorder such as bipolar I or II, or major depressive disorder. You may recall that having cyclothymia puts you at moderate risk for developing bipolar I or II disorders.

Research has shown that bipolar disorder may occur along with other mental illnesses such as obsessive-compulsive disorder, bulimia, panic disorder, some personality disorders, and alcohol or drug abuse (Strakowski et al. 1994). There is no reason to believe that cyclothymia would be any different.

LIVING WITH THE DIAGNOSIS

In my work with clients, I have found that some people really want to know their diagnosis and others do not. There are pros and cons to either choice. On the negative side, what some people don't like about receiving a diagnosis is that they feel labeled. It's as if they lose their own identity and become the disorder itself. You may notice that throughout this workbook, I am careful to refer to "those with cyclothymia" rather than "cyclothymics." It is a subtle yet important difference in the language. The former separates the person from the illness, while the latter identifies the person *as* the illness. I hope to stress that you are not your illness. Instead, you are a unique person who struggles with symptoms of an illness.

There is also the matter of the stigma that still exists with mental illness. Although this is very unfortunate, it is nevertheless a reality for many people. Knowing your diagnosis and possibly sharing it with others can bring on some unpleasant changes in how others react to you and how you think about yourself. In chapter 9, I will discuss how to help others understand your difficulties with cyclothymia so you can dispel myths and misunderstandings that contribute to this stigma.

Perhaps you fear asking for your diagnosis because of what you know of others' experiences with mental illness. If you have witnessed one or more of your own family members struggle with bipolar disorder or major depression, you may have lived through situations in which you felt frightened, lonely, hopeless, discouraged, or heartbroken. It can be quite scary to think that you might have a mental illness as well, and having a diagnosis can make the fear more real. For many people, the unpleasant events they remember occurred many years ago. It is important to keep in mind that treatments for mental illnesses are constantly improving. Even in recent years, medication for mood disorders has made tremendous advances. They are more effective and have fewer side effects than ever before. Despite the stigma that persists, more people these days are aware that mental illness is treatable, and more have become willing to seek help for it.

■ Maria

Maria has recently been thinking about going to her college counseling center, in part because she has had difficulties from time to time with concentration, motivation, and energy. Her grades have suffered a bit more this semester as a result. She has also thought it might be helpful to talk about problems she has had getting along with her mother, particularly since she'll soon be spending a whole week with her family on a vacation at the beach. She confided in her best friend, "I'm also trying to work up the courage to go find out that I don't have bipolar disorder like my mother." Maria took a self-assessment on a Web site for major depression and bipolar disorder. While she seemed to have a lot of the symptoms of both, the results of the assessment indicated that she should seek a further evaluation.

On the positive side, knowing your diagnosis can help put a name to the struggles you have endured. Cyclothymia is recognizable and treatable. It can be reassuring to know that you are not alone, that you are one of millions of people who have lived with the mood swings and disruptions this illness can cause. You did not bring cyclothymia on to yourself. It is not your fault. It is not a character flaw or something you could will away if you were just "strong enough." Having cyclothymia doesn't make you weak, defective, or "crazy."

Cyclothymia is an illness, much like diabetes is an illness. We don't think of those with diabetes as being weak willed or flawed in character. We don't tell them to just "snap out of it" or "get over it." We recognize that the fact they have the illness is not under their control, and we know that to function at their best, they need proper diagnosis and treatment.

Knowing your diagnosis is also an important part of choosing your treatment approach. Clinical depression is treated differently than anxiety, which is treated differently than ADHD, which is treated differently than cyclothymia. You may want to be very involved in managing your illness and choosing a treatment that is suitable for you. If you had a stroke, developed a tumor, or were in the early stages of heart disease, you would likely want your physician to tell you your diagnosis. Identifying your illness can help get you started in making informed decisions about your medical treatment, learning how you can take good care of yourself, and managing the symptoms that affect your life.

Seeking a diagnosis is a key first step toward managing and preventing symptoms. Once you know you have cyclothymia, you can learn the symptoms that are characteristic of this illness. Learning the symptoms gives you areas to focus on for management strategies and alerts you to warning signs that can prompt you to intervene before symptoms become worse. Since cyclothymia puts you at risk of developing a more severe bipolar disorder, learning strategies for management and prevention of symptoms may be critical. We will explore a number of such strategies in depth in part 2 of this workbook.

No matter the issue that affects our lives, it is generally advantageous to become an informed consumer in today's society. Knowing that you have cyclothymia allows you to seek information from your doctor, national organizations, publications, and reputable Web sites. It can help you feel empowered, hopeful, and in control of things that can sometimes feel very much out of your control.

Summing Up

In this chapter, I have tried to demystify the diagnostic process as well as present some of the difficulties that can arise in making an accurate diagnosis. Determining whether you have cyclothymia requires a thorough evaluation by a trained professional. The adage "Don't try this at home" is appropriate here. Getting a proper diagnosis can be complicated and requires a complete clinical and medical evaluation. It also requires years of training and experience on the part of the clinician.

In the next chapter, we will look more closely at the impact cyclothymia has on everyday life. I'll address how it may affect you personally as well as your partner, family, friends, and coworkers. I'll examine some special issues, including alcohol and drug use and the problem of suicide with mood disorders.

CHAPTER 4

How Does Cyclothymia
Affect You?

The purpose of this chapter is to help you gain a broader perspective on how cyclothymia affects your life aside from the main symptoms I have already discussed. I would like to emphasize three things. First, I want to help you understand that you are not alone in your illness, you are not "crazy" or defective, and your mood swings are a part of an illness and not who you are as a person. Second, I hope to help you gain an awareness of how other people might perceive your behaviors, your feelings, and your illness in general. Being mindful of this can help you manage difficulties in relationships, particularly as they may be related to your illness. These first two issues are important as you step outside of yourself and your symptoms to better understand how cyclothymia affects you and those you care about.

The third goal of this chapter is to help you recognize patterns so that you can identify red flags and learn how to prevent future difficulties. By patterns I mean those situations or events that seem to come up time and time again. Becoming good at spotting those red flags will allow you to act to head off a negative outcome.

I will address two additional topics associated with mood disorders that you should be aware of: suicide and alcohol and drug use. Both occur at high rates in those who have bipolar disorder, and may be issues for those with cyclothymia as well.

THE EXPERIENCE OF CYCLOTHYMIA

In your struggles with cyclothymia, you may have experienced thoughts at one time or another like the following:

- *I am the only one with this problem.*

- *No one understands what I am going through.*

- *I'm defective, bad, no good, crazy, a loser, etc.*

- *Will I ever be normal?*

- *Why do I have this problem?*

It can feel like a real battle at times to sit with such thoughts or questions that are hard to answer. Sometimes the internal struggle can be as difficult as, if not more difficult than, the outward manifestations of your illness. This is all the more reason to remember that you are not alone, that there are millions of others who have similar struggles and experiences.

You are not "crazy" or defective, and *you are not your illness.* It is the illness of cyclothymia that can make you feel, think, and behave in certain ways. No one really chooses to have devastating mood swings and problems in relationships, just as no one chooses to live with the effects of diabetes or other medical illnesses. A person must learn to manage and live with the impact of a medical illness, and the same is true for cyclothymia.

What Are Your Experiences?

I have provided lists below of common thoughts, feelings, and behaviors you might experience if you have cyclothymia. They are labeled "common" for a reason. I hope to demonstrate that the experiences you have are a typical outcome of your illness.

Keep in mind that these common thoughts, feelings, and behaviors can happen not only when you experience symptoms but at any other time as well. One of the devastating effects of the ups and downs of cyclothymia is that it can damage your sense of self. By this I mean that it can be hard to see yourself as having a consistent personality. The highs of hypomania can allow you to feel on top of the world, full of self-esteem and confidence, while the lows of the depressive symptoms can lead you to doubt everything, particularly yourself. No wonder it can be hard to feel consistently good about yourself! I hope that knowing that this variability in how you think about yourself is typical of cyclothymia will help you to understand and manage it better.

EXERCISE 4.1 COMMON THOUGHTS

Below are some common thoughts you might have. Check off any and all that apply to you. If you can think of other thoughts that go through your mind, write them in at the bottom.

_____ I am no good.

_____ No one understands.

_____ I hate myself.

_____ Why try?

_____ Nothing will get better.

_____ Others are incompetent.

_____ I'll never be "normal."

_____ Something is wrong with me.

_____ I can't handle it.

_____ I'm not good enough.

_____ It's everyone else's fault.

_____ I can't do anything right.

_____ Only bad things happen.

_____ People are out to get me.

_____ I am such a failure.

_____ I am completely to blame.

_____ I only make mistakes.

_____ No one loves/likes me.

_____ I am ugly.

_____ I don't deserve to live.

_____ I can't trust anyone.

_____ I always mess up.

_____ I can do anything I want.

_____ If people knew the real me, they wouldn't like me.

If you have a hard time recognizing thoughts you have about yourself, this is not unusual. It might be helpful for you in the coming days and weeks to "listen" to how you speak to yourself internally. Pay attention to your inner thoughts. This is difficult to do at first and takes some practice, but it will be important that you learn to do this well. I will talk about how your thoughts affect your feelings and behaviors in chapter 7.

EXERCISE 4.2 COMMON FEELINGS

Below are some common feelings you might experience. Check off the ones that apply to you. If you know of other feelings you'd like to include on this list, write them in at the bottom.

_____ miserable	_____ overwhelmed	_____ hopeless
_____ useless, worthless	_____ regretful	_____ afraid
_____ defective	_____ angry, enraged	_____ upset over "little things"
_____ apathetic	_____ frustrated, irritable	_____ anxious, nervous
_____ numb	_____ uninterested	_____ lonely
_____ guilty	_____ helpless	_____ overconfident
_____ ecstatic	_____ creative	_____ invincible
_____ physical pains	_____ unmotivated	_____ empty
_____ self-loathing	_____ apprehensive	_____ euphoric

_____ _____   _____ _____   _____ _____

_____ _____   _____ _____   _____ _____

_____ _____   _____ _____   _____ _____

_____ _____   _____ _____   _____ _____

_____ _____   _____ _____   _____ _____

_____ _____   _____ _____   _____ _____

_____ _____   _____ _____   _____ _____

EXERCISE 4.3 COMMON BEHAVIORS

Below are some common behaviors you might engage in. Check off the ones that apply to you. If you know of other behaviors that cause you difficulties, write them in at the bottom.

____ talk too much	____ take risks, do something dangerous	____ make poor judgments
____ isolate myself	____ put on a "mask"	____ have a short temper
____ get hyperactive, energetic	____ overspend money	____ forget to eat
____ act overly outgoing	____ behave obnoxiously	____ laugh too much
____ behave childishly	____ behave inappropriately	____ say mean things
____ act impulsively	____ am easily influenced	____ distrust others
____ take on too much	____ behave selfishly	____ get impatient
____ commit social indiscretions	____ get too focused on sex	____ behave irresponsibly
____ behave self-destructively	____ get very ambitious	____ am overly alert
____ cause disruptions	____ damage relationships	____ do things that damage my career
____ let someone down, don't follow through on a commitment	____ act carelessly	____ get quiet
____ get restless	____ get melancholic	

____ _____   ____ _____   ____ _____

____ _____   ____ _____   ____ _____

____ _____   ____ _____   ____ _____

____ _____   ____ _____   ____ _____

____ _____   ____ _____   ____ _____

■ Maria

Maria tends to keep her thoughts and feelings to herself, but she revealed her inner turmoil to her college counselor. "People think I have it all together. They have no idea how crappy I feel and how I always tell myself I'm a big, ugly, stupid failure. When I feel like this, I tend to snap at people. I have a hard time keeping my frustrations to myself. Sometimes it's a good idea if I just stay away from my friends for a while." Maria realizes she is beginning to recognize a cycle of thoughts, feelings, and behaviors that all seem to go together during those times when she is struggling.

HOW OTHERS MAY PERCEIVE YOU

People who have cyclothymia tend to feel things strongly. The more strongly you feel things, the harder it can be to step outside of yourself and see others' viewpoints. Therefore, you may have difficulty understanding how others see you. Nevertheless, if you value your relationships, then it is important to become aware of your impact on others. Doing this will allow you to decide whether your behaviors are acceptable to you or whether you believe some change may be in order.

EXERCISE 4.4 OTHERS' STATEMENTS

Think for a moment about how your cyclothymia affects others, how your behaviors affect the various relationships you have at home, at work, and with friends. Have you heard any of the following statements from people around you? Perhaps too many times?

☐   I have to walk on eggshells around you.

☐   You make me responsible for how you feel.

☐   I feel I have to keep things stress free.

☐   I have to predict your feelings and behaviors.

☐   I can tell when I need to steer clear of you.

☐   You won't let me help you.

☐   I don't know what to do to help you.

☐   I don't understand your moodiness.

☐   You are so sensitive.

☐   You take things personally.

☐   I have difficulty trusting you.

☐   You blame me for all our problems.

☐   You embarrass me.

What else have you heard people tell you about your moods, behaviors, and thoughts?

_____

_____

_____

_____

_____

_____

_____

EXERCISE 4.5 OTHERS' DESCRIPTIONS

How else might people describe you? Check any of the following that apply. You might even write in ones that are not listed here.

____ quick to yell	____ hot-tempered	____ easily frustrated
____ overly sensitive	____ verbally abusive	____ makes things my fault
____ reckless	____ too optimistic	____ minimizes problems
____ arrogant	____ wants a quick fix	____ misunderstands me
____ moody	____ unpredictable	____ inconsistent
____ unreliable	____ shows off	____ knows it all
____ overspends money	____ embarrassing	____ takes big risks

____ _____ ____ _____ ____ _____

____ _____ ____ _____ ____ _____

____ _____ ____ _____ ____ _____

____ _____ ____ _____ ____ _____

■ Marcus

For the past year or so, since he broke up with his girlfriend of four years, Marcus has been doing some soul-searching to figure out why many of his relationships with women have gone sour. "After my ex-girlfriend and I had some time apart, I asked her to be honest with me about what she thought went wrong in our relationship. She said I was hot-headed and unpredictable. Apparently she felt on edge around me, not knowing what would make me angry. I never knew that until we talked." Marcus also had an opportunity to talk with his best friend about how other people see him. His friend told him that people sometimes find him hard to approach and get to know because he seems irritable and quiet much of the time.

To get even more information about how other people respond to your cyclothymia, it can be incredibly fruitful to sit down and speak with a trusted friend. Consider asking someone who you know will be honest with you. Tell this person you are interested in becoming more aware of your impact on others. You might ask questions like the ones listed on the next page. Write down what your friend tells you in the workbook so you'll have it for future reference. Use an additional sheet of paper if you need more room.

EXERCISE 4.6 INFORMATIONAL INTERVIEW

How would you describe my personality? My behavior? My feelings?

_____

_____

_____

_____

How do you think I affect other people? What do they think of my behaviors and mood?

_____

_____

_____

_____

What are some good and not-so-good qualities about me that you think it would be useful for me to know?

_____

_____

_____

_____

What have I done that has led you to feel frightened, embarrassed, angry, frustrated, helpless, and so on?

_____

_____

_____

_____

RECOGNIZING PATTERNS AND RED FLAGS

Have you noticed that very similar things seem to happen time and time again? You might ask yourself, "Why does this always happen to me?" Or, "Why do people always do this to me?" It is common for all of us, whether we have cyclothymia or not, to have recurrent themes in our lives. Sometimes we recognize these themes or patterns as something in which we play a role. Other times, this becomes evident only after much soul-searching. *The point is not to start blaming yourself for unpleasant things that happen but rather to take responsibility for changing them.*

■ **Jerry**

Jerry has spent some years exploring themes in his life that tend to lead to problems in his relationships. A common pattern for Jerry involves getting too stressed out at work. When this happens, he becomes more irritable in general. He takes his frustration home and lashes out at his wife, often saying mean and degrading things to her that he later regrets. His wife has almost left him twice over cruel remarks he has made. While he later deeply regrets his behavior and apologizes to his wife, damage has already been done to the relationship. This pattern culminates in Jerry thinking he is a "no-good loser" and feeling depressed for the next several days.

While it may not feel good to acknowledge the role you play in patterns that recur in your life, there is certainly a great advantage to doing so. It means that you have some power to change them. The ultimate goal of recognizing patterns is to help build a framework for preventing them. Here is how this works. The first step is to identify recurrent patterns that lead to difficulties for you. The second step is to acknowledge the part you play in these patterns. The third step is to identify the precursors, or red flags, that signal the pattern is about to occur again. The fourth step is to develop a plan for preventive measures that you will use whenever you notice the red flags happening again. As you proceed through the next few sections, fill in your own information in exercise 4.7. This chart is also available online at www.CyclothymiaWorkbook.com.

EXERCISE 4.7 RECOGNIZING YOUR PATTERNS

Your Patterns	Your Role	Your Red Flags	Your Prevention Plan
When I get stressed out at work, my wife and I get into arguments	*I take my frustrations out on my wife. I say mean things, start fights*	*overwhelmed at work, feel stressed, irritable, drive too fast, slam doors*	*stress management, cool down before going home, exercise, warn my wife*

Step 1: Recognizing Your Own Patterns

Before you go further, I want to emphasize again that the purpose of this section is not to blame you or find you at fault for problems in your life. That would neither be fruitful nor do you or anyone else any good. In fact, overwhelming yourself with blame and self-criticism may just perpetuate what does not work well for you in your life. It can lead to feelings of depression, frustration, and discouragement. What can be very useful, however, is to honestly examine events in your life for the purpose of figuring out what you can do differently the next time, to give yourself the opportunity for satisfaction rather than disappointment.

You may already be thinking of several unpleasant patterns that occur time and again for you. If so, go ahead and write them in the first column of your "Recognizing Your Patterns" worksheet. If you have difficulty identifying recurrent patterns in your life, you might refer back to your frank discussion with a trusted person. You may also find it useful to respond to the following questions by filling in the blanks with some of the first things that come into your mind.

EXERCISE 4.8 YOUR PATTERNS

People always _____

_____

I don't ever seem able to _____

_____

People usually say I _____

_____

People think I am _____

_____

Whenever I try to , _____

it seems to always turn out that _____

_____

For years I have struggled with _____

_____

Step 2: Identifying Your Role

The extent of influence you have in patterns in your life varies. You may be completely responsible (for example, by regularly picking fights with people for no apparent reason). You might maintain patterns (for example, by never expressing your true feelings to your partner and continually suffering feelings of inadequacy and low self-esteem as a result). You may also exacerbate patterns (for example, adding to your difficulty making friends by disrespecting your coworkers). It is also possible to play a role in patterns simply by being passive. This can happen, for example, if you are in abusive relationships and have difficulty getting out of them for whatever reason.

If you are able to identify patterns in your life, it is likely that you do have some amount of responsibility in them. Again, the good news is that you will also have some amount of power to change them for the better. However, it requires being honest with yourself. Do you take things out on other people? Do you engage in risky or outrageous behaviors? Do you let stress get out of hand before you do anything about it? Do you take constructive feedback as negative criticism? Are you passive-aggressive if you don't get your way? If you need some help with recognizing your roles, you might take a look back over your responses to the worksheets in this chapter. When you identify your roles, write them in your worksheet for exercise 4.7.

Step 3: Spotting Your Red Flags

Identifying your red flags is an important and perhaps challenging step in this process. Look at the chart you are filling in for exercise 4.7. Pick the pattern that has happened most recently. In your mind, go back in time and recall what events, feelings, or behaviors occurred just before the pattern took place and just before you engaged in your role in the pattern. These are the red flags or triggers that can let you know that the pattern is beginning again. Some examples include

- getting yelled at by your boss

- beginning a new project with a tight deadline

- getting a headache

- feeling fidgety, restless

- arguing with your partner

- believing someone wronged you

- going to a party, staying out late

- having your plans fail to work out as expected

- getting cut off in traffic

- feeling stressed out

- not getting enough sleep

- drinking too much alcohol

- feeling anxious, tense

- receiving feedback

- having your car break down

- catching a cold or other illness

Here, you are looking for things that seem to play a part in "setting you off," leading you to feel irritable or depressed, or otherwise triggering the pattern you have identified. I hope you will take your time considering this, since it is easy to overlook some useful red flags. For instance, you might notice that you clench your fists just before you yell at your partner. You might slam a book down on the table, lose your appetite for dinner, wake up too early in the morning, spend all evening working on a project in the garage to get away from your family, feel that your future is looking very bleak, and so on. You can learn to recognize these important precursors to your patterns in the very moment they occur.

Even if you are able to list all kinds of red flags for yourself, it still may be helpful to pay close attention to what happens the next time a pattern emerges. Really notice every detail of the event, particularly your own feelings and behaviors. You might be surprised that you learn something new you can list in your red flags column.

 **Helen**

Helen likes to joke, "I have really learned over the years what my red flags are. I've had plenty of problems and plenty of time to figure that out! One of the biggest warning signs that my mood could plummet is when my brother calls and asks for money. I get into this whole thing about wanting to help him on the one hand and wanting him to take responsibility for his own problems on the other. I've learned that I have to limit the amount of time I speak with him on the phone if I want to have a peaceful evening with my family. Another big red flag for me is when I start thinking that someone might be mad at me, like my husband. I can really start doubting everything and feeling anxious. The last time this happened, my husband came home and was really quiet all evening. I kept bugging him

to tell me what was wrong, which made things worse. It turned out he was just feeling overworked at his job and he didn't feel like talking as much as usual."

Step 4: Your Plan for Prevention

Up to this point, you have worked hard to be honest with yourself about patterns that recur in your life, the role you play in them, and the red flags that can signal their onset. Your work thus far may encourage you to begin thinking about ways you can prevent the patterns from happening again. If you do have some ideas, go ahead and write them on your chart for exercise 4.7. I don't mean to leave you hanging at this point, but I will be discussing a number of strategies in part 2 of this workbook that will give you all kinds of wonderful ideas about preventing unpleasant patterns and otherwise help you to manage your symptoms. So, I hope you will be patient with me for just a bit and keep your chart handy as we proceed through the rest of the workbook. In chapter 10, you will bring everything together you have learned, and you should be able to complete the last column of your chart with no trouble.

To peek ahead just a bit, strategies you'll write in your last column could include specific ideas for managing depressive or hypomanic symptoms, anger, and problems in relationships. You may also want to increase your social interactions, use good communication skills, and evaluate your diet, sleep patterns, and exercise. Learning to improve your mood through modifying negative thinking is another important strategy I will address in detail in chapter 7.

MOOD DISORDERS AND SUICIDE

I turn now to address other issues that can affect the lives of those with cyclothymia. You may recall that one of the diagnostic criteria for a major depressive episode is thoughts of death or suicide, or suicide attempt. Mood disorders in general are associated with an increased risk of suicide. Bipolar disorders in particular have one of the highest rates of suicide among all mental disorders. According to the DSM, the rate of suicide of those with bipolar disorder is 10 to 15 percent (American Psychiatric Association 2000). In their review of thirty studies evaluating suicide rates among patients with bipolar disorder, Goodwin and Jamison (1990) found that an average of 19 percent died by suicide. Among patients with bipolar disorder, 25 to 50 percent attempted suicide on at least one occasion.

Goodwin and Jamison further showed a gender difference in the rates of attempted and completed suicides. Approximately 15 to 48 percent of women who have bipolar disorder attempt suicide, while 4 to 27 percent of men attempt it. While women are two to three times more likely to try to kill themselves, men are two to three times more likely to complete a suicide.

There is less information about suicide rates of those with cyclothymic disorder. Remember that cyclothymia is often not brought to the attention of medical or mental health professionals unless a person wishes to seek treatment or the condition becomes severe enough to warrant hospitalization. In the latter case, it is likely that cyclothymia has progressed into a more severe bipolar disorder. This is all the more reason to take steps to keep the symptoms of cyclothymia from becoming worse.

It is not uncommon for people to have fleeting thoughts about death or suicide from time to time. What becomes a problem is when thoughts about suicide lead to plans to carry out the act, or when behaviors become impulsive or otherwise create a risk of death.

Situations that may put people at risk for suicide include prior suicide attempt, impulsivity, loss of an important relationship, adverse life events, access to lethal means of suicide, family history of suicide or mental illness, and exposure to physical or sexual abuse or violence. According to the National Institute of Mental Health (2001), other signs that may be associated with suicidal thoughts and feelings include

- talking about feeling suicidal or wanting to die

- feeling hopeless, that nothing will ever change or get better

- feeling helpless, that nothing you do makes any difference

- feeling like a burden to family and friends

- abusing alcohol, drugs, or both

- putting your affairs in order (for example, by organizing your finances or giving away possessions to prepare for your death)

- writing a suicide note

- putting yourself in harm's way or in situations where there is a danger of being killed

---

Please note: If you have thoughts of death or suicide, make plans for suicide, or engage in behaviors that could create a risk of death, you need to seek assistance from a trained medical or mental health professional immediately. Here are some things to remember:

You can call your doctor, your local emergency room, or emergency services (911).

Don't remain alone; seek out family or friends and let them know how you're feeling.

Get rid of items that you could use to harm yourself. Ask someone you know to help you with this.

ALCOHOL AND DRUG ABUSE

Alcohol and substance abuse is another common problem associated with mood disorders, and it occurs frequently among those with bipolar disorder. In one study of patients diagnosed with bipolar disorder, at least 50 percent had a history of substance abuse, with rates being higher for men than women (Regier et al. 1990).

While the particular relationship between bipolar disorder and substance use or abuse is unknown, it has been hypothesized that the use of alcohol and drugs may serve at least two functions. First, substance use may be an attempt to "self-medicate." In other words, if a person feels stressed out, upset, lonely, angry, or otherwise distressed, it is not unusual to want to have an alcoholic drink to "settle the nerves." You already know that people with bipolar disorder or cyclothymia tend to struggle frequently with distressing feelings. If you get in the habit of reaching for a substance to manage your moods, then you may put yourself at risk for developing an addiction, only exacerbating the problem. In commenting on his research on cyclothymia,

Hagop Akiskal (1996) noted that 50 percent of his patients engaged in *polysubstance abuse* (using more than one type of substance; for example, both alcohol and cocaine). He concluded that this was mainly due to the desire to self-medicate.

The second reason people with bipolar disorder and cyclothymia may abuse alcohol and drugs is to enhance the highs of mania or hypomania. Recall that one of the diagnostic criteria for hypomania is a tendency to engage in risky behaviors. Certainly, substance abuse qualifies as a risky behavior. People with cyclothymia enjoy the highs of hypomania and like to make it last. They feel good, on top of the world, and indestructible. Put these things together and you may have a recipe for a substance abuse problem.

Substance abuse has obvious problems in that it is detrimental to your physical and mental well-being. It can also make diagnosis and treatment much more difficult. Cyclothymia is already a tricky condition to diagnose accurately, and the effects of substances can create symptoms that look like both depression and hypomania. Treatment is compromised, since substances can create unpleasant mood states and lead to other self-destructive behaviors. Alcohol and drugs may also affect any mood-stabilizing drugs that have been prescribed for you by your doctor, making them less effective in the long run.

Again, this information about alcohol and drug abuse is offered in the spirit of letting you know what to look out for as you consider your own experiences and work toward developing your plan for managing your symptoms. If you have been diagnosed with cyclothymia, you may be at increased risk for substance abuse problems. Knowing this ahead of time can help you take a different path and head off potential problems that might otherwise be devastating.

Summing Up

In this chapter, we went more in depth into the impact cyclothymia has on your life. You had the opportunity to do some self-exploration into your everyday experiences and to examine how others might be affected. You looked at the unpleasant patterns that occur in your life, as well as the role you may have in these patterns. You also began to identify the precursors or red flags that signal the need to take action to prevent difficulties or keep them from getting worse. I wrapped up this chapter by addressing the devastating effects of suicide and substance abuse, two issues that occur at high rates in people with bipolar disorder.

I hope you were able to spend some thoughtful time with the activities in this chapter. If you weren't, please come back to them again before too long. There is the possibility for some key self-discoveries here that can shape your development of strategies in later chapters. Likewise, if you think of additional information that should be added to any of the worksheets in this chapter as we go along, go back and add the information as soon as you can so you won't forget it.

CHAPTER 5

What Treatments Are Effective for Cyclothymia?

If you wish to seek professional treatment for your cyclothymia, there are some good options available to you. In this chapter I will address what research has shown to be effective for treating cyclothymia and bipolar disorder, as well as how to go about finding professional help.

As you have learned, both cyclothymia and bipolar disorder tend to be chronic conditions that often begin in early adulthood and last a lifetime. While people with more severe bipolar disorder may require life-long treatment to manage symptoms, those with cyclothymia may not. Instead, they may function well for periods of time, perhaps benefiting from available treatments every so often.

Because the symptoms of cyclothymia tend to affect every part of your life, it can be useful to get assistance with managing not only the symptoms but the fallout of the symptoms as well. You might find that a self-help workbook such as this provides some of the basic things you need to cope with your cyclothymia, but if you would like to seek out further assistance, the information in this chapter might prove useful.

Since there has been more research on effective treatments for bipolar disorder than for cyclothymic disorder, I will combine this information here and use the terms rather interchangeably. It is generally understood that treatments found to be beneficial for bipolar disorder are also appropriate for cyclothymia (Howland and Thase 1993). The primary goals of treatment include increased mood stability and improved overall functioning. Within these goals, specific targets of therapy can include enhancing social interactions and important relationships, learning to function better at work, learning how to gain support from partners or family, and recognizing stressors that can lead to problems with mood (Rivas-Vazquez et al. 2002). You may have additional goals such as improving communication with your partner, learning how to manage stress more effectively, dealing with a history of trauma or abuse, or doing some marriage counseling.

PSYCHOTHERAPY

There are various forms of *psychotherapy*, or "talk therapy," that have been shown to be useful for the treatment of bipolar disorder. Common ones include cognitive behavioral therapy, family therapy, psychoeducation, and interpersonal and social rhythm therapy. Many of the strategies and activities in part 2 of this workbook are built upon principles inherent in these approaches. These types of psychotherapy are briefly described for you below.

■ Helen

Helen has been seeing her psychologist, Dr. Evans, for about four months. While they met weekly in the beginning, Helen now meets with him every other week. She reports, "I really find it helpful to meet with Dr. Evans. It gives me a place to go to talk about my problems and figure out how to fix them. He's so supportive." Helen began taking medication (an antidepressant and a mood stabilizer) about two months ago, and she has found it very helpful. She says, "The medication seems to take the edge off of things. I feel like I can handle problems without getting too upset or depressed."

Cognitive Behavioral Therapy

Cognitive behavioral therapy, or CBT, has been shown to be effective for treating a number of mental health issues, including major depressive disorder and many of the anxiety disorders. It is a structured therapy that emphasizes focusing on identified problems in your present life. A cognitive behavioral therapist will be more directive than some other therapists in working with you to plan what you will discuss in your session, assigning homework for you to complete between meetings, and measuring your progress along the way. Little time is spent on things like childhood events or unconscious motives unless they have direct bearing on current issues.

CBT is based on the premise that how you perceive and think about the world directly influences how you feel and behave. Many of the strategies of CBT are aimed at addressing your *automatic thoughts*, or thoughts you have automatically in reaction to events that occur around you. Negative thoughts like *I am such a failure* or *No one likes me* inevitably lead to unpleasant feelings like shame, fear, guilt, or depression. Using the techniques of CBT, you can learn to identify and modify negative thoughts before they lead you down a path of distress.

The principles and strategies of CBT are used widely in the mental health field because of their effectiveness. They can be readily learned in a self-help workbook and used throughout your life in a variety of situations. I will spend all of chapter 7 discussing these principles in great detail.

■ Maria

"I had to get up some nerve to go to my college counseling center, but I'm glad I did it," Maria says. "My therapist was understanding and knowledgeable about mood problems. She reassured me that my condition is not as severe as my mother's. But I did find out that I am at risk for more severe problems because of my family history. I want to do whatever I can to keep things from getting worse for me, because I've seen how bad it can get. An interesting thing I learned is that some of the most famous writers and artists have struggled with mood problems, including bipolar disorder. Since I'm a writer, maybe I can tap into the creativity but keep the bad stuff from happening."

Family Therapy

Family, marital, or couples therapy for bipolar disorder is based in the premise that your illness has an impact on the life of your family and, in turn, your family affects you and your illness. While it is beneficial for you to understand the effects of your illness, it is also quite helpful to educate those around you. Educational interventions for families and partners of those with bipolar disorder include teaching them about symptoms, the course of the illness, treatment approaches, and relapse prevention.

As you may have found in your own life, interactions between you and your family or partner can be problematic whether or not you are experiencing symptoms of cyclothymia. Studies have suggested that stressful family environments may be related to more problems in the course of bipolar disorder, while supportive environments can help people recover more quickly from depressive or manic episodes (Johnson et al. 1999).

Family-focused psychoeducational treatment (FFT) is one type of family therapy that has received support from research (Miklowitz and Goldstein 1997). This program is offered in twenty-one sessions over a nine-month period (twelve weekly sessions, six biweekly, and three monthly) for those with bipolar disorder and their families. It has three components:

Education about bipolar disorder. Information is provided about symptoms, causes, treatment, risk factors (such as irregular sleep patterns and drug use), and helpful factors (such as social and emotional support).

Communication skills training. Members are taught skills such as active listening and giving appropriate feedback, and they are encouraged to role-play during sessions and to complete homework assignments between sessions.

Problem-solving skills training. Individuals learn to identify and evaluate problems, brainstorm solutions, follow through on a solution, and respond to signs of symptom relapse.

■ Jerry

Since his two previous marriages had failed, Jerry decided that he wanted to do some couples counseling with Sue before they got married. Sue thought this was a good idea as well, and they saw a therapist for about six meetings. Jerry says, "We thought it was really helpful to talk about what hadn't worked well in both our other relationships. I also wanted Sue to know more about my cyclothymia and hear from a professional about the effects it has on relationships. Sue was understanding, and she had some of her own things that we had to work out, too."

Psychoeducation

Psychoeducation simply means educating people with mental illnesses about various aspects of their condition. Structured, multiple-session education programs help people to make improvements in a number of areas. People are taught to recognize early warning signs and take preventive action as soon as possible. Such programs have helped people improve social and occupational functioning, increase time between their manic (Perry et al. 1999) and depressive episodes, and reduce number of hospitalizations and lengths of stay, even after two years (Colom et al. 2003).

Topics commonly covered in psychoeducational programs may include

- general education about the symptoms and effects of bipolar disorder

- learning to identify warning signs or red flags that indicate the onset of a manic or depressive episode, often through reviewing your past history of mood difficulties

- developing and practicing an action plan to avert the escalation of symptoms, including seeing a chosen therapist or psychiatrist

- recording symptoms on worksheets with the goal of understanding the difference between problematic mood symptoms and normal mood fluctuations

- complying with treatment recommendations

- coping with symptoms

- managing stress

- avoiding substance abuse

- regulating lifestyle behaviors such as sleep, exercise, and nutrition

- preventing suicidal behavior

- learning about and coping with the social consequences of past and future mood problems

- improving interactions in relationships

- improving quality of life and general well-being

Some of these topics should seem familiar to you by now. Most of them will be very familiar to you by the time you complete this workbook!

Interpersonal and Social Rhythm Therapy

Interpersonal and social rhythm therapy (IPSRT) is a structured, present-oriented approach developed by Frank and colleagues (1994) focusing on behaviors that help maintain stable daily routines. IPSRT is based on the premise that certain events in the life of a person with bipolar disorder can trigger problems with mood by disrupting circadian rhythms and daily routines. IPSRT has two main goals: (1) to help people understand and solve problems in their social environment that are related to mood symptoms, and (2) to help people understand the impact of social interactions and events on their circadian rhythms, and to bring these rhythms back into order to manage mood swings.

This approach uses the *social rhythm metric*, a chart developed by Monk and colleagues (1991) for daily monitoring of activities such as what time you go to bed, what time you get up, when you have meals, your social interactions, and other routines associated with exercise and work. The point of keeping such a record is to demonstrate how changes in your mood can be related to variations in basic routines and patterns of social stimulation, and in turn how these situations are affected by your mood. After monitoring your cycles for some time and understanding these relationships, you may find that you can stabilize your routines and rhythms, thereby regulating your mood.

In chapter 6, you will use a slightly modified version of the social rhythm metric to monitor your own daily rhythms and social interactions. You will be able to see for yourself how or whether these factors influence your own difficulties with mood.

Another portion of IPSRT focuses on exploring and working to resolve one or more issues identified early on in therapy. Each issue is conceptualized as falling within one or more of the following areas:

- grief over death of a loved one, or other type of loss

- interpersonal disputes (continual conflicts in important relationships)

- role transitions (changes in personal, familial, social, or occupational situations)

- interpersonal skill deficits (problems with social skills, getting along with others)

The IPSRT approach identifies specific strategies to use in exploring each of these areas. You and your therapist will use these strategies toward addressing your concerns.

What You Can Expect from Psychotherapy

If you choose to participate in psychotherapy, you will likely meet with your therapist weekly or every other week. Your first meeting will probably be an information-gathering session. Your therapist will explain confidentiality, discuss the process of counseling, and inform you of treatment options that are available. You may be asked about goals you have for counseling, and you will have the opportunity to ask questions. Sometimes people feel a bit nervous meeting with a therapist for the first time, so if you do have questions, you might want to write them down and bring them with you so you won't have to worry about forgetting them.

You should always feel free to speak honestly with your therapist about what is on your mind. For instance, if you are not pleased about some aspect of your treatment, you should let your therapist know. Your therapist will want to make therapy as useful as possible for you and should be very receptive to concerns you have. It is okay for you to ask how long treatment may last, what your therapist can do to help you, and how you can measure your progress along the way. Getting your questions answered can help you feel more comfortable with the therapeutic process, perhaps a necessary ingredient in making your venture worthwhile.

You will need to take an active part in your therapy if you want to experience improvement. The more motivated you are to address issues honestly, do homework exercises from week to week, and practice skills you learn outside of the therapist's office, the more you will benefit in the long run. The more responsibility you take for making changes in your life through therapy, the better you will feel about your accomplishments.

Please be aware that the therapeutic process takes time. You might need to remind yourself to be patient with the work that you're doing. It took a lifetime to develop the issues that brought you to counseling, and it will take a little time to realize improvement in them. Toward the end of this chapter, I'll offer some thoughts about how to find a good mental health professional.

MEDICATIONS

If you choose to look into the option of medication to treat your cyclothymic symptoms, you should gather as much information as you can. When you purchase a medication, it often comes with an informational insert describing the drug, how you should take it, and possible side effects. Be sure to tell your doctor about all other prescription and over-the-counter medications you are taking. You should also report what you are taking in the way of vitamins, minerals, and herbal supplements. Any substance you take has the potential to affect mood and behavior and to interact negatively with prescribed medication, so it will be important for your doctor to know what you are taking.

Make sure you ask your doctor any questions you have about your medication. It's important that you feel comfortable about trying a new medication and know what to expect as a result of taking it. Your doctor should explain how long it may take for your medication to be effective and what you might experience as your body gets used to it. Many medications will take some time to reach a therapeutic level in your body. It is not uncommon for people to feel a bit impatient, perhaps discontinuing their medication before it has a chance to be effective simply because they believe it isn't working for them.

Occasionally, the process of finding the right medication and the right dosage for a person takes some time. It's not always an exact science. I would encourage you to be patient with the process and work closely with your doctor about how your medication is working for you. You should never discontinue taking your medication suddenly, since this may cause some unpleasant side effects. It is also very important that you take your medication exactly as it is prescribed. Never double up on it or take more than you are supposed to. If you believe your medication isn't working or you have other concerns about it, speak with your doctor as soon as you can. Most concerns can be managed quite easily.

Mood Stabilizers

Medications used to treat cyclothymia and bipolar disorder are often referred to as *mood stabilizers*. Because little research has been done to assess the effectiveness of certain medications in the treatment of cyclothymia, your doctor will consider medications that have been shown to be effective in treating bipolar disorder.

The drug most widely used to treat bipolar disorder is lithium. Lithium was approved by the Food and Drug Administration in 1970 for the treatment of mania, and it has proven to be effective in preventing the recurrence of depressive and manic episodes (National Institute of Mental Health 2001). It is common for a doctor to prescribe lithium in addition to another mood-stabilizing drug such as Tegretol (carbamazepine) or Depakote (valproic acid) since lithium alone does have some limitations in its effectiveness. While lithium is commonly used to treat bipolar disorder, your doctor may or may not choose to prescribe it for your cyclothymia. There are other medications that can provide similar effects.

Table 5.1 lists several classes of drugs with specific medications that are commonly used to treat bipolar disorder.

Table 5.1   Medications Used to Treat Bipolar Disorder

Antipsychotic Medications

Generic Name	Trade Name
clozapine	Clozaril
olanzapine	Zyprexa
quetiapine	Seroquel
risperidone	Risperdal
ziprasidone	Geodon

Anticonvulsants, or Antimanic Medications

Generic Name	Trade Name
carbamazepine	Tegretol
divalproex sodium (valproic acid, valproate)	Depakote
gabapentin	Neurontin
lamotrigine	Lamictal
topimarate	Topamax

Antidepressant Medications

Generic Name	Trade Name
bupropion	Wellbutrin
citalopram	Celexa
fluoxetine	Prozac
paroxetine	Paxil
sertraline	Zoloft
imipramine	Tofranil
venlafaxine	Effexor

Benzodiazepines, or Antianxiety Medications

Generic Name	Trade Name
clonazepam	Klonopin
lorazepam	Ativan

Side Effects

It is not unusual to experience some side effects after you begin taking a new medication. Many side effects are tolerable and will go away within a few days or weeks, once your body has had a chance to get used to the drug. The more common side effects include nausea, weight gain, tremor, anxiety, dizziness, dry mouth, headache, and reduced sexual drive or performance (National Institute of Health 2002). If you experience side effects, be sure to tell your doctor. Sometimes changing the dosage, the time of day you take it, or the medication itself can relieve the problem. Remember not to change the way you take your medication or stop taking your medication without guidance from your doctor.

COMBINING PSYCHOTHERAPY AND MEDICATION

For the more severe bipolar disorders, medication is definitely the first treatment of choice. However, medication alone is not enough to prevent symptoms or episodes from recurring. While the effects of today's medications can vastly improve the lives of those with bipolar disorder compared to decades ago, there is no medication that can "cure" this illness. People still may experience manic or depressive episodes that greatly disrupt their lives. Something more is often needed. It is becoming more widely accepted that a combination of medication and psychotherapy may be the best approach for long-term symptom-free periods.

Psychotherapy has also been found to be useful with *medication compliance,* or taking medication as it is prescribed by your doctor. Psychotherapy can help people understand the reasons for taking their medication and manage problems that sometimes come up with taking it. This can help people stick with taking their medication as prescribed by their doctor, thereby improving their outcome with treatment.

Kay Redfield Jamison, a psychiatrist and leading researcher of bipolar disorder, says, "Lithium moderates the illness, but therapy teaches you how to live with it" (1995, 83). Jamison has struggled herself with bipolar disorder for most of her adult life.

HOW TO FIND PROFESSIONAL HELP

Whether you wish to seek psychotherapy or medication or both, you will want to find good professional help. One way to begin this process is to ask people within the medical community who they know that specializes in treating mood disorders. You can ask your family physician, a nurse, a psychologist, a psychiatrist, or a social worker. You can call your local hospital, community mental health services, or mental health professionals in private practices for recommendations. Another method for finding good professional help is to call your local chapters of the National Alliance for the Mentally Ill or Depression and Bipolar Support Alliance. See the Resources section for contact information. You will likely receive referrals for experienced professionals such as psychiatrists or psychologists.

People have often heard of psychiatrists and psychologists, but many don't know the differences between them. A psychiatrist is a medical doctor, similar to your family physician, who has had training diagnosing and treating mental illnesses. Psychiatrists have gone to medical school and fulfilled internship and residency requirements, including specialization in mental health treatment. A psychiatrist can prescribe medication and carry out biomedical treatments. Psychiatrists are also trained to provide psychotherapy, although many do not provide regular psychotherapy for their clients. A psychologist is a doctoral-level practitioner also trained in diagnosing and treating mental illnesses. Psychologists have completed training and internship experiences, often through a university program. Psychologists do not prescribe medication, but they have extensive training in providing psychotherapy. They often spend much of their time providing psychotherapy to their clients.

If you are not limited by insurance restrictions, you should consider "shopping around" for a good mental health provider. It is okay to ask how much experience providers have had in treating cyclothymia or bipolar disorders, how long they have been in practice, what kinds of treatment approaches they consider, and so forth. You should feel free to ask any questions you have of your provider so that you can feel comfortable with the treatment process.

■ Marcus

"I saw a counselor last year to help me control my anger better, especially at work. I get frustrated pretty easily with my coworkers, then I get angry and say things without thinking, and then it just causes a lot of problems," Marcus says. *"I went to counseling about eight or ten times, and it was helpful. My counselor talked about using cognitive therapy, and it helped me to look at situations a little differently. I learned how to use an automatic thought record and change my thinking about some things so I wouldn't get so worked up. I still have problems sometimes, but it's better than it was."*

Summing Up

In this chapter, I have addressed psychotherapies and medications commonly used to treat cyclothymia and bipolar disorder. Certainly, whether you seek any of these treatments is a personal choice for you to make. Some people enjoy therapy and find it useful, while others do not wish to work with a therapist. Similarly, medications can be very effective in managing symptoms, but not everyone chooses that option either. I believe it is important that you are aware of treatment options available to you so that you can make your own informed decision. If you have an interest in seeking more specific information about treatment, you might check out the Resources section.

The end of this chapter on treatments for cyclothymia marks the end of part 1 of your workbook. You have been building your knowledge base about cyclothymic disorder and exploring the impact of this illness on your life along the way. The work you have done thus far has prepared you for part 2, the heart of the workbook, where you will learn practical ways to manage your mood swings and lead a balanced life.

PART II

Managing Cyclothymia

In the first part of this workbook, I have presented information on a number of topics to help provide a context for the work you will be doing in the second part. You have learned about the nature of cyclothymic disorder, its causes, diagnosis, and treatments. You have also spent time doing some self-exploration. The work you did identifying your symptoms, creating your genogram, recording stressors, and recognizing common thoughts, feelings, and behaviors will soon be put to good use.

What lies ahead in the remaining chapters is the "work" part of this workbook! Before we move forward, I would like to offer a few thoughts.

Be patient with yourself. Trying new things can be frustrating at first, but with practice, perseverance, and patience, you will likely experience a rewarding payoff.

Change is a process. Bringing change into your life is a process of moving among breakthroughs, insights, setbacks, disappointments, and triumphs. There are many ups and downs, but inevitably you can reach your goals. What you can achieve is often well worth the challenges you face along the way.

Change takes time. By the time you reach a place in your life where you decide you need to do something about your problems, you have likely struggled with them for quite a long time. You may have had cyclothymia for many years. It will take some time to learn to manage it well. Be careful about wanting a quick fix or rapid results. Try not to get down on yourself if you don't think you are progressing as fast as you want to.

Change can be scary. Human beings are interesting creatures. Even though we may live with difficulties and want something different, that something different is unknown to us. It is frightening. What we know well is the difficulties. Oftentimes, we tend to gravitate toward what we know, even if it is something undesirable, rather than choose to face the unknown.

Did I suggest "Be patient with yourself"? Some of the activities that lie ahead will be frustrating; some will require some time. There may be moments when you want to put this workbook down and walk away. That's okay! If you find yourself getting too frustrated, take a break. Don't do too many things at once. Pace yourself. Take it slow. You'll get there!

CHAPTER 6

Monitoring Your Mood

In this chapter, I offer several charts for monitoring your mood, your social interactions, daily rhythms, stress, sleep, and exercise. Recall from my discussion about the causes of cyclothymic symptoms that problems in these areas can put you at risk for experiencing difficulties. While I focus on monitoring aspects of your life in this chapter, upcoming chapters will focus more on strategies for you to adopt as you wish. You can record the effects of those strategies with the charts you will find here.

GOOD REASONS FOR KEEPING CHARTS

If you have ever participated in counseling or therapy, you may know that it is common for therapists to assign homework for their clients to complete between sessions. Indeed, this gives people insight into their struggles and the opportunity to practice strategies outside of the therapist's office, in the real world, where it really counts.

To make these charting activities beneficial for you, it is important that you try to buy into the reasoning behind doing them. The following are some very good reasons for you to monitor aspects of your life through charting.

- It can give you the opportunity to learn much more about how your illness affects you. Charting allows you to see for yourself what kinds of variability you have in your mood and identify patterns over time.

- It can help you learn your red flags, or warnings that tend to signal increased problems. This allows you to head off difficulties or prevent symptoms before they get out of hand.

- It can help you monitor the extent to which what you are doing for yourself is helpful. Because progress is often slow and gradual, it can be difficult to detect when things are improving. Keeping charts gives you tangible evidence that what you are doing is actually having an effect.

- It helps you implement changes and practice your strategies regularly. It can help motivate you to keep a consistent routine by filling out your chart at the same time each day. It is a good reminder of what you are trying to accomplish.

- If you are receiving counseling, it can enhance the progress you make in therapy. It can also help your therapist or doctor to understand the nature of your illness when addressing goals for counseling or prescribing medication.

- It can allow you to gain control over something that has likely felt very much out of control.

COMMON OBSTACLES TO KEEPING CHARTS

Whether it is in therapy or with self-help workbooks such as this, it isn't uncommon for people to have some difficulty completing activities for a variety of reasons. Below I have offered common things people say about the problems they have in doing the kind of work you will encounter in this and upcoming chapters. I have also offered some things to think about if you find yourself struggling.

"It's too much to do. It takes too long. It's too complicated."

Whenever you start doing something new, it can seem overwhelming until you get used to it. You might remember your first day on a new job. Things probably seemed a bit complicated at first. After a time, however, you were likely doing tasks more easily, forgetting that they once seemed difficult. With more time and practice, you probably had to think less about how to do things. Instead, you did them rather routinely, with more skill and effectiveness.

Doing these self-help activities will be a lot like that first day on the job. Things will seem hard at first. It will feel like a lot to keep track of. With some time and practice, however, these activities will seem second nature. Once you get the hang of it, you can expect to spend between ten and fifteen minutes each day on charting. Eventually, you will integrate some of the techniques into your life in such a natural way that you hardly notice you are even using "strategies" anymore.

Try to be patient with yourself, letting yourself accept that these tasks are indeed difficult in the beginning. Give yourself several weeks or more before you conclude they are too much to do. Before you came across this workbook, were the things you were doing for yourself working well? Were they improving your life? If not, then give yourself a good chance to do something that may give you what you want.

"Doing it reminds me of all my problems."

Has avoiding problems really worked well for you in the long run? The tougher your struggles are, the harder they are to face head-on. Avoiding problems has never been an effective way to solve them. Doing so only serves to let the problems become more embedded in your life. Facing them is the only way to begin managing them.

Yes, it may be painful at first to face your illness and the struggles it has caused for you. However, addressing these things in a straightforward manner will help you feel more in control, give you more self-confidence, offer a sense of achievement, and improve practical aspects of your life. Are these things worth it to you?

"I don't believe it will help."

Some of the things you will do in the remainder of this workbook can seem deceptively simple. It is easy to dismiss such things very quickly. However, remember that these activities are based upon research about what is effective in treating mood disorders. What have you got to lose?

"I've tried that technique before, and it didn't work."

Most of the time, when people say this, one of several things has actually taken place. One, the technique was not really done properly. It may have been done poorly or without proper instruction. Two, the technique was not practiced or used long enough to work. It was abandoned prematurely. Three, the technique was not practiced enough before it was tested in a critical moment. Techniques are skills that must be practiced, much like learning to ride a bike. You cannot go from being able to stay steady on two wheels to racing competitively in a short span of time.

"It's not helping quickly enough."

These days, people are very used to quick fixes and easy solutions, and often expect nothing less. This expectation may be reasonable in many situations. However, when it comes to something as complicated as a mood disorder, such expectations are often inappropriate. They can lead to disappointment and frustration. In short, there are no quick fixes for cyclothymia.

Anything you have been struggling with for a long time will take some more time to remedy. You have likely been coping with your symptoms for years, experiencing many difficulties along the way. It will take a little while for you to have some good results. It's kind of like those fad diets that don't really have any lasting effect. You can lose some weight in the short run, but it always comes back. Sometimes you gain even more weight than you lost. The best way to really lose weight is to maintain a steady routine of proper diet and exercise over a long period of time. It may take a lot longer to lose weight, but the results are much more stable and long lasting. Similarly, the activities you will do here will take time to be beneficial to you. The changes that can happen over time are much more valuable than any short-term quick fixes will ever be.

"I forget to do it."

Incorporating a new routine in your life does take some time. You may forget to fill out a chart once in a while at first. After a time, however, charting can become a habit. Try doing it at the same time each day. Pick a time when you can arrange to have some privacy with no distractions. Allow sufficient time so you won't feel rushed and can be sure to do the exercises properly.

Another suggestion is to pair your charting with an existing habit. Some people find it convenient to do their charts for the previous day while they are having breakfast in the morning. Other people prefer doing them in the evening just before going to bed. So, you could do your charts while having coffee, during a regular break in the day, after watching the evening news, before turning the lights off for bed, or with any other daily habit.

You might also put your charts and other materials in a place where you have easy access to them. You could carry them in a purse, notebook, briefcase, or book bag that you have with you frequently. If you see your materials regularly, you will be reminded frequently about doing them. You could also put them out in a place at home where you see them easily. Be careful about tucking them away in a drawer, leaving them on a shelf, or otherwise putting them where they are easily forgotten.

"I have trouble with motivation."

You don't have to feel motivated to do your charts. Just do them! I know that may sound a bit harsh, but there is some truth to it. You should expect that you won't feel motivated each time you sit down to complete your charts. In fact, sometimes you'll think it's just a hassle. However, when you see your efforts paying off, when you experience the rewards of your work , you will feel better about a number of things, including your motivation. Some of the suggestions I have made above about remembering to do your charts can help with motivation as well.

"I don't want to have to do this forever."

I hope you haven't assumed that you will have to do these activities for the rest of your life, because that isn't the case at all. You will learn a lot about yourself by keeping these charts. You will also learn what works well for you and what does not. When you become adept at noticing these things, you'll find you won't have to lean on your charting nearly as much. You will catch yourself noticing your red flags sooner, you'll implement preventive strategies without much thought, you'll recognize when your daily rhythm is getting off, and so forth. You'll know when you can put your charts aside and when you might need to pick them up for review again.

AN OVERVIEW OF THE CHARTS

I hope you are now considering the idea that keeping charts may be useful for you and letting any negative thoughts about charting fall by the wayside. In this chapter, I provide instructions for using three different charts:

Mood Chart. This is where you will rate and record your daily moods, the amount and level of stress you experienced, the amount of sleep you got the night before, whether you took your medications as prescribed, your alcohol or drug use, and whether you exercised.

Rhythm Chart. This chart is a little more involved. You will record when you did certain daily routines and your level of involvement with other people. You will also calculate a daily rhythm score.

Monthly Mood and Rhythm Chart. This chart is a tool for helping you recognize patterns in mood, stress, sleep, and daily rhythms—all things that can influence cyclothymic symptoms. You will transfer your scores from your Mood Chart and your Rhythm Chart to this one, giving you a visual representation of some important factors.

CHARTING YOUR MOOD SWINGS

Figure 6.1 is an example of a Mood Chart for Marcus. Notice that this chart covers February 8 through 14, and it is the second week Marcus has been keeping a Mood Chart. He filled in this basic information, including the dates corresponding to the days of the week.

Down the left side of the chart, you see labels in bold for the main topics he rated, including mood, stress, sleep, medications, alcohol and drugs, and exercise. Mood is broken down into several areas: depression, hypomania, irritability, and anxiety. While I have discussed issues of depression and hypomania, irritability and anxiety are valuable moods to rate as well since they can often be precursors to more serious problems with mood. So, you want to be sure to rate those, too.

Making Ratings

At the end of each day, arrange to have about ten minutes of quiet, undisturbed time so you can fill in your charts. It works much better if you spend a little time each day on this activity rather than try to catch up at the end of the week. If you wait, your information will be much less accurate and you will be more likely to get frustrated with having to recall so many ratings. Excessive frustration could make you feel like giving up before you have a chance to see whether these activities can be useful to you.

On Marcus's Mood Chart, notice the rating system at the top. When you rate your experiences on your own chart, use this scale by choosing a number between 0 (none at all) and 10 (extreme amount). If you fluctuate throughout the day on your rating, go ahead and give yourself an average rating for the day. As you think about how to choose a rating, it may be helpful to think in terms of your previous experiences with the particular factor. With regard to depression, for instance, a full 10 could be equivalent to the worst, most difficult experience you have ever had with depressive symptoms: a time when you really struggled with down or depressed mood; impairment in your daily functioning; problems with energy, sleep, concentration; or other depressive symptoms like those listed in the "Depression and Hypomania" section of chapter 1. A rating of 0 would be a complete absence of these symptoms, while a 5 would be halfway in between. As you did with your 10 rating, think of a past experience that would reflect a midpoint rating of 5 so that you will have a consistent frame of reference for rating future experiences with depression. Marcus rated his depressive symptoms for Sunday, February 8 as a 5.

For hypomanic mood, refer again to the "Depression and Hypomania" section of chapter 1 to review those symptoms. As with your depression ratings, consider your most *extreme* experience with hypomania as rating a 10. This may not be the most *distressing* experience you have had with hypomania (remember that many people are not necessarily distressed by hypomanic symptoms). A rating of 0 signifies no symptoms of hypomania, and something in the middle rates a 5. Again, think of a specific experience with hypomania that reflects a 5 so you will have a reference point for future ratings. Marcus rated his hypomanic symptoms for the day on the lower end, giving himself a 3.

For your ratings of irritability and anxiety, here are some definitions to consider:

Irritability: Being easily annoyed, bothered, or frustrated; having a bad temper; being snappy or disagreeable; reacting to situations and people in an overly sensitive manner. Feelings of irritability can be internal (kept inside) or external (acted upon).

Anxiety: Feeling uneasy, distressed, restless, apprehensive, or fearful about things that have not yet happened or about threats that may be unclear. There is frequently a component of worry or great concern that contributes to feelings of distress or discomfort.

For your ratings of irritability, anxiety, and stress, do what you did with depression and hypomania. Think of specific situations in which you felt a 10 (extreme amount) and a 5 (moderate amount) to help you scale your ratings. Under your stress rating, include a brief statement about the nature of the stress you have been experiencing. On Marcus's chart, you can see that he felt increasingly stressed over the week as he prepared for a presentation at work that took place on Thursday, February 12.

For the sleep item, simply record the total hours of sleep you got the night before. Please note that the number of hours you record for sleep is on a different kind of scale than the other topics. While high ratings on other topics suggest greater difficulties, the number of hours you sleep does not necessarily work this way. In some cases, too little sleep will indicate a problem. At other times, too much sleep may be a problem. This is what you will be trying to find out.

For the medication item, if you are taking a prescription, indicate whether you took it as directed that day. Marcus is not on medication, so he put "n/a" for this item across the week. If you drank alcohol, put the type and number of drinks. If you did drugs, put the type and amount. Record some notes about what led to your alcohol or drug use. Marcus recorded his alcohol and drug use, noting that he used them because he felt tense and wanted to relax.

In the exercise row, record how well you stayed with your exercise plan. Marcus has a goal to work out four days a week, on Sundays, Tuesdays, Thursdays, and Saturdays. He met his goal well on Sunday (0) and Saturday (2) but not on Tuesday (10) and Thursday (8). I will encourage you to consider creating an exercise plan in chapter 8. Note that the scale for this item may seem intuitively backward. A rating of 10 for exercise means you did not stick with your plan at all, while a 0 means that you did it exactly as planned. This is to reflect that higher scores on all your ratings (except sleep) will indicate problems or difficulties, while lower scores suggest that things are going well.

And finally, in the bottom row, you will write a few comments about things that happened that day, your reaction to events, or other notes about things that may affect your mood, daily activities, interactions with other people, and so forth. These notes will help cue you to what has happened throughout the week that may be related to certain ratings or scores on all your charts. It's hard to remember details like this unless you write them down.

Following Marcus's Mood Chart is a blank Mood Chart (exercise 6.1) for you to use. Make eight to twelve photocopies of this chart to start you off for a few months. (This chart is also available online at www.CyclothymiaWorkbook.com.) Use one copy of this chart to practice making your ratings for today. Make sure these instructions are clear to you before moving on. I will discuss how to interpret this chart and what to do with your ratings when we get to the Monthly Mood and Rhythm Chart.

Mood Chart

Name: _____Marcus_____   Month: _____February_____   Week: _____2_____

At the same time each day, fill in this week's chart. For the mood and stress ratings, use the scale at the top of the chart. Make notes in the spaces provided to describe the nature of your stress, the situation around alcohol or drug use, and other aspects of the day.

Base your ratings below on a scale from 0–10:   0 = None at all;   5 = Moderate amount;   10 = Extreme amount

		Sun 8	Mon 9	Tues 10	Wed 11	Thurs 12	Fri 13	Sat 14
Mood Ratings	Depression (0–10)	5	6	6	5	2	3	2
	Hypomania (0–10)	3	3	3	6	6	7	9
	Irritability (0–10)	3	3	7	8	8	7	6
	Anxiety (0–10)	0	2	4	5	5	0	0
Stress Rating	Stress (0–10)	3	5	7	7	8	4	3
	Notes		prepare for presentation	prepare for presentation	prepare for presentation	prepare for presentation		
Sleep	How many hours of sleep did you get?	8	7	7	5	4	5	4
Meds	Medications taken as prescribed? (yes/no)	n/a	n/a	n/a	n/a	n/a	n/a	n/a
Alcohol, Drugs	Number of drinks; type and amount of drug(s)	0	0	0	3 beers	3 beers	0	6 drinks 2 cocaine
	Notes				feeling tense, want to relax	tough day, need to relax		deserve to relax
Exercise	How well did you stick to your exercise plan? 0 = Right on target 5 = Moderately well 10 = Not at all	0	n/a	10	n/a	8	n/a	2
Daily Notes	Make notes about things that impact your mood, daily activities, interactions with others, etc.	lunch with sister and her husband	worked on presentation with group	argued w/group about project direction	fought w/group members; have to fix program by tomorrow	presentation went fine, irritated with coworkers, snappy	couldn't sleep, irritated w/coworkers, snapped at boss	couldn't sleep, woke up early, wired

Figure 6.1 Marcus's Mood Chart

EXERCISE 6.1 MOOD CHART

Name: _____   Month: _____   Week: _____

At the same time each day, fill in this week's chart. For the mood and stress ratings, use the scale at the top of the chart. Make notes in the spaces provided to describe the nature of your stress, the situation around alcohol or drug use, and other aspects of the day.

Base your ratings below on a scale from 0–10:   0 = None at all;   5 = Moderate amount;   10 = Extreme amount

		Sun	Mon	Tues	Wed	Thurs	Fri	Sat
Mood Ratings	Depression (0–10)							
	Hypomania (0–10)							
	Irritability (0–10)							
	Anxiety (0–10)							
Stress Rating	Stress (0–10)							
	Notes							
Sleep	How many hours of sleep did you get?							
Meds	Medications taken as prescribed? (yes/no)							
Alcohol, Drugs	Number of drinks; type and amount of drug(s)							
	Notes							
Exercise	How well did you stick to your exercise plan? 0 = Right on target 5 = Moderately well 10 = Not at all							
Daily Notes	Make notes about things that impact your mood, daily activities, interactions with others, etc.							

CHARTING YOUR DAILY RHYTHMS AND SOCIAL INTERACTIONS

You may recall the discussion of interpersonal and social rhythm therapy (IPSRT) from chapter 5, when I talked about treatments for bipolar disorder. This approach emphasizes the importance of maintaining stable daily routines, since disruptions in these routines can upset your circadian rhythm and trigger mood problems. The IPSRT approach uses the social rhythm metric for monitoring daily activities.

In a moment I will talk about using a modified version of this metric, the Rhythm Chart. First, take a moment to look at another of Marcus's charts, the Average Time of Activity Chart (figure 6.2). This chart is generally filled out just once, unless you have significant changes in your home, school, or work schedule. You will use it to compare with your Rhythm Chart, which you will fill out daily. Note that Marcus carefully recorded the average time he engages in seventeen different activities each day of the week. He works during the week at a full-time job, so his average times look similar on Monday through Friday.

Following Marcus's chart is a blank Average Time of Activity Chart (exercise 6.2) for you to fill in with your own scheduled times. If you need more copies, make a photocopy of this chart or retrieve one from www.CyclothymiaWorkbook.com. Think about your daily schedule and fill in the chart with the typical time you engage in each of the seventeen activities—or, if your schedule tends to be irregular, with the time you believe you need to do them in order to maintain a consistent, healthy daily rhythm. You may find it useful to make modifications in an irregular schedule to create daily consistency and keep your circadian rhythm on track. It is important to have similarly scheduled routines each day, including over the weekend. Any significant deviation from your regular routines on the weekends—such as staying out very late or getting excessive amounts of sleep—can throw off your circadian rhythm, even though it may seem like an enjoyable thing to do.

AVERAGE TIME OF ACTIVITY

Name: _____ *Marcus*

In the chart below, indicate the average time you typically start each activity, or the time you believe you need to start it in order to maintain a good, healthy daily rhythm. Be sure to include a.m. or p.m. For example, "Monday—Out of bed—7:00 A.M." You will use these times to determine your daily rhythm ratings on your Rhythm Chart (Exercise 6.3).

Activity	Sunday	Monday	Tuesday	Wednesday	Thursday	Friday	Saturday
Out of bed	9:00 A.M.	6:00 A.M.	6:00 A.M.	6:00 A.M.	6:00 A.M.	6:00 A.M.	9:00 A.M.
First contact (in person or by phone) with another person	12:30 A.M.	8:00 A.M.	8:00 A.M.	8:00 A.M.	8:00 A.M.	8:00 A.M.	12:30 A.M.
Have morning beverage	9:30 A.M.	6:30–7 A.M.	6:30–7 A.M.	6:30–7 A.M.	6:30–7 A.M.	6:30–7 A.M.	9:30 A.M.
Have breakfast	10:00 A.M.	6:30–7 A.M.	6:30–7 A.M.	6:30–7 A.M.	6:30–7 A.M.	6:30–7 A.M.	10:00 A.M..
Go outside for the first time	12–1:00 P.M.	7:00 A.M.	7:00 A.M.	7:00 A.M.	7:00 A.M.	7:00 A.M.	12–1:00 P.M.
Start work, school, housework, volunteer activities, child/family care	12:30 P.M.	8:00 A.M.	8:00 A.M.	8:00 A.M.	8:00 A.M.	8:00 A.M.	12:30 P.M.
Have lunch	1:00 P.M.	12:00 P.M.	12:00 P.M.	12:00 P.M.	12:00 P.M.	12:00 P.M.	1:00 P.M.
Take an afternoon nap	2–3:00 P.M.	n/a	n/a	n/a	n/a	n/a	
Have dinner	6–7:00 P.M.	7:00 P.M.	7:00 P.M.	7:00 P.M.	7:00 P.M.	7–8:00 P.M.	6–7:00 P.M.
Physical exercise	anytime	n/a	6:30-7:00	n/a	6:30-7:00	n/a	anytime
Have an evening snack/drink	8–11:30 P.M.	8–11:30 P.M.	8–11:30 P.M.	8–11:30 P.M.	8–11:30 P.M.	8–11:30 P.M.	8–11:30 P.M.
Watch evening TV news	10:00 P.M.	10:00 P.M.	10:00 P.M.	10:00 P.M.	10:00 P.M.		
Watch another TV program	8–11:00 P.M.	8–11:00 P.M.	8–11:00 P.M.	8–11:00 P.M.	8–11:00 P.M.		
Activity A	2–4:00 P.M.	7–10 P.M.	7–10 P.M.	7–10 P.M.	7–10 P.M.	6–10:00 P.M.	2–4:00 P.M.
Activity B							6–10:00 P.M.
Return home (last time)	8–9:00 P.M.	6–9:00 P.M.	6–9:00 P.M.	6–9:00 P.M.	6–9:00 P.M.	10–12:00 P.M.	10–12:00 P.M.
Go to bed	10–11:00 P.M.	10–11:00 P.M.	10–11:00 P.M.	10–11:00 P.M.	10–11:00 P.M.	11P.M.–1A.M.	11P.M.–1A.M.

A social rhythm chart. Adapted by permission of Ellen Frank from Monk et al. 1991.

Figure 6.2 Marcus's Average Time of Activity

EXERCISE 6.2 AVERAGE TIME OF ACTIVITY

Name: _____

In the chart below, indicate the average time you typically start each activity, or the time you believe you need to start it in order to maintain a good, healthy daily rhythm. Be sure to include a.m. or p.m. For example, "Monday—Out of bed—7:00 A.M." You will use these times to determine your daily rhythm ratings on your Rhythm Chart (Exercise 6.3).

Activity	Sunday	Monday	Tuesday	Wednesday	Thursday	Friday	Saturday
Out of bed							
First contact (in person or by phone) with another person							
Have morning beverage							
Have breakfast							
Go outside for the first time							
Start work, school, housework, volunteer activities, child/family care							
Have lunch							
Take an afternoon nap							
Have dinner							
Physical exercise							
Have an evening snack/drink							
Watch evening TV news							
Watch another TV program							
Activity A							
Activity B							
Return home (last time)							
Go to bed							

A social rhythm chart. Adapted by permission of Ellen Frank from Monk et al. 1991.

Using a Rhythm Chart

Now I'll talk about how to use a Rhythm Chart. Figure 6.3a is a portion of a Rhythm Chart that Marcus has filled out. At first glance, you'll notice that some of it looks familiar. You see the seventeen daily activities listed down the left side. These are common activities that many people have in their daily routines. They are also activities related to maintaining your circadian rhythm. While the list of activities may seem like a natural order of progression throughout the day, you should know that you do not need to complete them in the order they are shown here.

If you look across the top of the chart in the gray shaded area, you'll see that Marcus has filled in the numbered day of the month ("8"). Just below that you see three shaded columns. The first is labeled "Check If Did *Not* Do." You will check this column next to an activity only if it something that you *didn't* do during the day. If you completed the activity, leave the space blank. On Sunday, Marcus didn't watch the evening TV news, but he did everything else on his schedule.

For "People Present": 0 = You were alone 1 = With your spouse/partner 2 = With your children 3 = With other relatives 4 = With other(s) a = Just present b = Actively involved **Activity**	Sun 8 . Check if did *not* do	Clock Time (A.M./P.M.)	People Present	Mon 9 . Check if did *not* do	Clock Time (A.M./P.M.)	People Present
Out of bed		9 A.M.	0			
First contact (in person or by phone) with another person		1 P.M.	3b			
Have morning beverage		10 A.M.	0			
Have breakfast		10 A.M.	0			
Go outside for the first time		12 P.M.	0			
Start work, school, family/child care, volunteer activities, housework		12 P.M.	4a			
Have lunch		1 P.M.	3b			
Take an afternoon nap		2 P.M.	0			
Have dinner		6 P.M.	4b			
Physical exercise		3 P.M.	4a			
Have an evening snack/drink		8 P.M.	4b			
Watch evening TV news	✓					
Watch another TV program		9 P.M.	0			
Activity		date	4b			
Return home (last time)		9 P.M.	0			
Go to bed		10 P.M.	0			

Daily Rhythm Score: ____1____   _____

A social rhythm chart. Adapted by permission of Ellen Frank from Monk et al. 1991.

Figure 6.3a Marcus's Rhythm Chart

The second shaded column is labeled "Clock Time (a.m./p.m.)." In the space provided for each activity, write in the time that you started doing it. You may want to be more precise than Marcus and indicate whether your activity started on the quarter hour or half hour. These are the times that you will compare with your Average Time of Activity Chart later on.

Filling in the "People Present" column will be slightly more challenging at first, but you'll get used to it. Take a look at the top left of the chart and notice that a key is provided for you. If you were alone during that activity, you will record a 0. If you were with other people during your activity, then select the description (1–4) that characterizes that person's relationship to you. If you were involved with people from more than one category (for example, partner and child), you need only record one of them. Also indicate how involved you were with that person by choosing "a" (just present) or "b" (actively involved). For instance, notice on Marcus's chart the activity "Have lunch." If you follow across to the right, you see he wrote in "3b." It turns out that Marcus had an enjoyable lunch with his sister and her husband. So, he was "with other relatives" (3), and he was "actively involved" (b) with them. Figure 6.3b is Marcus's full Rhythm Chart.

It is useful to record "People Present" on your Rhythm Chart for at least two reasons. One, many activities you do are dependent on having someone to do them with; otherwise they might not occur at all. Two, having someone to share an activity with can affect how much you enjoy doing it. When people feel depressed, they may withdraw, avoiding people in general. However, being involved with people can help the depression from becoming worse, or help lift a depression that already exists. Conversely, people experiencing hypomania may become overinvolved with others in ways that are problematic. Arguments, conflicts, sexual indiscretions, and the like are not uncommon. It can be telling to see the extent to which involvement with others plays a role for you in maintaining daily rhythms.

Your Daily Rhythm Score

At the bottom of Marcus's Rhythm Chart for Sunday, February 8, he has recorded a daily rhythm score of 1. Here is how you determine this score: Give yourself one point for each activity you did *not* do (count the check marks). Give yourself another point for each activity that you did not start within forty-five minutes of the time you indicated on your Average Time of Activity Chart. You might circle the ones that apply so you can simply count them. Also, if you were actively involved with only one person during the day, give yourself one point; if you were not actively involved with anyone, give yourself two points. Instructions for calculating this score are summarized on your blank chart for your reference.

On Marcus's chart for Sunday, he did not do one activity, "Watch evening TV news." That's one point. If you compare times on his Average Time of Activity Chart (figure 6.2) with the ones he recorded on his Rhythm Chart, you'll see that he actually did start them all within forty-five minutes of his scheduled time. He receives no extra points here, so he still has only one point. Marcus also had active involvement with others on five occasions for this day. Again, he received no extra points. His total score for Sunday, February 8 is 1 point.

In figure 6.3c, I have used Marcus's chart as an example of how to calculate your daily rhythm score. I have circled items on Wednesday and Thursday that should be given one point. So that you'll have some practice, take a pencil and circle items on Friday and Saturday that should also receive points. See if you can find a score of 6 for Friday and 9 for Saturday.

The higher your daily rhythm score, the more you are deviating from your normal circadian rhythm. The more this happens, the more you may be at risk for developing increased problems with mood. If you look at Marcus's full Rhythm Chart (figure 6.3b), you'll see his daily rhythm score increasing over the week. You may recall from his Mood Chart that he was feeling stressed about a presentation. At a glance, you may notice more check marks, meaning that he did not do some important daily activities. Also, the times he started his activities began to deviate as the week progressed. These are just a few observations. We'll take a closer look at how to interpret scores in the next section.

Make eight to twelve photocopies of the blank Rhythm Chart (exercise 6.3; this chart is also available online at www.CyclothymiaWorkbook.com) and take a few moments to record information about your day today. If you find yourself struggling with some aspect of filling out your own chart, you might review some of the information above.

RHYTHM CHART

Name: __Marcus__   Month: __February__   Week: __2__

At the same time each day, fill in the chart below. For "People Present" use the rating system at the top left to record who you were with and their involvement with you. Calculate your "Daily Rhythm Score" at the bottom: give yourself 1 point for each activity you did NOT do, and ones that were NOT started within 45 minutes of your "Average Time." Give yourself 1 point if you were only "Actively Involved" with one person; two points if not "Actively Involved" with anyone.

For "People Present":
0 = You were alone
1 = With your spouse/partner
2 = With your children
3 = With other relatives
4 = With other(s)

a = Just present
b = Actively involved

Activity	Sun 8 — Did not do	Clock Time	People Present	Mon 9 — Did not do	Clock Time	People Present	Tues 10 — Did not do	Clock Time	People Present	Wed 11 — Did not do	Clock Time	People Present	Thurs 12 — Did not do	Clock Time	People Present	Fri 13 — Did not do	Clock Time	People Present	Sat 14 — Did not do	Clock Time	People Present
Out of bed		9 A.M.	0		6 A.M.	0		6 A.M.	0		7 A.M.	0		7 A.M.	0		7 A.M.	0		6 A.M.	0
First contact (in person or by phone) with another person		1 P.M.	3b		8 A.M.	4b		8 A.M.	4b		8:30 A.M.	4b		8:30 A.M.	4b		9 A.M.	4b		7 A.M.	4b
Have morning beverage		10 A.M.	0		6:30 A.M.	0		6:30 A.M.	0	✓			✓				7:30 A.M.	0		6:15 A.M.	0
Have breakfast		10 A.M.	0		6:30 A.M.	0		6:30 A.M.	0	✓			✓			✓			✓		
Go outside for the first time		12 P.M.	0		7 A.M.	0		7 A.M.	0		7:30 A.M.	0		7:30 A.M.	0		8 A.M.	0		6:30 A.M.	0
Start work, school, family/child care, volunteer activities, housework		12 P.M.	4a		8 A.M.	4a		8 A.M.	4a		8:30 A.M.	4a		8:30 A.M.	4a		9 A.M.	4a		7 A.M.	4a
Have lunch		1 P.M.	3b		12 P.M.	4b		12 P.M.	4b		12 P.M.	4b		12 P.M.	4b		12 P.M.	4b		1 P.M.	3b
Take an afternoon nap		2 P.M.	0																		
Have dinner		6 P.M.	4b		7 P.M.	0		7 P.M.	0		7 P.M.	0		7 P.M.	4b		7 P.M.	4b		8 P.M.	3b
Physical exercise		3 P.M.	4a					✓							7 A.M.	0					7 A.M.	4a
Have an evening snack/drink		8 P.M.	4b		8 P.M.	0		11 P.M.	0		11 P.M.	0		11 P.M.	0		11 P.M.	4b		11 P.M.	4b
Watch evening TV news	✓				10 P.M.	0		10 P.M.	0	✓			✓								
Watch another TV program		9 P.M.	0		8 P.M.	0		12 P.M.	0		12 P.M.	0		12 P.M.	0							
Activity		date	4b		project	0		project	0		project	0		coworker	4b		coworker	4b		party	4b
Return home (last time)		9 P.M.	0		6 P.M.	0		6 P.M.	0		6 P.M.	0		10 P.M.	0		1 A.M.	0		4 A.M.	0
Go to bed		10 P.M.	0		11 P.M.	0		2 A.M.	0		3 A.M.	0		2 A.M.	0		12a	0		4 A.M.	4
Daily Rhythm Score:	**1**			**0**			**3**			**6**			**7**			**6**			**9**		

A social rhythm chart. Adapted by permission of Ellen Frank from Monk et al. 1991.

Figure 6.3b Marcus's Rhythm Chart

For "People Present":
  0 = You were alone
  1 = With your spouse/partner
  2 = With your children
  3 = With other relatives
  4 = With other(s)

  a = Just present
  b = Actively involved

Activity	Wed 11 Check if did not do	Clock Time (A.M./P.M.)	People Present	Thurs 12 Check if did not do	Clock Time (A.M./P.M.)	People Present	Fri 13 Check if did not do	Clock Time (A.M./P.M.)	People Present	Sat 14 Check if did not do	Clock Time (A.M./P.M.)	People Present
Out of bed		7 A.M.	0		7 A.M.	0		7 A.M.	0		6 A.M.	0
First contact (in person or by phone) with another person		8:30 A.M.	4b		8:30 A.M.	4b		9 A.M.	4b		7 A.M.	4b
Have morning beverage	✓			✓				7:30 A.M.	0		6:15 A.M.	0
Have breakfast	✓			✓			✓			✓		
Go outside for the first time		7:30 A.M.	0		7:30 A.M.	0		8 A.M.	0		6:30 A.M.	0
Start work, school, family/child care, volunteer activities, housework		8:30 A.M.	4a		8:30 A.M.	4a		9 A.M.	4a		7 A.M.	4a
Have lunch		12 P.M.	4b		12 P.M.	4b		12 P.M.	4b		1 P.M.	3b
Take an afternoon nap												
Have dinner		7 P.M.	0		7 P.M.	4b		7 P.M.	4b		8 P.M.	3b
Physical exercise					7 A.M.	0					7 A.M.	4a
Have an evening snack/drink		11 P.M.	0		11 P.M.	0		11 P.M.	4b		11 P.M.	4b
Watch evening TV news	✓			✓								
Watch another TV program		12 P.M.	0		12 P.M.	0							
Activity		project	0		coworker	4b		coworker	4b		party	4b
Return home (last time)		6 P.M.	0		10 P.M.	0		1 A.M.	0		4 A.M.	0
Go to bed		3 A.M.	0		2 A.M.	0		12a	0		4 A.M.	4

Daily Rhythm Score: ___6___   ___7___   ___6___   ___9___

Figure 6.3c Marcus's Rhythm Chart

A social rhythm chart. Adapted by permission of Ellen Frank from Monk et al. 1991.

EXERCISE 6.3 RHYTHM CHART

Name: _____   Month: _____   Week: _____

At the same time each day, fill in the chart below. For "People Present" use the rating system at the top left to record who you were with and their involvement with you. Calculate your "Daily Rhythm Score" at the bottom: give yourself 1 point for each activity you did NOT do, and ones that were NOT started within 45 minutes of your "Average Time." Give yourself 1 point if you were only "Actively Involved" with one person; two points if not "Actively Involved" with anyone.

For "People Present":
0 = You were alone
1 = With your spouse/partner
2 = With your children
3 = With other relatives
4 = With other(s)

a = Just present
b = Actively involved

Activity	Sun Check if did not do	Sun Clock Time (A.M./P.M.)	Sun People Present	Mon Check if did not do	Mon Clock Time (A.M./P.M.)	Mon People Present	Tues Check if did not do	Tues Clock Time (A.M./P.M.)	Tues People Present	Wed Check if did not do	Wed Clock Time (A.M./P.M.)	Wed People Present	Thurs Check if did not do	Thurs Clock Time (A.M./P.M.)	Thurs People Present	Fri Check if did not do	Fri Clock Time (A.M./P.M.)	Fri People Present	Sat Check if did not do	Sat Clock Time (A.M./P.M.)	Sat People Present
Out of bed																					
First contact (in person or by phone) with another person																					
Have morning beverage																					
Have breakfast																					
Go outside for the first time																					
Start work, school, family/child care, volunteer activities, housework																					
Have lunch																					
Take an afternoon nap																					
Have dinner																					
Physical exercise																					
Have an evening snack/drink																					
Watch evening TV news																					
Watch another TV program																					
Activity																					
Return home (last time)																					
Go to bed																					

Daily Rhythm Score: _____   _____   _____

A social rhythm chart. Adapted by permission of Ellen Frank from Monk et al. 1991.

CHARTING YOUR MONTHLY PROGRESS

At the end of each week, after you have worked hard to record ratings and scores on your Mood Chart and Rhythm Chart, it will be time to put that good work to use. You will have gathered valuable data about your mood states, behaviors, rhythms, interactions with others, and more. You will be ready to plot your data on a chart that will give you a visual representation of your patterns, your red flags, and your progress.

First, I'll talk about how to plot this information, then I'll discuss how to interpret it. To begin, take a look at Marcus's Monthly Mood and Rhythm Chart (figure 6.4). You see a large grid with a scale for ratings down the left side and the days of the month labeled across the bottom. There is also a key at the bottom with six topics. Four of these topics (depression, hypomania, stress, and sleep) are from the Mood Chart, and one (the daily rhythm score) is from the Rhythm Chart. In addition, women should note when they have their menses, since some changes in mood may be influenced by the menstrual cycle. You can do this simply by circling the days of your menses at the bottom of the chart.

For each of the five topics in the key, I suggest that you find a thin colored marker or pencil so you can plot a color-coded graph. This will help you to easily distinguish among the lines that you draw on your chart. In Marcus's graph, I have used a different type of line to represent each topic. When you find your colored markers or pencils, go ahead and draw a short line next to each topic with the color that will represent it so you can remember which color goes with which topic.

You remember that Marcus's sample charts were from his second week of keeping charts, but on this monthly chart, you'll see data for both weeks. I know it seems like a lot to look at, but if you sit with it for a moment, you will be able to make out which line represents which factor. Take a few moments to compare Marcus's charts you have seen with the data points and the lines that connect them. Remember, you'll start on February 8, since those are the charts that we have been looking at.

On Marcus's Mood Chart, you see that on Sunday, February 8 he rated depression as a 5. In order to plot this point, he went to the vertical line at the bottom of the chart that represents the eighth day of the month. Then he went straight up on the chart until he reached the horizontal line that represents the rating of 5. That is where Marcus drew a point for the depression rating for that day. After he did the same thing for the other depression ratings for the week, he connected the dots by drawing lines between them.

Make photocopies of the blank Monthly Mood and Rhythm Chart (exercise 6.4) for your own use. This chart is also available online at www.CyclothymiaWorkbook.com. If you practiced making some ratings on the Mood Chart and Rhythm Chart earlier, go ahead and plot those scores on your Monthly Mood and Rhythm Chart.

Monthly Mood and Rhythm Chart

Month: ___*February*___   Year: ___*2004*___

Each week, plot your ratings for each day below. From your Mood Chart, record your mood and stress ratings and your number of hours of sleep. From your Rhythm Chart, record your daily rhythm score. So that you can easily see patterns, use different colored markers for each topic. If you are a woman, also circle the days of your menses.

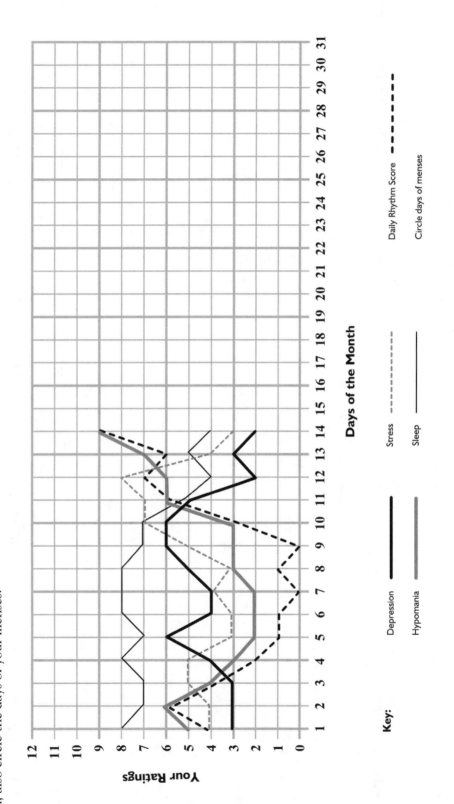

Figure 6.4 Marcus's Monthly Mood and Rhythm Chart

EXERCISE 6.4 MONTHLY MOOD AND RHYTHM CHART

Month: _____   Year: _____

Each week, plot your ratings for each day below. From your Mood Chart, record your mood and stress ratings and your number of hours of sleep. From your Rhythm Chart, record your daily rhythm score. So that you can easily see patterns, use different colored markers for each topic. If you are a woman, also circle the days of your menses.

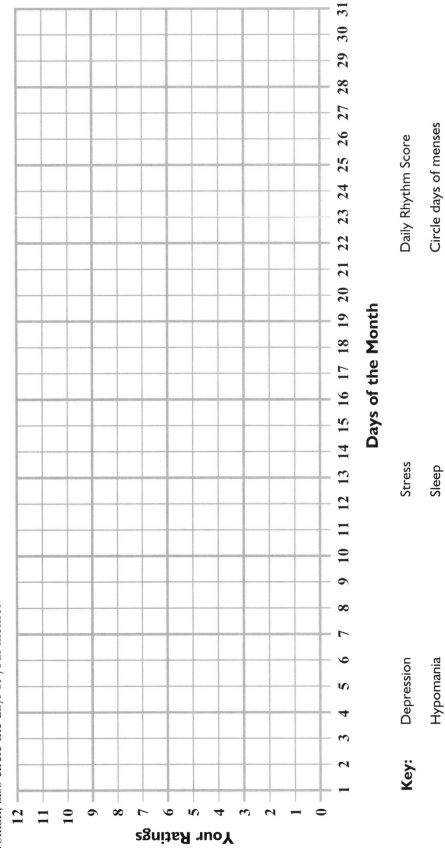

Days of the Month

Key:

Depression	Stress
Hypomania	Sleep
	Daily Rhythm Score
	Circle days of menses

INTERPRETING YOUR CHARTS

There are several ways to interpret your weekly Mood Charts and Rhythm Charts and your Monthly Mood and Rhythm Chart. In general, you will be looking for patterns, red flags for problems, and obstacles to your daily rhythms. While you will likely begin to get a good idea of patterns that affect you after keeping your charts for just a few weeks, you will probably need to keep them for about eight to twelve weeks (two or three months) in order to get some useful, consistent information.

Recall that high ratings on all the factors (except sleep) not only indicate immediate problems but can also signal upcoming difficulties with other factors. Conversely, lower scores (except for sleep) may suggest that things are going well for you. The amount of sleep you record on your charts needs to be interpreted a little differently. Most people do well with seven or eight hours of sleep each night, while more or less sleep can signal some problems. Getting a lot less sleep can indicate problems with depression or hypomania, and sleeping much more might be related to depression.

To interpret the data you have gathered, consider taking the following steps:

1. Start with the big picture or overall view by looking at your Monthly Mood and Rhythm Chart. See if you notice any general trends about the relationships among factors.

2. Once you have drawn some conclusions about these relationships or raised questions for yourself, take a closer look at the weekly charts for more information about specific influences on the main factors from the monthly chart. For instance, notes you made about stress or other daily occurrences can refresh your memory about what happened days or weeks ago and help you clarify things.

3. Dig a little deeper into the other factors on your weekly charts that you did not graph on your monthly chart. This can be particularly useful in helping you learn more about influences on your mood. Digging deeper is also useful if you find it hard to spot red flags or patterns, or if there don't seem to be other clear relationships among the main factors.

I'll demonstrate these steps by reviewing Marcus's charts in some detail. Then I'll guide you as you examine your own charts.

The Big Picture

On Marcus's Monthly Mood and Rhythm Chart (figure 6.4), let's begin by looking at the graphed line representing his depression factor. Marcus started off the month with some consistent days on the low end of the scale, with a small spike on the fifth day of the month. After going down a little bit, his ratings increased again in the early part of the second week but dipped down into the low range toward the end of the two weeks. Marcus's depression ratings, at a glance, are more variable than his hypomania ratings. Also, it appears that for at least these two weeks, his depression and hypomania had an *inverse relationship*. That is, when depression increased, hypomania decreased, and when depression decreased, hypomania increased. While Marcus experienced some midrange depression during this two-week period, he did not report having significant difficulties with this factor.

Marcus's hypomania ratings started at the middle of the range at the beginning of the month, then dropped until the beginning of the second week. His ratings jumped up quickly beginning on the eleventh day and stayed high until the end of the week. As you may recall, and as you can see from his stress ratings, Marcus had an important presentation at work toward the end of the second week. It is interesting to note that his stress and hypomania ratings seem to mirror each other until the very end of the two weeks. Even though his stress level diminished after he completed his presentation, his hypomania rating stayed quite high. Perhaps stress is an important red flag for Marcus. As his stress level increases, so may his hypomania. It might also be that when stress drives his hypomania to a certain level, the hypomania may continue despite the stress being reduced. Or perhaps he does not tend to be as focused on stress once the highs of hypomania kick in, causing him to make lower stress ratings. These are questions to be addressed with data from more charts over time.

Marcus's stress ratings seemed fairly mild until a few days into the second week. His stress increased sharply as the date of the presentation at work approached, then took a dive on the last two days of the week. Stress appeared to be an important factor for Marcus. As it increased, several other factors increased as well. Hypomania and his daily rhythm score increased, while sleep decreased. Stress ratings increased *before* changes in these other factors happened, making stress a big red flag for Marcus.

Whether problems with less sleep caused difficulties with daily rhythm scores and hypomania or whether it is a by-product of these other factors remains to be seen. More weekly and monthly charts might provide some clearer answers. Nevertheless, there appears to be some relationship here.

Marcus's daily rhythm scores at the beginning of the month were moderately high, but they dropped nicely for a number of days. Marcus maintained his daily activities and interpersonal interactions quite well. However, as the second week progressed, his scores jumped up quickly and stayed high through the end of the week. This was quite apparent after the scores were plotted on his monthly chart.

A Closer Look

Now that we have looked at the big picture, it's time to look a bit more closely at some of the details that affected the trends on the monthly chart by examining Marcus's weekly charts. A sharp increase in daily rhythm scores like the one I was just talking about can happen for a variety of reasons. On Marcus's Rhythm Chart (figure 6.3b), look at the specific items that contributed to his high scores. On Wednesday through Friday, Marcus got up later than usual in the morning. He also missed his morning breakfast and beverage several times and got in to work late on Friday. Marcus also stayed up much later than usual, reducing the amount of sleep he got.

It seems that for Marcus, a disruption in his daily rhythm can cause a chain reaction. Staying up late one night leads to less sleep and starting the next day later, which leads to missing exercise workouts and other routine activities like having breakfast and coffee. He might not be able to fall asleep as easily the next night, or he might feel energized to do other things that delay when he gets home and goes to bed. Marcus's notes on his Mood Chart indicate that he stayed up very late at night on purpose in order to fix some programming for his presentation.

Some people can get into the mind-set that once they've "blown it," they might as well keep going. Perhaps this is what happened for Marcus toward the end of the week. It can be disheartening to see your daily rhythm scores climb, but it's important to take a step back and consider this in a different way. With cyclothymia, you *will* occasionally have high scores. Allow yourself to accept this fact. That's what cyclothymia is all about. In a way, high scores can be useful, because this is where you will gain information about how to manage your illness. If you didn't have some high scores from time to time, you wouldn't be able to learn about your patterns and red flags.

Dig a Little Deeper

There are a number of factors from the Mood Chart that were not graphed on the Monthly Mood and Rhythm Chart simply because it would get too confusing to have so many lines there. Nevertheless, these are important factors that can have powerful influences on some of the ones I have addressed already.

For Marcus, irritability appears to play a role in his difficulties this week. If you look at the numerical ratings he gave to irritability on his Mood Chart (figure 6.1), you notice that they spike quickly beginning on Tuesday. In fact, irritability jumped up more quickly than hypomania. Irritability could also be an important red flag for Marcus. Anxiety ratings moved up just a bit midweek but went down again at the end of the week. With what transpired this week, anxiety may not be as significant as some other factors.

With regard to alcohol and drug use, you see that Marcus had a few beers for the first time on Wednesday night. What is interesting about this is the note that he made about it. Marcus wrote that he had some beers because he felt tense and wanted to relax. Could it be that other methods of stress reduction, such as exercise, would have been more useful to Marcus? Did having some beers affect his ability to sleep, thereby contributing to the chain reaction? Marcus had more drinks on Saturday and used cocaine twice that evening at a party. In his notes for Saturday, he wrote that he deserved to relax. For many people, experiencing the hypomanic symptoms of cyclothymia can lead to feeling uninhibited about drug and alcohol use. It can be easier to give yourself permission to use, while you might not make that decision if you weren't feeling hypomanic. It goes without saying that increased drug and alcohol use can cause significant problems with regard to mood, conflicts with others, getting arrested for driving under the influence or drug possession, health concerns, and so forth.

Marcus also made notes on his Mood Chart about daily occurrences related to feeling stressed. He wrote about experiencing stress around having to prepare for a presentation at work. He made this note four days in a row, including the day of the presentation, and his stress ratings increased significantly as the week progressed. In his daily notes, Marcus wrote about frustrations with his group and the project on which they were working. He also noted that he got into some conflicts with people, even snapping at his boss on Friday. It might be helpful to know which Marcus found more stressful: the project itself or the problems he had with his coworkers.

Also, it appears that as Marcus's stress increased, his exercise plan fell by the wayside. Exercise can be a great way to reduce stress. Whether sticking to his exercise plan would have helped Marcus reduce his stress this week is unknown to us. More data from future weekly and monthly charts would help answer some of the questions we have raised for Marcus.

What Have We Learned about Marcus?

Now that we have reviewed Marcus's weekly and monthly charts in some detail, what have we learned?

Marcus's Patterns

- Increased stress may be related to increases in hypomania and daily rhythm scores and decreases in sleep.

- Even after stress is reduced, hypomania may stay high or even increase.

- Increased irritability may predict hypomania and lead to difficulties in managing stress.

- Feeling tense may lead to unhelpful ways of managing stress, such as alcohol and drug use.

- Increased hypomania may impair decision making about drug and alcohol use.

- Alcohol and drug use may interfere with the ability to sleep well.

- Increased stress and irritability may interfere with the ability to stick with an exercise plan.

- A decrease in number of hours of sleep may exacerbate problems with daily rhythm and hypomania.

- Increased stress or irritability may lead to problems in relationships (such as conflicts with coworkers).

Marcus's Red Flags

- stress

- reduced hours of sleep

- irritability

- alcohol and drug use

- conflicts, arguments, being snappy with others

- pressure or stress at work

- feeling tense

- not sticking to an exercise plan

Marcus's Daily Rhythms

- When Marcus maintains his daily rhythms, stress, mood, and sleep generally stay within good, manageable ranges.

- Increased daily rhythm scores signal increased problems in other areas.

- Marcus does a good job with being actively involved with people each day.

- If Marcus has problems with his daily rhythm, it tends to start with him staying up too late at night.

- Marcus has had stretches of time when he has been quite good at maintaining his daily rhythms.

Note that we need a lot more data over time to answer some questions that were raised for Marcus, as well as to confirm information about his patterns, red flags, and daily rhythms.

Now It's Your Turn

To help you with interpreting information on your charts, I have provided some questions to help you notice patterns, red flags, and obstacles to your daily rhythms.

EXERCISE 6.5 INTERPRETING YOUR CHARTS

Look at your Monthly Mood and Rhythm Chart (exercise 6.4). Write down the general trends you initially notice with each of your factors.

Depression _____

_____

_____

Hypomania _____

_____

_____

Stress _____

_____

_____

Sleep _____

_____

_____

Daily rhythm scores _____

_____

_____

Do two or more lines tend to rise or fall together? Do some factors or symptoms seem to occur together? If so, you may be able to determine red flags, or factors that seem to lead to problems with others.

_____

_____

_____

_____

When one line rises, does another rise shortly afterward? Again, this may alert you to some red flags for the occurrence of other problems.

_____

_____

Do some lines go down while others go up? For instance, if you get less sleep, does your hypomania line go up?

_____

_____

Are some lines fairly steady, while others seem to jump all over the page?

_____

_____

If you are female, what did you notice about the relationship between various factors and your menses?

_____

_____

_____

Look at your Mood Chart (exercise 6.1). What daily notes or information about stress help you understand the movement of other factors?

_____

_____

_____

_____

How do ratings of irritability or anxiety influence other factors?

_____

_____

_____

_____

What impact does medication, alcohol and drug use, or exercise have on other factors?

_____

_____

_____

Look at your Rhythm Chart (exercise 6.3). What tends to happen when you experience an increase in your daily rhythm scores?

_____

_____

_____

_____

Which daily rhythm activities are more difficult to maintain than others?

_____

_____

_____

With increased daily rhythm scores, what happens in your interactions with others? (Look at the "People Present" column.)

_____

_____

_____

_____

What other factors seem to lead to increased daily rhythm scores?

_____

_____

_____

_____

_____

What other conclusions can you draw from your charts?

_____

_____

_____

_____

_____

What questions do you still have about information in your charts?

_____

_____

_____

_____

_____

After several weeks or months of keeping charts, do you notice other overall trends?

_____

_____

_____

_____

_____

_____

_____

EXERCISE 6.6 YOUR PATTERNS, RED FLAGS, AND DAILY RHYTHMS

What have you learned about your patterns? In exercise 4.7, you began to identify patterns and red flags for yourself. You might go back to that chapter and transfer your findings to that chart.

_____

_____

_____

_____

_____

_____

List your red flags below.

_____

_____

_____

_____

_____

_____

What have you learned about your daily rhythms?

_____

_____

_____

_____

_____

Summing Up

This has been a complex yet important chapter. You have learned about the usefulness of keeping Mood Charts, Rhythm Charts, and Monthly Mood and Rhythm Charts. I talked about good reasons for keeping these charts and common problems that can get in the way. I went step-by-step over how to record information and how to interpret your data. You have seen a lot of charts and a lot of examples in this chapter. I hope you agree that it's useful to keep these charts, and I hope you understand how to make them work for you. Don't forget to transfer your findings about your patterns to exercise 4.7. Remember that you will need to keep your weekly and monthly charts for at least eight to twelve weeks before you can really draw solid conclusions. I encourage you to be patient with the process of keeping your charts. Make it a habit each day. All your hard work will pay off as you learn about your patterns, your red flags, and your daily rhythms. This information is key in making plans for managing and preventing cyclothymic symptoms. In the next chapter, you'll continue the work of learning how to manage cyclothymia as we take a close look at how powerful your thoughts can be in influencing your mood and behaviors.

CHAPTER 7

Cognitive Behavioral Strategies

Research on mood disorders has shown two very interesting things. First, your mood states can cause you to think in characteristic ways. Second, how you think can influence your mood states. This is good news because it gives you the opportunity to change how you feel by changing how you think.

This chapter will help you continue the work you have been doing to understand and manage your cyclothymia by offering a new way to think about your thoughts. Most people have never been taught to really consider the types of thoughts they have about things, yet thoughts can be terribly powerful. I will discuss how your thoughts affect your mood and behaviors and how cyclothymic symptoms of depression and hypomania influence your thoughts as well. I will also explain a number of effective strategies you can use to manage your mood.

COGNITIVE BEHAVIORAL PRINCIPLES

The strategies I will be discussing in this chapter have their roots in cognitive behavioral therapy (CBT). I discussed this approach briefly in chapter 5, when I talked about effective treatments for mood disorders. CBT is based on the premise that how you perceive and think about the world directly affects how you feel and behave. You can see this concept illustrated on the next page. Thoughts, feelings, and behaviors all influence and are influenced by each other. Cognitive behavioral strategies typically intervene at the thought level to change feelings, but some strategies target the behavioral level as well.

I'll try to provide an example of how thoughts can influence feelings. For a few moments, let yourself think about a recent event that elicited a strong emotional reaction for you. It could be something that was embarrassing or exciting, or something that led you to feel angry, sad, or frightened. Put this book down, then close your eyes and think about this event in some detail for at least one or two minutes. Be sure to notice what you feel when you do this. After you spend a little time thinking about this event, recall what you experienced. Did you notice feeling even slightly different than you did before this exercise? What emotions or physical sensations did you have? Did your thoughts cause you to do anything like fidget, clench your fists, smile, frown, or furrow your eyebrows?

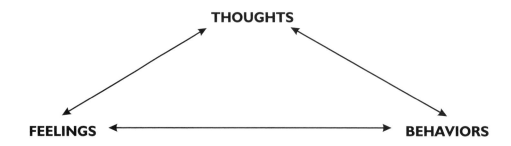

THOUGHTS

FEELINGS ← → **BEHAVIORS**

Other examples that demonstrate the power of thoughts are suddenly remembering something important you forgot to do or remembering something you have to do sometime soon that you are really dreading. Thoughts like these can elicit feelings of apprehension, fear, guilt, anger, or sadness. Thinking about sexual activity, having to speak in front of a large group, going back to work on Monday morning, giving a gift to someone special to you, winning the lottery, and so forth can all elicit some change in how you feel emotionally and physically.

The common theme among all these examples is that simple thoughts alone can cause changes in how you feel. You were just sitting where you are, not really experiencing the events themselves. It was the thought about the event that caused the feeling. If these examples didn't seem to do it for you, consider the following scenario.

In chapter 4, Helen said that one of her red flags is when she thinks that someone might be angry with her, particularly her husband. When this happens, she says, "I can really start doubting everything and feeling anxious." Imagine that Helen's husband has told her that he needs to work late one evening and that he would call her by 8:00. However, at 8:35, Helen's husband has not called. What might she think? How might she feel? Below are two examples, response A and response B. For each that I've described, first notice the thoughts that Helen has about her husband not calling on time. Then notice the feelings and the behaviors associated with the thoughts. See if it makes sense to you that the kinds of thoughts Helen has would likely generate the types of feelings and behaviors listed as well.

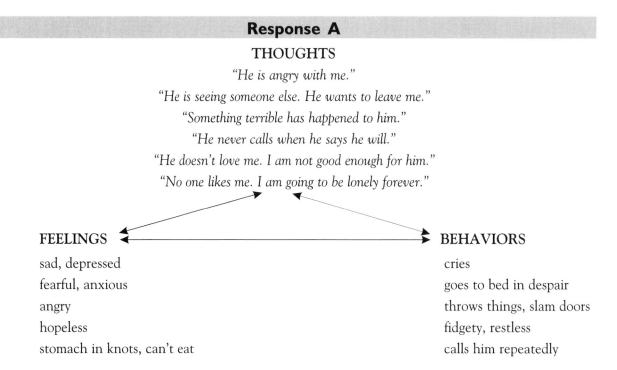

Response A
THOUGHTS
"He is angry with me."
"He is seeing someone else. He wants to leave me."
"Something terrible has happened to him."
"He never calls when he says he will."
"He doesn't love me. I am not good enough for him."
"No one likes me. I am going to be lonely forever."

FEELINGS ← → **BEHAVIORS**

FEELINGS	BEHAVIORS
sad, depressed	cries
fearful, anxious	goes to bed in despair
angry	throws things, slam doors
hopeless	fidgety, restless
stomach in knots, can't eat	calls him repeatedly

Response B

THOUGHTS

"Something came up and he will call me when he can."

"He innocently forgot."

"He misplaced his phone, the battery ran low, etc."

"He has a lot of work to do. It took longer than he expected."

FEELINGS ←――――――――――→ **BEHAVIORS**

FEELINGS	BEHAVIORS
mildly concerned for his welfare	calls once or twice, leaves a message
slightly annoyed	goes on with her regular routine
no strong or disturbing feelings or physical reactions	calls a friend
	watches a TV show, waits for him

What are some differences between the types of thoughts listed in response A and response B? Given that Helen and her husband are not having any significant problems in their relationship, which thoughts seem more balanced or realistic? Does it make sense that the more extreme thoughts in response A would lead to more distressing feelings and behaviors than the types of thoughts in response B?

Of course, we don't know everything about Helen's situation with her husband. We don't really know if he is angry with Helen, or if something terrible has happened to him, or if his oversight in calling her is innocent. So we can't really know which are the more realistic, accurate thoughts for her situation. These examples are really just to illustrate how certain types of thoughts can lead to certain types of feelings and behaviors. For instance, it would seem quite strange for Helen's thoughts in response A to generate the more mild feelings of response B. Instead, it makes more sense that those strong or extreme thoughts would generate the more distressing feelings listed in response A.

Think back to some situations you have experienced that were similar to Helen's. Have you ever gotten very upset about something, certain that a terrible event had happened, only to find out that you were totally off base? Have you ever misinterpreted someone's intentions or actions as a reaction to you, only to discover that it had nothing to do with you at all? Have you ever jumped to a conclusion about something and later found out that your assumptions were inaccurate? Certainly, most people can easily answer "yes" to all these questions. Sometimes faulty thinking doesn't cause too many problems, but then again, sometimes it does.

Helen has learned over time that she has a tendency to jump to drastic conclusions or become frightened by thinking about outcomes that are unlikely to happen. Sometimes this leads her to become angry quickly and verbally lash out at her husband. Other times she feels sad and withdraws quietly to her room. Shortly, I will use Helen's situation to illustrate some specific CBT strategies. First, I need to cover a few more ideas about the CBT approach.

Thoughts Cause Feelings, Not Events

Here is a concept that you may think is a bit strange at first. Like most people, you probably believe it is an *event* that happens around you which causes you to feel emotions. In reality, it's not the events themselves that cause you to feel certain emotions. Instead, it is your *thoughts about the events* that cause feelings. You have to make meaning out of a situation before you can feel an emotion about it. This can be difficult to believe, since there is often just a split second between an event and an emotion.

Imagine you are at a grocery store trying to decide which brand of cereal to purchase. You are facing the cereal boxes with your back to the aisle. As you are looking at them, you are suddenly hit from behind with a shopping cart. Even before you can turn around, what is your very first thought about this event? Many people might think something like *What an inconsiderate so-and-so!* or *They should be looking where they are going!* or *They hit me on purpose!* or *They don't respect me.* Again, before you can turn around, what feelings might you have? Some people might feel anger or rage at being hit with a shopping cart. So, in a split second, you have made some meaning of this situation and experienced a feeling about it.

Suppose you turn around and discover that the person who hit you was a small, elderly woman who hasn't realized what she has done until you turn around. She seems to struggle as she walks, and it's clear that she's having trouble managing her cart. As you turn toward this woman who looks up at you with surprise and begins to apologize, what new thoughts and feelings do you have about this event? You might immediately change your thought to something like *Oh, it was an accident* or *She didn't mean it.* What would happen to your feelings of anger or rage? Those strong feelings might turn quickly to forgiveness or a much milder form of irritation. The event itself has not changed, but your thoughts about it have. The different thoughts you had about the same situation before and after you turned around generated very different feelings.

Automatic Thoughts

Thoughts about events happen almost instantaneously. Whether they are rational or not doesn't matter. They just come automatically. In fact, in the world of CBT, an *automatic thought* is just that: a thought or an image that comes to mind in response to an event. In order to make all the other CBT strategies effective for you, you will need to learn to recognize your automatic thoughts. This is often a challenging task at first, but with some practice, you will get the hang of it. The thoughts in Helen's responses A and B are good examples of automatic thoughts. You might think of automatic thoughts as being in the form of phrases or sentences.

Automatic thoughts are the link between events and feelings.

Event	Automatic Thought	Feeling
A car is coming toward you	*I am in danger!*	fear, anxiety

This situation shows how automatic thoughts and their subsequent feelings and behaviors can be very useful, even protective. If you were in this situation, your behavior would be to quickly jump up onto the curb and get out of danger. Sometimes, however, our automatic thoughts can lead to feelings that are not so useful. For example, let's revisit Helen's situation.

Event	Automatic Thought	Feeling
Helen's husband hasn't called	*He is angry with me.*	sadness, fear

Helen has jumped to a conclusion without really knowing the facts of the situation. She is feeling distressed with sadness and fear, perhaps needlessly so.

Sometimes Thoughts Are Not Realistic

Most of us have never really been taught to evaluate how we think about things. We just simply think things. In fact, lots of thoughts go swimming around in our minds all the time. Sometimes we notice them, but many times we do not. We certainly don't tend to grab a thought and ask, *Is that thought realistic?* We generally just assume that all our thoughts are realistic and accurate.

You may have gathered by now that CBT suggests we don't always think in realistic ways. Sometimes our thoughts are exaggerated, sometimes they are self-defeating, sometimes they reflect our worst fears, and sometimes they are not as fair or balanced as they could be.

Rethink Your Thinking and Change Your Mood

One of the most interesting things about CBT is that *you can change how you feel by changing the way you think.* I know that may sound a bit strange at first, but it's true. You can actually improve your mood by modifying your automatic thoughts. You will learn how to do that shortly.

If you find yourself thinking *There's nothing wrong with my thinking,* stick with this discussion a little longer and see what you think. The concepts of CBT can take some getting used to, but if you hang with it and work on applying the principles to your own life, you just may be surprised at how you can modify your thinking and change your mood all at the same time.

Thinking Styles

Consider Helen's automatic thought *He is angry with me.* Does it seem to you that she may be trying to read her husband's mind or personalizing his behavior as some sort of reaction to her? Again, while Helen's husband may indeed be angry with her, we just do not have that information. For all we know, it may be more likely that he simply forgot to call.

Those who have studied cognitive behavioral concepts over the years have categorized certain types of thinking that are irrational or inaccurate, or otherwise lead to problems with mood. These kinds of thinking go by many names, including *cognitive distortions, maladaptive thinking,* and *dysfunctional thinking.* They all refer to the same thing: errors in thinking or thoughts that lead to negative mood states. I tend to prefer the term *thinking styles,* as it seems a little less judgmental.

I have provided a list of twenty thinking styles in exercise 7.1 below. As you read over them, remember that everyone thinks in these ways from time to time. The task for each of us is to recognize which thinking styles we engage in ourselves. I know what mine are. I hope you can determine which ones you do, too.

These styles in thinking can be subtle yet very powerful in causing needless emotional distress. Interestingly, the more distressed you become, the more your thinking can become narrowed and focused, making it difficult to think in balanced ways. Many times, simply identifying which thinking style you are using can be very liberating, allowing you to break free from narrow, unhealthy thinking patterns.

EXERCISE 7.1　IDENTIFY YOUR THINKING STYLES

Read through the following list of thinking styles and determine whether any apply to you. For each one that does, check whether you do it sometimes or often in the columns on the right. Just so you know, it is not at all unusual for people to find that they do most or all of these styles of thinking from time to time.

Thinking Styles		I do this . . .	
		some-times	often
All-or-nothing	Events are only good or only bad. They are black or white, with no gray areas or middle ground between the extremes. If something falls short of perfection, then you see it as a complete failure. *My work today was a total waste of time.*		
Overgeneralizing	You draw general conclusions based on one event or a single piece of evidence. If something bad happens one time, you see it as an unending cycle of defeat. *People are always mean to me.*		
Mind reading	You believe you know what people think and feel about you, as well as why they behave the way they do toward you, even though they have not told you. *He thinks I'm stupid.*		
Catastrophizing	You expect things to turn out badly. *If I ask my boss for a raise, he will yell at me.*		
Chain reaction	You continue down the chain, link by link, with one bad thing leading to another, ending in a larger bad outcome with regard to an overall goal. *If I fail this test, I won't pass this class, then I will fail out of school, then I won't graduate, then I won't get a good job, then I will be unhappy in a dead-end job forever.*		
"What-ifs"	You ask questions about bad or fearful things that could possibly happen in the future, while being unsatisfied with any answers. *What if something happens to her?*		
Personalizing	You think that things people say or do are in reaction to you, or you believe you are responsible for things people do or say. *He looked at his watch because I'm boring.*		
"Shoulds"/"musts"	You have strict rules about how you and others should or must feel and behave. You feel angry if others break these rules and guilty if you break them. *I shouldn't take any time off. I must work hard all the time.*		
Filtering	You magnify or dwell on the negative details of a situation while ignoring all the positive ones. *Look at all the things I have done badly.* If your mood is more hypomanic, you may do the opposite by magnifying the positive details of a situation while ignoring all the negative ones. *I'm going to quit my job and start up a new business I have an idea for.*		

Jumping to conclusions	You make illogical leaps in believing that A causes B without enough evidence or information to support your conclusions. *My boyfriend was late picking me up. He doesn't really want to go out with me tonight.*		✓
Comparisons	You compare yourself to other people, trying to figure out who is better, smarter, more attractive, and so on. *She is so talented. I'll never amount to anything.*		
Discounting positives	You automatically discount or reject positive actions or events as if they don't matter. If you did something well, you tell yourself that it doesn't count, it wasn't good enough, or anyone could have done it as well or better. You don't allow yourself to enjoy even small accomplishments. *If I had spent more time preparing for my presentation, it could have been better.*		✓✓
Maximizing/ minimizing	You maximize your problems or blow the effects out of proportion to the situation. Or, you minimize the value of your positive qualities. *This is the worst thing that could happen. I'll never be able to manage it.*		✓✓✓
Blaming	You blame yourself for things that are not in your control. Or, you hold others responsible for your misfortunes. *It's my fault that my husband drinks. If I were a better wife, he wouldn't do that.*		✓✓✓
Emotional reasoning	You automatically believe that what you feel is true for you. If you feel strange, boring, or stupid, for example, then you believe you *are* these things. *I feel embarrassed. I am so awkward and foolish.*		✓✓✓
Name calling	You use negative labels to define yourself, your feelings, or your behaviors. Or, if other people irritate you, you label them as if you are commenting on their character rather than simply their actions. *I'm a loser* or *He is such a jerk!*		✓✓✓
Being right	You are always trying to prove that your opinions and behaviors are the right ones. You cannot accept that you might be wrong, and you will go to great lengths to prove that you are right or others are wrong. *You don't know what you're talking about. We have to do it my way, or it won't work.*		
Reward fallacy	You expect to receive rewards or payoffs as a result of your own deeds or sacrifices, as if someone is keeping score. You feel angry or resentful if your actions do not reap rewards. *I spent all that time fixing a nice dinner, and no one appreciated it.*		
Change fallacy	You believe that if you pressure people enough, they will change to suit you. You also believe they *must* change, since you let your happiness depend on them. *If she told me she loved me more often, then I could feel happy.*		
Fairness fallacy	You believe you know what is fair, but since others don't agree with you, you feel resentful or angry. *I deserve a day off from work because I worked hard over the weekend, but my boss won't allow it.*		

Here are some of Helen's automatic thoughts, along with the thinking styles that describe them:

He is angry with me.	mind reading, personalizing
Something terrible has happened to him.	catastrophizing
He never calls when he says he will.	overgeneralizing
He doesn't love me. I am not good enough for him.	mind reading, personalizing, blaming
He is seeing someone else. He wants to leave me.	catastrophizing, mind reading, chain reaction
No one likes me. I am going to be lonely forever.	

As you can see, some thoughts reflect more than one thinking style. This is not uncommon. It seems that some of Helen's most common thinking styles are mind reading, personalizing, and catastrophizing.

At this point, you have learned some basic principles of CBT:

■   Our thoughts can influence our moods in powerful ways.

■   Thoughts, feelings, and behaviors are closely related, influencing each other.

■   Thoughts, not events, cause feelings.

■   Automatic thoughts about events may be realistic, unrealistic, or somewhere in between.

■   There are characteristic styles of thinking that can lead to unnecessary distress.

KEEPING AN AUTOMATIC THOUGHT RECORD

An important part of CBT is keeping a record of your automatic thoughts. I've created a one-page chart (exercise 7.2) that allows you to capture key pieces of information about situations to which you can apply CBT strategies. The purpose of keeping this record is to help you catch your automatic thoughts, recognize the feelings that go along with them, and work on balancing out your thinking toward modifying your mood.

Doing this well takes some patience and practice, but if you stick with it, I think you will be very pleasantly surprised at the results you can get. People often initially express doubt that this technique will work for them. They say things like, "How can this possibly help me to feel better?" or they otherwise express disbelief that it is possible to change their moods at all. However, many people who work with this technique become quite adept at catching their automatic thoughts, responding to them, and modifying their mood without even needing to use the record any longer.

The time to record your automatic thoughts is when you notice your mood become worse. When you do, it is helpful to ask yourself what you are thinking and feeling right now. You want to capture what is going through your mind just as soon as you can and get it down onto paper. If you wait hours or days to fill out your Automatic Thought Record, you will lose precious information, as the details of the moment will certainly fade away.

I will explain step-by-step how to properly record your automatic thoughts. Make some photocopies of the blank Automatic Thought Record (exercise 7.2) for yourself. This record is also available online at www.CyclothymiaWorkbook.com. It may look like there are a lot of things to do on this chart, but we'll take it a step at a time. It will take a little patience, and perhaps some fumbling through from time to time, but you can do it.

Automatic Thought Record

As soon as you feel your mood worsening, fill in the chart below by asking yourself, "What am I thinking and feeling right now?"

Time, Date	Situation	Automatic Thoughts	Feelings	Your Response	Results
	• What event led to the distressing feelings?	• Record the thoughts or images that went through your mind • Rate how strong you believed each thought (0–100%). • Which thinking styles apply?	• What feelings did you have? • How intense were they (0–100%)?	• Respond to each thought using questions below. • Rate how strong you believe each response (0–100%).	• Rate intensity of feelings. • Rate belief in thoughts. • Write a more balanced thought. Rate your belief in this thought (0–100%).
2/4 8:35 P.M.	My husband didn't call when he said he would	"He is angry with me" 90% (personalizing, mind reading, jumping to conclusions) "Something terrible has happened to him" 65% (catastrophizing) "He never calls when he says he will" 45% (overgeneralization)	anxious 90% sad 55% frightened 50% angry 40%		

Respond to each of your automatic thoughts using the following questions. (See table 7.1 for additional strategies)

(1) What is the evidence your thought is true? Not true? (Two sides should total 100%)   (4) What's the worst thing that could possibly happen? The best? The most realistic?

(2) Would others agree that your thought is true?   (5) If a friend in this situation had this thought, how would you respond?

(3) What are some alternative explanations for your thought?   (6) What are the benefits of this thought? The costs? (Two sides should total 100%)

Figure 7.1 Helen's Automatic Thought Record

EXERCISE 7.2 AUTOMATIC THOUGHT RECORD

As soon as you feel your mood worsening, fill in the chart below by asking yourself, "What am I thinking and feeling right now?"

Time, Date	Situation	Automatic Thoughts	Feelings	Your Response	Results
	• What event led to the distressing feelings?	• Record the thoughts or images that went through your mind • Rate how strong you believed each thought (0–100%). • Which thinking styles apply?	• What feelings did you have? • How intense were they (0–100%)?	• Respond to each thought using questions below. • Rate how strong you believe each response (0–100%).	• Rate intensity of feelings. • Rate belief in thoughts. • Write a more balanced thought. Rate your belief in this thought (0–100%).

Respond to each of your automatic thoughts using the following questions. (See table 7.1 for additional strategies)

(1) What is the evidence your thought is true? Not true? (Two sides should total 100%)

(2) Would others agree that your thought is true?

(3) What are some alternative explanations for your thought?

(4) What's the worst thing that could possibly happen? The best? The most realistic?

(5) If a friend in this situation had this thought, how would you respond?

(6) What are the benefits of this thought? The costs? (Two sides should total 100%)

Step 1: Recording Your Situation, Automatic Thoughts, and Feelings

Figure 7.1 is an example of Helen's record, although only a portion of it is filled out for now. Notice that in the first column, she has briefly described her situation. She has also recorded some of her automatic thoughts, the thinking styles that characterize her thoughts, and her feelings. Essentially, she has taken some of the information in the cognitive triangle at the beginning of the chapter and put it into her Automatic Thought Record.

For now, I'll focus on the first four columns. Let me offer a few guidelines for how to respond so that the information you gather will be useful to you when you get to the specific CBT strategies.

Time, Date. Be as specific as possible about the time and date. Stay away from entries like "morning," or "when I got home." Sometimes, the actual time is key in understanding aspects of the situation.

Situation. Write a brief statement, no more than a few sentences, that summarizes the situation. You may be tempted to describe your situation in great detail, as if you were making a case to justify your reactions. If you do this, you will tend to include thoughts and feelings, when those should be saved for their own columns. All you need to do here is write a simple description that helps you remember the situation later on.

Automatic Thoughts. Writing your thoughts is actually a little trickier than it looks. It takes practice to write them in such a way that you can respond effectively to them later on. I will explain more about this as we go along. For now, consider the following suggestions:

- Write one thought at a time. Sometimes people put several thoughts together in the same statement. It will be easier to respond to them later if you break them up into single statements. This can also illustrate for you the fact that it's possible to have a multitude of thoughts all at the same time around a single event.

- Don't write questions. Reframe them as statements, even if the statement feels a little strong. For example, *Why does he do this to me?* should be written as something like *He doesn't respect me*, or *He makes me angry*, or *He shouldn't do this.*

- Stay away from exclamatory statements like *Oh darn!* or *Crap!* or *Oh great!* Instead, identify the underlying thought expressed by the exclamatory statement. It is better, for instance, to write something like *I can't handle this!* or *This always happens to me!* or *She doesn't like me anymore!*

- Save feelings for the feelings column. Thoughts are not feelings, and feelings are not thoughts. It is common for people to include feeling words in their thought statements. For instance, *Things are hopeless now* could be written as a thought like *Things will never get better*, and "hopeless" could be entered into the feelings column.

- Automatic thoughts can be images that come to mind. Some people tend to think more in images than with words. For instance, instead of noticing a thought like *My boss will yell at me*, a visual person might vividly imagine the boss yelling, glaring, and waving a finger. For the automatic thoughts column, you can go ahead and describe the image, but also try to write out what the image means to you in a thought or statement form.

Feelings. If you are not used to recognizing your feelings or putting words to them, you might find this challenging at first. Some common feeling words are listed below. Make sure you write down what feelings you experience for each separate thought. It may be only one feeling, or it could be several. Notice that for her first thought, *He is angry with me,* Helen has recorded two feelings, "anxious" and "sad."

<u>Frightened</u>	<u>Ashamed</u>	<u>Angry</u>	<u>Sad</u>	
afraid	embarrassed	annoyed	abandoned	hopeless
anxious	guilty	disgusted	alone	inadequate
apprehensive	humiliated	enraged	defective	incompetent
full of dread	insulted	frustrated	dejected	inferior
edgy	invalidated	grouchy	depressed	insecure
horrified	regretful	filled with hate	despairing	isolated
nervous	remorseful	hostile	disappointed	lonely
overwhelmed	shamed	irritated	discouraged	neglected
panicked		jealous	empty	rejected
scared		mad	filled with grief	unhappy
tense		outraged	helpless	worthless
		resentful		

Step 2: Rating Your Thoughts and Feelings, Identifying Thinking Styles

The next step is to rate how strongly you believe your thoughts and how intense your feelings are. If you look again at Helen's Automatic Thought Record, you see that she has put ratings next to each thought and each feeling.

On a scale from 0 to 100 percent, rate how strongly you believe each thought. As you might imagine, 0 percent would be absolutely no belief in the thought, while 100 percent indicates that you completely and wholeheartedly believe that the thought is true. It's not unusual to have a variety of thoughts about any situation, but you'll likely find that some thoughts are stronger than others. Helen's strongest thought was *He is angry with me;* she rated her belief in it as 90 percent. She rated her belief in *Something terrible has happened to him* as 65 percent and *He never calls when he says he will* as 45 percent.

Helen then rated the intensity of her feelings of anxiety (90 percent) and sadness (55 percent). These ratings are similar to the ones you used in the last chapter when you rated moods such as depression and hypomania. Your most intense experience with the feelings you list will be considered 100 percent. As with each of your thoughts, make sure you give each feeling its own rating of intensity.

With regard to thinking styles, look at each automatic thought you recorded, then go to the thinking styles list (exercise 7.1) and try to identify which one describes each thought. Sometimes only one thinking style characterizes a thought, while at other times two or even three thinking styles seem appropriate. Go ahead and write each one that applies next to each thought. You may find that simply recognizing the thinking styles you are engaging in is helpful. It signals an error in thinking. This signal is a good first step to reducing your belief in a negative thought and the intensity of the distressing feelings it causes.

Step 3: Responding to Your Automatic Thoughts

Now you are getting to the heart of learning how to modify problematic automatic thoughts and improving your mood. The strategies for balanced thinking in table 7.1 are powerful CBT strategies for modifying thoughts that cause distress. Take a few minutes to read over them. I will be demonstrating some of them as Helen responds to her first automatic thought, *He is angry with me.*

Table 7.1 Strategies for Balanced Thinking

After you have identified your automatic thoughts and recognized the thinking styles you tend to use, try these practical strategies for balancing out your thinking. Don't move through them too quickly. Sit with each strategy for several minutes until you truly exhaust all possibilities. It can be useful to have someone help you brainstorm responses to your thoughts using these strategies. The first six strategies are cued for you on your Automatic Thought Record, but the remaining ones are just as likely to be powerful in responding to your automatic thoughts.

What is the evidence *for* your thought? *Against* it? This is where you need to put on your "scientist's cap" and really look objectively at the evidence you have that your automatic thought is *true* and the evidence you have that it is *not true.* Don't worry about how valid or ridiculous your evidence might seem at first, just write it down. Rate the group of evidence that supports your thought as true, and then rate the group that supports it as not true. The two ratings should total 100 percent. Don't rate the two sides purely on how many statements you have for and against. Each item will likely have a different weight for you based on its importance or validity. Just make a judgment call based on how valid you think each side is.

Would others agree that your thought is true? Try to step outside of yourself as you answer this question. It can be very tempting to quickly answer, "Of course others would agree!" But would they really? Think of several family members or friends who, if they were right there with you, could give their opinions about whether your thought is true. Why might they disagree with you? Be careful about letting your thoughts be influenced by your emotions and about using only certain pieces of evidence to support your arguments.

What are some alternative explanations for your thought? Again, with the "scientist's cap" on, let yourself come up with a list of probable or even not-so-probable alternative explanations for your thought. The longer you sit with this list, the more alternatives you are likely to generate.

What's the worst thing that could possibly happen? The best? The most realistic? You may become very distressed by events if you don't consider them in context with other things that could possibly happen. Your distress can seem like it's the worst thing you have ever felt, but if you compare it with something like experiencing nuclear holocaust, or death, the intensity of your feelings can diminish in comparison. Then ask yourself whether you could live with the worst outcome. The answer is likely to be yes.

If a friend in this situation had this thought, how would you respond? Remove yourself slightly from the situation for a moment by imagining your friend has come to you with the very same situation, thoughts, and feelings. As a compassionate person, what would you tell your friend? Would you conclude that your friend is right and should feel distressed? What keeps you from being compassionate with yourself?

What are the benefits of this thought? The costs? Here you are looking at the pros and cons. How beneficial is it to believe the thought, and how beneficial is it not to believe the thought? Rate each side so that the two total 100 percent. Again, rate them not by how many items you have for each side but by how much weight they hold for you.

Set up an experiment. In the spirit of trying to test the validity of your thoughts, you can arrange an "experiment" to gather data and evaluate the outcome. For instance, if you believe *I never do anything right*, then for several days in a row, you can record all the things you do right. Such things could include "got the kids off to school," "drove safely to the store," "was nice to the clerk," "called to check on a friend," "took a walk to get some fresh air," "helped kids with homework," and "went to bed at a reasonable hour."

Define your terms. When you label yourself or another person as a failure, a loser, or something else, take a moment to define exactly what the label means as if it were a dictionary entry. You'll likely find that no one really meets such definitions. This technique is useful for modifying a name-calling thinking style.

Examine the logic. Do your automatic thoughts have you jumping to conclusions that don't logically follow from the situation? For example, you might conclude that you're a terrible artist because your painting didn't win first place in a competition. What would be a more logical thought to have based upon the situation? Perhaps something like this: *I'm a good artist. There were lots of entries in this competition, and the judges liked the winning entry best. The fact that the winning entry is good doesn't mean my painting is bad or that I'm a bad artist. I may place higher in a different competition.*

Recognize limited information. Do your automatic thoughts have you jumping to conclusions without enough information to back them up? You might find you are only looking for evidence that backs up your thought and ignoring evidence that doesn't support it or even refutes it.

Examine shades of gray. Instead of thinking about events in extreme terms, consider putting them on a scale from 0 to 100, with 100 being the worst possible outcome. What really is a 0, and what outcome would really be worthy of a 100 rating? Where does your thought fit in? What other situations would also be on this scale? Rather than think about your experience as a total failure, let yourself acknowledge that it is a partial success. This technique is useful for modifying an all-or-nothing thinking style.

Examine your language. Listen to how you speak to yourself, and examine the language of your automatic thoughts. Try using words that are less dramatic and emotionally laden. For instance, if you say to yourself, *I must get As on all my tests*, you might substitute *I would like to do well in my classes. I will do the best I can.* This technique is useful for modifying "shoulds" and "musts."

Examine your attributions. Instead of blaming yourself or someone else for things that don't work out well, consider all the outside factors that have contributed to the situation. Rather than focusing on blame and guilt, let yourself work on solving the problem. This technique is useful for modifying a blaming thinking style.

Take a poll. Ask other people their opinions on an issue reflected by your thought. See if the evidence supports or refutes your thought. For instance, if you believe it is shameful and strange to feel shy or embarrassed in groups of people you don't know, ask a handful of your friends and family if they have ever felt shy when meeting new people.

Distinguish between people and behaviors. Be careful about taking one behavior, situation, or feeling and letting that determine who you believe you are as a person. For instance, losing a competition doesn't make you a loser as a person.

Accept that cyclothymia naturally causes variations in your thoughts, mood, and behavior. To expect consistency in these things is unrealistic and sets you up to feel discouraged. Variability is expected and "normal" for cyclothymia; be patient with yourself.

Be your own defense lawyer. Pretend that you have hired yourself to defend yourself (that is, make a positive case for you), and write down the strongest case you can think of in your own favor. It doesn't matter whether you believe it or not.

Helen's responses using some of the strategies for balanced thinking are shown in figure 7.2 (on the next page). I have zoomed in on a portion of the Automatic Thought Record for this example. You might find you need to have several copies of a blank Automatic Thought Record in order to effectively respond to your own thoughts. Although I have included some strategies for disputing thoughts at the bottom of the record, don't forget to consider using the other strategies listed in table 7.1.

Note that Helen rated her belief in each of her responses to her automatic thought. Please don't skip this step. Rating your responses is very important because it gives you the opportunity to evaluate your thought at a deeper level. It is a key part of being able to help yourself think in more balanced ways.

Automatic Thoughts	Feelings	Your Response
• Record the thoughts or images that went through your mind • Rate how strong you believed each thought (0–100%). • Which thinking styles apply?	• What feelings did you have? • How intense were they (0–100%)?	• Respond to each thought using questions below. • Rate how strong you believe each response (0–100%).

"He is angry with me"
90%
(personalizing, mind reading, jumping to conclusions)
	anxious
	90%
	
	sad
	55%
		1. Evidence that my thought is
		   TRUE (30%)
		   • he didn't call on time
		   • he has been angry at me before
		   NOT TRUE (70%)
		   • he has forgotten to call before
		   • we have been getting along well
		   • he seemed to be in a good mood earlier
		   • there's nothing he would be mad about
		2. Would others agree that my thought is true?
		   PROBABLY NOT (50%)
		3. Alternative explanation: (70%)
		   • he just innocently forgot to call
		   • he got really busy and hasn't been able to
		   • he's on his way home
		   • he's on a business call right now
		4. The worst thing: he is angry with me (80%)
		   Can I live with it? yes (100%)
		   The best thing: he's not angry at all (40%)
		   Most realistic: probably not angry (50%)
		5. If a friend had this thought, I would say...
		   • don't worry, nothing is wrong (40%)
		   • you are overreacting (65%)
		   • wait until you really know (60%)
		   • if he is angry, you can deal with it (95%)
		   • you haven't done anything wrong (95%)
		6. Benefits of believing he is angry: (25%)
		   • I can prepare for how to handle it
		   Costs of believing he is angry: (75%)
		   • I'm anxious/sad, maybe over nothing
		   • I can't get anything done this evening

Respond to each of your Automatic Thoughts using the following questions. (See Table 7.2)

(1) What is the evidence your thought is true? Not true? (Two sides should total 100%)

(2) Would others agree that your thought is true?

(3) What are some alternative explanations for your thought?

(4) What's the worst thing that could possibly happen? The best? The most realistic?

(5) If a friend in this situation had this thought, how would you respond?

(6) What are the benefits of this thought? The costs? (Two sides should total 100%)

Figure 7.2   Helen's Responses

Step 4: Getting Results, Changing How You Feel

As you do the work of responding to your automatic thoughts on your own Automatic Thought Record, you may notice your mood changing, if only slightly. For many people, just getting their thoughts down on paper and reading them back is a powerful experience. It makes a big difference to see your thoughts more objectively. Sometimes, reading what you wrote allows you to see your thoughts in a new way even before you get to the work of using strategies to modify them.

Now it's time for Helen to evaluate the results of her work. Figure 7.3 shows her entire completed Automatic Thought Record. In the last column, you see she was asked to revisit her belief in her original automatic thought and the intensity of her feelings. Helen recognized that she still feels some anxiety and sadness, although the intensity of those feelings has dropped to 60 and 25 percent respectively. She also rerated her belief in her automatic thought *He is angry with me* at 65 percent. While she still has this thought, Helen's belief in it has dropped a moderate amount from her original rating of 90 percent. Because her belief in her thought has diminished, so has the distress she initially experienced.

After all her efforts in responding to her automatic thought, Helen was able to generate a more balanced thought. She wrote, *There could be many reasons why my husband hasn't called yet. It might not have anything to do with me.* She rated her belief in this thought as 70 percent. Helen did a nice job evaluating her original automatic thought fairly and objectively. Her narrow focus on the belief that her husband was angry with her led Helen to feel needless distress at a time when she really had no practical information about the situation.

This is a good time to talk about appropriate expectations for how much you will be able to modify your thoughts and feelings. The goal here is not to keep from having distressing automatic thoughts or feelings ever again. They won't go away completely. To believe they will is unrealistic and will just lead to frustration and discouragement. Instead, an appropriate goal is to be able to modify your thoughts and feelings slightly to moderately. With more practice, you may be able to do much more. For many people, though, even small changes can mean the difference between being able to function despite having strong feelings and being immobilized by them. Reducing the intensity of your feelings by modifying your thoughts can have an amazing impact on your daily life.

Along the same lines, an appropriate goal is to be able to respond more quickly and more effectively to your automatic thoughts with practice. This will allow you to manage your emotions before they become overwhelming to you. You will also be able to recognize your thinking styles much more quickly. Sometimes people even find humor in their use of thinking styles. The realization *There I go personalizing again!* can take the sting out of a situation very quickly.

Troubleshooting

If you find you are having trouble reducing the intensity of your mood using Automatic Thought Records, consider the following questions:

Have you accurately identified and described the distressing situation? Sometimes, being inaccurate or vague about the situation that initiated the distressing feelings makes it difficult to take the next steps. Try recording specific information about the event. If you have trouble identifying it exactly, think back to the time when your distress began. What had been going on around that time? Who had you been talking to? What were you doing? You might have to retrace your steps a bit.

AUTOMATIC THOUGHT RECORD

As soon as you feel your mood worsening, fill in the chart below by asking yourself, "What am I thinking and feeling right now?"

Time, Date	Situation	Automatic Thoughts	Feelings	Your Response	Results
	• What event led to the distressing feelings?	• Record the thoughts or images that went through your mind • Rate how strong you believed each thought (0–100%). • Which thinking styles apply?	• What feelings did you have? • How intense were they (0–100%)?	• Respond to each thought using questions below. • Rate how strong you believe each response (0–100%).	• Rate intensity of feelings. • Rate belief in thoughts. • Write a more balanced thought. Rate your belief in this thought (0–100%).
2/4 8:35 P.M.	My husband didn't call when he said he would	"He is angry with me" 90% (personalizing, mind reading, jumping to conclusions)	anxious 90% sad 55%	1. Evidence that my thought is TRUE (30%) • he didn't call on time • he has been angry at me before NOT TRUE (70%) • he has forgotten to call before • we have been getting along well • he seemed to be in a good mood earlier • there's nothing he would be mad about 2. Would others agree that my thought is true? PROBABLY NOT (50%) 3. Alternative explanation: (70%) • he just innocently forgot to call • he got really busy and hasn't been able to • he's on his way home • he's on a business call right now 4. The worst thing: he is angry with me (80%) Can I live with it? yes (100%) The best thing: he's not angry at all (40%) Most realistic: probably not angry (50%) 5. If a friend had this thought, I would say... • don't worry, nothing is wrong (40%) • you are overreacting (65%) • wait until you really know (60%) • if he is angry, you can deal with it (95%) • you haven't done anything wrong (95%)	Feelings: anxious 60% sad 25% Belief in original thought : 65% A more balanced thought : "There could be many reasons why my husband hasn't called yet. It might not have anything to do with me." 70%

Respond to each of your automatic thoughts using the following questions. (See table 7.1 for additional strategies)

(1) What is the evidence your thought is true? Not true? (Two sides should total 100%)   (4) What's the worst thing that could possibly happen? The best? The most realistic?

(2) Would others agree that your thought is true?   (5) If a friend in this situation had this thought, how would you respond?

(3) What are some alternative explanations for your thought?   (6) What are the benefits of this thought? The costs? (Two sides should total 100%)

Figure 7.3 Helen's Automatic Thought Record

Have you accurately identified, written, and rated your automatic thoughts? Writing automatic thoughts in a way that lets you respond effectively takes some practice. You may be tempted to write them out at some length, which makes them cumbersome to respond to. Try to boil your thought down to no more than a dozen words, getting to the heart of it as best as you can. You may also need to refer again to the suggestions in "Step 1: Recording Your Situation, Automatic Thoughts, and Feelings." Sometimes a problem exists in how people rate their thoughts. Complete belief or certainty in the thought equals 100 percent, while 0 percent is no belief in the thought at all. You might need to reflect on your experiences and identify a thought that would rate 50 percent belief and compare that to your belief in your current thought.

Are you responding to the automatic thought that generated the mood you wish to change? Look again at the automatic thoughts you listed and determine whether another thought might have greater influence on your mood than was originally apparent. You may find you need to respond to a different thought in order to notice some change in your mood.

Do you need to respond to more automatic thoughts around the situation? Each thought can lead to more than one mood, and the same mood may be caused by multiple thoughts. For these reasons, you may need to reevaluate whether your target mood is being caused by an additional thought. Responding to only one automatic thought may not be enough to bring a shift in your mood. You may need to work on more thoughts, particularly if they are related to some of your more distressing feelings. Also, consider whether you may have overlooked some important automatic thoughts when you first identified them. It might be fruitful to spend some extra time reflecting back on the situation to determine whether additional ones should be recorded and responded to.

Have you accurately identified and rated your feelings? Sometimes, people find it challenging to identify the mood they are experiencing. Refer again to the list of feelings provided in "Step 1: Recording Your Situation, Automatic Thoughts, and Feelings" and see if this helps you to accurately identify your feelings. Also, before you make your ratings, consider your frame of reference. Remember that 100 percent refers to the most intense experience of that feeling you have ever had. Fifty percent is the midrange. Think of examples of each so you can compare your current experience and rate it accurately.

Are your responses to your automatic thoughts valid, convincing, and complete? Have you moved too quickly through the strategies for balanced thinking? A common stumbling block to changing your mood is hoping for a quick fix. Becoming skilled at modifying your mood takes some patience and practice. Be careful about trying to move too quickly through the strategies for balanced thinking. Spend the time you need with each strategy until you exhaust all possibilities. Ask a person you trust and who knows you well to help you brainstorm responses to your thoughts using the strategies. Also consider that you may need to write another new thought in the results column that seems more credible to you.

Are you invested in maintaining your negative automatic thoughts and feelings? You may have mixed feelings about whether you wish to feel better. At times your distress may serve some purpose for you, whether it seems logical or not. For instance, if you seem to gain something from being sad or anxious, or you get your way by expressing anger, then it may be uncomfortable to think about getting your needs met in other ways. In such cases, it may be useful to create a list of advantages and disadvantages to feeling distressed.

Do you need to change your thoughts or do something else? Sometimes your distressing thoughts and feelings can be a signal that you need to take some action. For instance, if someone has done something inappropriate toward you, or you have done something you need to apologize for, it may be best to speak with the person to resolve the situation rather than focus on changing your thoughts and feelings about it. Taking this action may help improve your mood.

HOW DOES CYCLOTHYMIA AFFECT THINKING?

I've addressed at length how cyclothymia affects moods, but how does it affect your thoughts? As I discussed at the outset of this chapter, moods can affect thinking and thinking can affect moods. The ups and downs inherent in cyclothymia not only lead to different mood states but also affect how you think (Basco and Rush 1996). You can probably recall numerous situations in which you have been hot or cold about the same issue depending on your mood at the time. I'd like to give you more specific information here about how depressive and hypomanic symptoms likely influence your thinking.

Depressive Thoughts and Thinking Styles

Aaron Beck, a prominent researcher and theorist in the field of cognitive therapy (akin to CBT), conceptualized the *cognitive triad* of depression (Beck et al. 1979). He found that our thoughts when we are depressed are characteristically negative and pervasive, coloring our view of ourselves, our world, and our future. Here are some examples of such negative thoughts:

	"I am no good."
Self	"No one likes me."
	"I can't do anything right."
	"There's nothing out there for me."
World	"People are out to get me."
	"Things are just too hard."
	"Things will never get better."
Future	"I'm doomed to be miserable."
	"I won't be able to accomplish anything."

You may recall from chapters 1 and 3 that several of the symptoms of depression are related to thought processes. The thoughts and feelings of worthlessness or guilt brought on by depression reflect a negative sense of self. Similarly, thoughts of hopelessness suggest a belief that the future has nothing positive to offer. Depression also influences your thinking in that it often impairs your ability to concentrate, so you may have difficulty thinking clearly and making decisions.

EXERCISE 7.3 DEPRESSIVE THOUGHTS AND THINKING STYLES

While many of the thinking styles I discussed earlier can occur when you are depressed, the ones listed below are some of the most common. After each thinking style, write down examples from your own life when you thought that way. Try to think of at least one or two examples of each.

Filtering: You magnify or dwell on the negative details of a situation while ignoring all the positive ones.

_____

_____

_____

Jumping to conclusions: You make illogical leaps in believing that A causes B without enough evidence or information to support your conclusions.

_____

_____

_____

Overgeneralizing: You draw general conclusions based on one event or a single piece of evidence. If something bad happens one time, you see it as an unending cycle of defeat.

_____

_____

_____

Maximizing/minimizing: You maximize your problems or blow the effects out of proportion to the situation. Or, you minimize the value of your positive qualities.

_____

_____

_____

Personalizing: You think that things people say or do are in reaction to you, or you believe you are responsible for things people do or say.

_____

_____

_____

All-or-nothing: Events are only good or only bad. They are black or white with no gray areas or middle ground between the extremes. If something falls short of perfection, then you see it as a complete failure.

_____

_____

_____

Discounting positives: You automatically discount or reject positive actions or events as if they don't matter. If you did something well, you tell yourself that it doesn't count, it wasn't good enough, or anyone could have done it as well or better. You don't allow yourself to enjoy even small accomplishments.

_____

_____

_____

Hypomanic Thoughts and Thinking Styles

Hypomania can be a pleasant experience for people at times; their mood tends to improve and they feel optimistic and energized. They experience the opposite of Beck's cognitive triad, feeling quite positive—perhaps even overly positive— about themselves, their world, and their future. For others, however, hypomania can bring irritability and frustration. Either extreme can be troublesome, as you'll see.

If you revisit the symptoms of hypomania listed in chapters 1 and 3, you'll see several that pertain to a disturbance in thought processes. Increased self-esteem and grandiosity is common. This may be accompanied by increased self-confidence, an overestimation of personal abilities, and increased optimism such that possible negative consequences may be easily overlooked. You may be tempted to jump into situations that could be risky financially, professionally, or personally as your judgment is compromised. This is the flip side of the filtering thinking style: you tend to see only the positive details of a situation while overlooking the potential negatives.

Hypomania can also lead to racing thoughts and an increase in the flow of ideas. It's easy to become intrigued by new interests and plans, getting caught up in multiple projects that may or not be completed in the long run. Preoccupation with grand goals is not uncommon. Alternatively, hypomania can cause you to become more easily distracted, making it hard to concentrate or focus on any one thing at a time.

Basco and Rush (1996) identify nine errors in thinking that can happen for those in the early stages of hypomania or the manic phases of bipolar disorder. They are summarized here for you.

EXERCISE 7.4 HYPOMANIC THOUGHTS AND THINKING STYLES

Write down examples from your own life when you have had the thoughts below. Try to think of at least one or two examples of each.

He/she wants to have sex with me. Hypomania can lead to increased sexual interest, thoughts, and activities. Some sexual activities may be uncharacteristic for you and lead to problems with your relationships or your health. This increased interest in sex may cause you to misinterpret the intentions of others as you assume they are interested in you sexually as well.

_____

_____

_____

Everyone moves too slowly. The racing thoughts and ideas of hypomania, as well as general agitation or irritability, can lead you to believe that others are doing things too slowly. Frustration may increase, leading you to express your irritability to those around you.

_____

_____

_____

I want to speak to the person in charge. It can be tempting to go straight to the top of the chain of command when interacting with others. For instance, when you have a customer service concern or need a question answered, you may bypass those who can help you and request to speak to someone at the level of the company president.

_____

_____

_____

They think I'm funny. I'm a comedian. You might experience a heightened sense of humor or quick wit, enjoying the ability to amuse others. However, your humor may turn to sarcasm, becoming critical or otherwise inappropriate for the situation, and lead to problems in your relationships.

_____

_____

_____

They think I'm great. While hypomanic, you may misinterpret people's responses to you as being more positive than they were intended to be. For instance, if someone tries to tactfully give you feedback that something you have done is not acceptable, you may focus on the tactful aspects and interpret their feedback as an endorsement of your behaviors.

_____

_____

_____

Everyone else is boring. If others don't join in on your new ideas, your humor, your sexual drive, and so on, you may see them as being apathetic, dull, or lacking in imagination. You may judge the people closest to you this way when they are quick to notice your hypomania and react to your behaviors.

_____

_____

_____

I feel good. I don't need medication. It is easy to interpret feeling good as a sign that you have been "cured." You might tell yourself you no longer need medication. It's important to remember that if you are on medication, you will need it on both good days and bad days in order to stabilize your mood.

_____

_____

_____

I'm right, you're wrong. During hypomania, it's not unusual to experience a strong sense of conviction in your viewpoints. You may distrust others who don't agree with you, and you may get into unnecessary arguments with others even when they are more knowledgeable about the issue at hand.

_____

_____

_____

Live for today. Everything can look overly positive, causing you to believe you can't lose. This idealistic, overly optimistic attitude can override usual cues of caution and lead to indiscretions (such as gambling, spending, or infidelity) that reflect a deviation from normal moral behavior, as well as lead you to underestimate the potential risk in situations.

_____

_____

_____

Because the thoughts and feelings of depression are unpleasant, they tend to be much easier to recognize than the more enjoyable thoughts and feelings of hypomania—unless the hypomania involves feelings of agitation or irritability. The errors in thinking described for hypomania above can become wonderful red flags to let you know that you may be developing some changes in your usual perceptions and judgments. Recognizing these characteristic types of thoughts early can help you rein in hypomanic symptoms before they get out of hand.

Summing Up

You have continued some challenging work for yourself in this chapter as you have learned how thoughts and perceptions affect mood. You have seen how the concepts of cognitive behavioral therapy can help you to change your mood by responding to your automatic thoughts and changing the way you think. I hope you have identified which thinking styles tend to cause you excessive distress. I'd like to encourage you again to be patient with using your Automatic Thought Records. It takes a little time to get the hang of it, but I believe you can do it with some practice. You'll learn that you have the power to improve your mood!

I also talked about how mood shifts in cyclothymia can influence your thoughts. Some very different things happen with your thinking when you are depressed than when you are hypomanic. Depressed thoughts tend to be overly negative, while hypomanic thoughts tend to be overly positive, but both can create significant problems.

The material in this chapter complements what you learned in chapter 6 about monitoring your moods. While I'll come back to how to integrate all the topics in the workbook in chapter 10, you may already recognize a connection between this and the previous chapter. You can supplement your mood monitoring charts from chapter 6 with the details you record for yourself in specific situations using your Automatic Thought Records from this chapter.

You'll continue learning useful strategies for managing cyclothymic symptoms in chapter 8. I'll talk about additional ways to manage the mood swings of depression and hypomania, how to cope with anger and stress, how to maintain good sleep patterns, and how to develop a plan for exercise.

CHAPTER 8

Managing Mood Swings

In this chapter, I'll share more practical strategies you can use to manage your cyclothymic mood swings. We'll start off with things you can do when you notice yourself experiencing the red flags of depressive and hypomanic symptoms. I'll toss in some information about using daily activity scheduling, as well as how to regulate your sleep patterns. Next, I'll talk about how you can understand and manage your anger and irritability. Finally, we will revisit the topics of managing stress and developing an exercise plan. Recognizing red flags, practicing new skills for mood management, and implementing strategies as soon as possible to head off problems with mood will be the major themes of this chapter.

Spotting your red flags and taking immediate action is perhaps one of the very best things you can do to manage your mood swings. It's important to intervene as early as possible to keep symptoms from getting worse. Becoming adept at this kind of intervention takes time, patience, practice, and a healthy amount of trial and error.

Some of the strategies in this chapter are preventive; that is, doing them will help you ward off problems or certainly minimize the impact they could otherwise have on your life. Other strategies or skills will be helpful in the moment that problems arise, particularly if you practice them regularly. As you'll see, developing and practicing skills is very important. Think about this: A good basketball player will practice shooting dozens of free throws every day in the calm of a quiet gymnasium. When the pressure of the big game in front of the roaring crowd makes things tough, he or she will be prepared to step up and sink the winning basket. Without such preparation beforehand, there is little chance of winning the game.

Throughout this chapter, you will apply things you have already been working on, particularly with regard to your unique red flags that signal impending problems with mood. In chapter 4, you took some first steps in identifying your red flags as they relate to recurring patterns (exercise 4.7). You continued that work in chapter 6 with keeping charts on your mood and daily rhythms and recognizing additional red flags (exercises 6.1 through 6.6). In chapter 7, you learned to modify automatic thoughts that lead to distressing feelings (exercises 7.2 through 7.4). In exercise 7.1, you identified certain thinking styles you engage in that can also serve as red flags for problems with mood.

As you work through this chapter, you'll see lots of suggestions for things you can do to help alleviate problems with mood, anger, stress, and so forth. You might find it tempting to read quickly over some of these strategies and immediately dismiss them. You might decide that they are too simple, too difficult, too impractical, too silly, too patronizing, or too something else. I hope you will resist this temptation and give yourself a good chance to really try using these strategies. If they can help improve your mood state even a little, that could mean the difference between being able to function and feeling immobilized. People are frequently surprised that simple techniques can help improve how they feel.

MANAGING DEPRESSIVE SYMPTOMS

As I offer strategies for managing symptoms of depression, I'll first revisit the topic of red flags, specifically for depressed mood. Second, I'll provide a list of practical things you can do to help improve your mood. Third, I'll describe another cognitive behavioral strategy, daily activity scheduling, which can be very effective for alleviating depression. And fourth, I'll offer some thoughts on how to be compassionate with yourself if you find yourself struggling with depressive symptoms.

Your Red Flags for Depressive Symptoms

As you keep charts on your mood, rhythms, and thinking patterns, you will naturally begin to identify more and more of your early warning signs of oncoming depressive symptoms. Some red flags will be obvious to you. For instance, having an argument with your partner may be a consistent precursor to experiencing depressed mood. Other warning signs will be much more subtle. For example, the urge to listen to more melancholic music or certain songs on your stereo could signal a downward spiral in your mood. As you learn more about your red flags for depressive symptoms, make sure you record them in this workbook.

EXERCISE 8.1 RED FLAGS FOR DEPRESSION

Spend a few moments looking at some common red flags in the checklist below. If you notice you experience any of them prior to or while feeling depressed, go ahead and check them off. There is space at the end for you to add more red flags either now or in the future.

Emotional or Physical

- ☐ feel sad, down, empty
- ☐ feel more irritable
- ☐ don't feel like talking
- ☐ easily frightened
- ☐ hard to enjoy things, even if I try
- ☐ don't want to do anything anymore
- ☐ feel needy
- ☐ little interest in sex
- ☐ can't face daily tasks
- ☐ food tastes different, bland
- ☐ have nightmares

- ☐ lose interest in things
- ☐ feel guilty, regretful
- ☐ feel shaky
- ☐ feel numb
- ☐ everything is an effort
- ☐ feel low in energy, tired, fatigued
- ☐ feel alone, misunderstood
- ☐ feel agitated, anxious
- ☐ muscle aches, headaches
- ☐ crave certain foods
- ☐ have problems with skin and hair

Behavioral

- ☐ overeat or lose my appetite
- ☐ don't want to shower, get dressed
- ☐ stare at the television
- ☐ stop calling friends, avoid people
- ☐ withdraw, isolate myself
- ☐ cancel arrangements or appointments
- ☐ can't get up in the morning

- ☐ sleep longer than usual
- ☐ trouble sleeping, sleep less or more
- ☐ increase alcohol or drug use
- ☐ spend hours on the computer
- ☐ dress differently
- ☐ tearful, cry easily
- ☐ lie around the house

Cognitive

- ☐ difficulty concentrating
- ☐ worry a lot
- ☐ have thoughts about death
- ☐ want to give up
- ☐ more sensitive to others' comments
- ☐ low self-esteem, low self-confidence
- ☐ harder to think or make decisions
- ☐ attitude becomes sour
- ☐ things seem in slow motion
- ☐ feel confused or disorganized
- ☐ depressive thinking styles (from exercises 7.1 and 7.3)

_____

_____

Your Other Red Flags

- ☐ _____
- ☐ _____
- ☐ _____
- ☐ _____
- ☐ _____

- ☐ _____
- ☐ _____
- ☐ _____
- ☐ _____
- ☐ _____

As soon as you notice yourself experiencing any of these red flags, that's the signal to take action. In this chapter, I will discuss practical things you can do to help improve your mood, but don't forget about monitoring your mood and daily rhythms (chapter 6) and responding to negative automatic thoughts (chapter 7).

■ Helen

Helen says, "I've learned over time that when I start losing interest in things and feeling unmotivated, I'm going to start having some problems with depression. Last month I started getting back into gardening. I cleaned out the bed and planted a bunch of annuals. I used to enjoy gardening and found it relaxing, but I just got away from doing it. In the spirit of trying to do one pleasurable thing each day, I make time for myself every evening to go out and pull weeds, water, or add new plants—whether I feel motivated or not. I find that once I get out there, I usually enjoy it."

Strategies for Lifting Depressed Mood

Below you'll see a checklist of practical things you can do to help lift your mood. Perhaps you have done some of these things in the past and found them useful, or maybe you've only thought about giving them a try. I hope there will be at least a few ideas here that you have not considered before. Because you are a unique individual, you are likely to find that some of these strategies work for you while others do not. That's okay. Not everything will work for everyone.

EXERCISE 8.2 STRATEGIES FOR LIFTING DEPRESSED MOOD

As you look over these strategies, put two stars by ones that work well for you, put one star by ones you'd like to do more often, and circle ones that you would like to try for the first time. At the end of this list I encourage you to add other activities that have been pleasurable for you in the past.

- ☐ take a long, slow walk
- ☐ feed bread crumbs to birds
- ☐ write a poem about a pleasant time
- ☐ talk with a counselor, clergyperson, or trusted family member or friend
- ☐ do something nice for myself
- ☐ join a support group
- ☐ do some volunteer work
- ☐ go to a hobby store and pick out an arts and crafts activity to do at home
- ☐ eat a picnic lunch outside
- ☐ talk to a friend on the phone
- ☐ learn how to do something like needlepoint or woodworking
- ☐ make love with my partner
- ☐ nurture my spirituality
- ☐ take a long, hot bubble bath with candles and soft music

- ☐ donate a few dollars to charity
- ☐ reread a favorite book
- ☐ purchase a small gift for myself
- ☐ smile at a complete stranger, expect nothing in return
- ☐ cook a favorite meal
- ☐ join a club or organization
- ☐ start watching a television series
- ☐ go to a library and browse the children's books
- ☐ attend a presentation, event, or lecture
- ☐ spend some time outside
- ☐ purchase a packet of seeds and grow a plant in a small container
- ☐ take a drive in a new area
- ☐ visit a museum or art gallery
- ☐ take a road trip to a city I have never visited before

- ☐ get dressed in my favorite clothes, do my hair or makeup
- ☐ take a class in yoga, dance, or art
- ☐ draw or sketch something outdoors
- ☐ go window-shopping at the mall
- ☐ sing along with my favorite music
- ☐ clean out my closet
- ☐ rent a comedy
- ☐ go to a bookstore and sample music, browse through a stack of books at the coffee shop

- ☐ get *some* exercise, no matter what type or how brief
- ☐ start playing a sport I once enjoyed
- ☐ start keeping a journal or diary
- ☐ relax at a nearby park
- ☐ spend time playing with children
- ☐ donate household goods to charity
- ☐ surf the Internet for interesting topics
- ☐ write a letter to a friend and mention something I really appreciate about him or her

Other activities you find enjoyable

- ☐ _____
- ☐ _____
- ☐ _____
- ☐ _____
- ☐ _____

- ☐ _____
- ☐ _____
- ☐ _____
- ☐ _____
- ☐ _____

If you have trouble thinking of additional activities you find enjoyable, consider the following questions:

- ■ What kinds of things have you enjoyed doing in the recent or distant past?
- ■ What things have you enjoyed doing on your own?
- ■ What activities have you enjoyed doing with other people?
- ■ What things have you enjoyed doing that cost little or no money?
- ■ What activities have you always wanted to do?

Daily Activity Scheduling

Daily activity scheduling is another useful technique from cognitive behavioral therapy. You may have noticed that when you feel depressed, you don't really want to do very much. You may isolate yourself from people or otherwise disconnect from the outside world. Depression can make you want to withdraw from other people, which tends to perpetuate feelings of loneliness and despair. In fact, isolating yourself can make you more depressed. Anything you can do to stay connected with people will likely help improve your mood. Daily activity scheduling can be an effective method of helping you increase your contact with your environment so that you can begin to feel better.

With daily activity scheduling, you schedule just a few things that you need to accomplish throughout the day, as well as one or maybe two additional activities that are pleasurable. See the strategies listed in exercise 8.2 for ideas for pleasurable activities. Keep in mind, however, that if you feel very depressed, it may be necessary to think about scheduling only one pleasurable activity every other day or so, and you'll want to stick to activities that aren't too difficult. As you begin to feel better, you can move up to scheduling one or two pleasurable activities each day.

Engaging in pleasurable activities each day serves several purposes. One, they can be enjoyable. When you feel depressed, it can be difficult to enjoy doing anything. In fact, you may not do things that could be pleasurable because you don't believe they will bring any enjoyment at all. Feeling depressed actually makes you less likely to do things that will be positive for you. What you'll find, however, is that doing pleasurable activities can be at least more enjoyable than doing nothing at all. Two, these activities can distract you from experiencing the pain of your depressed mood and allow you to feel a different, more pleasurable emotion. If only for a short time, it can be helpful to give your mind a break from depressive thoughts and feelings and let it go to other things that can be more enjoyable. Three, doing pleasurable activities can give you a sense of mastery, purpose, and accomplishment. When you feel depressed, you may not feel very competent or capable. It can feel good to accomplish even small goals.

Figure 8.1 is a daily activity schedule for Jerry. Notice that all the days of the week are listed across the top, with most of the hours of the day provided down the left side of the page. Jerry has written in some activities that he needs to do each day, including going to his part-time job, picking up his two grandchildren, sleeping, and so forth. He has also scheduled one or two pleasurable activities to do each day. Those are marked with an asterisk. When Jerry completed this schedule, he was experiencing mild to moderate depressive symptoms. The types of activities he chose were appropriate for his mood state. Remember, if you are struggling with more severe depressive symptoms, you will likely want to schedule fewer and simpler activities. The goal is to allow yourself to do some enjoyable things, not to overwhelm yourself with very difficult tasks. The more depressed you feel, the more difficult things will be to accomplish.

A blank Daily Activity Schedule (exercise 8.3) is provided for you (this schedule may also be found online at www.CyclothymiaWorkbook.com). Your daily activity schedule will be complemented by information you record on your weekly Mood Chart (exercise 6.1). Recall that this chart asks you to record your moods (depression, hypomania, anxiety, and irritability) each day. At the end of one or two weeks, you can compare your mood ratings before and after implementing your daily activity scheduling to see if there is a difference. Unless you use your ratings, it will be quite difficult to determine whether scheduling pleasurable activities has any effect on your depressive symptoms. In fact, if you continue to feel somewhat depressed, you may be more likely to dismiss this activity as unhelpful rather than acknowledge that it helped improve your mood even a small amount. If you find that scheduling pleasurable activities helps improve your mood, then consider gradually adding a few more activities into your week.

If scheduling pleasurable activities does not seem to help improve your depressed mood, consider the following possibilities:

- ■   Are you scheduling activities that are too hard given your mood state? Perhaps they are too time consuming, require too much planning, or rely on things that are out of your control.

Daily Activity Scheduling

Name: ___Jerry___   Date: _____

Time	Sunday	Monday	Tuesday	Wednesday	Thursday	Friday	Saturday
7:00 A.M.	Get up	Get up	Get up	Get up	Get up	Get up	Get up
8:00 A.M.		Go to work	Pick up kids	Go to work	Pick up kids	Go to work	
9:00 A.M.	*Take walk with Sue	"		"		"	*Play golf
10:00 A.M.	"	"		"		"	"
11:00 A.M.		"		"		Go home	"
12:00 P.M.		"	Fix lunch for kids	"	Fix lunch for kids	*Lunch w/Sue	"
1:00 P.M.		"	*play game with kids	"	*play game with kids		
2:00 P.M.		"		"			
3:00 P.M.		"		"			
4:00 P.M.		"		"			
5:00 P.M.		Go home		Go home			
6:00 P.M.							
7:00 P.M.			*Woodworking project	*bowling	*Woodworking project		
8:00 P.M.	*Call Steve and Jill		"	"	"	*Go to the movies	
9:00 P.M.	"	*Read book				"	
10:00 P.M.		"					
11:00 P.M.	Go to bed	Go to bed	Go to bed	Go to bed	Go to bed	Go to bed	Go to bed
12:00 A.M.	"	"	"	"	"	"	"

Figure 8.1 Jerry's Daily Activity Scheduling

EXERCISE 8.3 DAILY ACTIVITY SCHEDULING

Name: _____   Date: _____

Time	Sunday	Monday	Tuesday	Wednesday	Thursday	Friday	Saturday
7:00 A.M.							
8:00 A.M.							
9:00 A.M.							
10:00 A.M.							
11:00 A.M.							
12:00 P.M.							
1:00 P.M.							
2:00 P.M.							
3:00 P.M.							
4:00 P.M.							
5:00 P.M.							
6:00 P.M.							
7:00 P.M.							
8:00 P.M.							
9:00 P.M.							
10:00 P.M.							
11:00 P.M.							
12:00 A.M.							

- Are you trying to do too many activities each day?

- Did you choose activities that you could really enjoy doing?

- Do you have an appropriate balance between things you *must* do and things you *want* to do?

Additional Thoughts about Managing Depression

Recall that in chapter 7, I talked about how people can be very critical of themselves when they feel depressed. They tend to think much more negatively about themselves, their world, and their future. For this reason, it is all the more important that you show compassion for yourself when you struggle with depressed mood. Sometimes it can be helpful to take the emphasis off of yourself and put it where it belongs: on the depression itself. Remember that cyclothymic disorder is an illness that affects how you feel, think, and behave. It is really no different than any other chronic medical condition, like diabetes or thyroid problems. You wouldn't blame people for being diabetic or having the difficulties with energy and mood that thyroid problems cause, would you? You would likely have compassion for them. You might recognize that they are not to blame for the occurrence of their conditions while acknowledging that they can take action to help manage their symptoms. Don't forget to have compassion for yourself as well.

Here are some other thoughts to consider as you work to manage your symptoms of depression:

- Intervene just as soon as you notice the smallest hint of a red flag. The sooner you act, the better off you will be in managing your mood. If you wait to take action, things can become difficult quickly, particularly since cyclothymia can bring rapid changes in your mood.

- Remember that depressed mood is temporary, particularly with cyclothymia. While the world can seem bleak when you feel depressed, these dark times do pass. They have passed before and they will pass again.

- If you feel overwhelmed, break large tasks down into smaller ones. Look at only one piece at a time. You can only accomplish one thing at a time, anyhow.

- Don't expect more from yourself than you are able to do while you feel depressed. Expecting too much from yourself will only lead to continued frustration and discouragement. Make sure you give yourself credit for even the smallest of accomplishments.

- Remember that depressed mood will affect your ability to think and concentrate, your energy level, your motivation, your ability to sleep, your appetite, and more. This is all the more reason to be compassionate with yourself when you are struggling.

- If your depressed mood becomes worse than you have experienced before, it doesn't seem to lift within two weeks, or you begin to have thoughts about suicide or death, you should seek professional help from your physician, a psychiatrist, or a psychologist. See chapter 5 for how to find professional help.

MANAGING HYPOMANIC SYMPTOMS

As I have said before, many people enjoy the energy and euphoria of hypomania. There can be some positive things about hypomania that you do not wish to change, and that is certainly fine. If, however, you experience problems with hypomania—and most people eventually do—then you may want to have some strategies ready for managing it. With cyclothymia, you may not be able to prevent hypomanic symptoms from happening, but you can have some control in how intense they become and put the brakes on many problems they cause.

Your Red Flags for Hypomanic Symptoms

You began identifying your red flags for hypomania in the activities in chapter 6. In this section, I will offer more typical red flags for hypomania so you can determine whether any apply to you. We'll also look at strategies for moderating hypomanic symptoms, revisit the importance of sticking to your daily rhythms, address the problem of alcohol and drugs, and talk about how to regulate your sleep patterns.

EXERCISE 8.4 RED FLAGS FOR HYPOMANIA

Here are some common red flags people experience when they find themselves becoming hypomanic. Check off any that you notice you experience, and write in your other ones in the blanks at the bottom. You might also ask your family and friends what they have noticed about you when you become hypomanic. This can be a wonderful way to get more information about symptoms you have overlooked before.

Emotional or Physical

- ☐ on a high
- ☐ want to live for today
- ☐ easily frustrated with small things
- ☐ restless, fidgety, can't sit still
- ☐ need less sleep
- ☐ feel sped up
- ☐ elated, euphoric
- ☐ senses seem more sharp
- ☐ feel more religious, spiritual
- ☐ feel "in another world"
- ☐ feel very important

- ☐ impatient, intolerant
- ☐ overactive
- ☐ irritable, grouchy
- ☐ physical aches and pains
- ☐ can't get to sleep
- ☐ feel more angry toward others
- ☐ inspired, motivated
- ☐ feel more creative
- ☐ energized
- ☐ feel powerful, strong
- ☐ fear "going crazy"

Behavioral

- ☐ increased alcohol or drug use
- ☐ increased libido (sexual drive)
- ☐ sexual indiscretions
- ☐ feeling more outgoing or gregarious
- ☐ driving faster or more recklessly
- ☐ argumentative, inflexible
- ☐ behave irresponsibly
- ☐ embarrass myself and others
- ☐ draw attention to myself
- ☐ more talkative

- ☐ people comment on behavior change
- ☐ more active
- ☐ arrogant, obnoxious
- ☐ spending money more readily
- ☐ can't slow down, even if I want to
- ☐ intrusive, inappropriate toward others
- ☐ more aggressive, mean, cruel
- ☐ domineering, controlling
- ☐ giving in to impulses
- ☐ talking faster or louder

☐ work harder, longer hours

☐ going out more, partying more

☐ outbursts, anger toward others

☐ acting like I know everything

☐ being outrageous, uninhibited

☐ involved in numerous projects

Cognitive

☐ poor judgment or decision making

☐ urge to jump into new projects

☐ thinking seems much more clear

☐ make snap decisions, act thoughtlessly

☐ overly optimistic, grandiose

☐ racing thoughts, ideas flowing fast

☐ can't concentrate or focus

☐ new ideas for projects

☐ more sensitive to others' comments

☐ increased confidence, self-esteem

☐ more thoughts at the same time

☐ have strange or bizarre thoughts

☐ feel more intelligent

☐ lose trust in others

☐ easily distracted

☐ believe my thoughts are controlled

☐ hypomanic thinking styles (from exercises 7.1 and 7.4)

☐ _____

☐ _____

Your Other Red Flags

☐ _____

☐ _____

☐ _____

☐ _____

☐ _____

☐ _____

If you have trouble thinking of additional red flags, think about answers to the following questions:

■ What kinds of changes do you experience in your energy and activity levels when you begin to feel hypomanic?

■ How do you relate to other people differently?

■ What happens with your thinking and perception?

■ Are there changes in your sleep patterns? If so, what are they?

■ Do you begin to do things you wouldn't normally do when you don't feel hypomanic?

Strategies for Moderating Hypomania

Let's begin with some simple strategies for managing hypomanic symptoms.

EXERCISE 8.5 STRATEGIES FOR MODERATING HYPOMANIA

Take a look at the list of strategies below for moderating your hypomanic symptoms. As you did previously, check off ones you have done before. Put two stars by ones that work well for you, put one star by ones you'd like to do more often, and circle ones that you would like to try for the first time. There is space at the end for you to add other strategies that are not already listed.

☐ take a long, slow walk

☐ get some *mild* exercise, no matter what type or how brief

☐ relax at a nearby park

☐ spend time outdoors

☐ play a musical instrument

☐ join a support group

☐ do some volunteer work

☐ go to a hobby store and pick out an arts and crafts activity to do at home

☐ eat a picnic lunch outside

☐ write letters or poetry

☐ do some relaxation exercises

☐ make love with my partner

☐ nurture my spirituality

☐ sit in a quiet room with little stimulation

☐ avoid alcohol and illicit drugs

☐ take a class in yoga, dance, art

☐ draw or sketch something outdoors

☐ cook a favorite meal

☐ talk with a counselor, clergyperson, or trusted family member or friend

☐ reread a favorite book

☐ do some household cleaning

☐ rent a movie

☐ use my energy creatively

☐ listen to my favorite music

☐ go to a library and browse the children's books

☐ spend time with friends

☐ arrange to be with people

☐ take steps to get more rest

☐ avoid caffeine, sugar, processed foods

☐ visit a museum or art gallery

☐ avoid stimulating places and events

☐ stay in familiar surroundings

☐ start keeping a journal or diary

☐ stay at home, resist going out

☐   don't overextend myself

☐   stick to daily rhythms I know are use-
      ful for me

☐   reduce stress

☐   let someone hold my credit cards and
      checks for me

Other strategies for moderating your hypomania

☐   _____

☐   _____

☐   _____

☐   _____

☐   _____

☐   _____

☐   _____

☐   _____

☐   _____

☐   _____

Stick to Your Daily Rhythms

Although I discussed the importance of daily rhythms in chapter 6 in some detail, it is worth revisiting. Monitoring your mood and regulating your daily rhythms using the charts provided in chapter 6 will go a long way to help you recognize your red flags before they become full-blown problems. You recall that Marcus had changes in his schedule, his sleep, his stress level, and his mood before he began to have further problems that culminated in excessive alcohol and drug use. If he had taken some action in the early stages, he might have been able to head off the more severe problems he ultimately experienced.

Use Daily Activity Scheduling

Daily activity scheduling (exercise 8.3) can be very useful in managing hypomania as well as depression. When you feel hypomanic, it can be very tempting to take on a number of activities or suddenly get involved in a variety of new things. It can also be harder to stick with one task at a time without getting distracted and feeling scattered among activities.

Daily activity scheduling when you feel hypomanic can help you stay focused long enough to get something accomplished. It can help you stay on track and use your energy and creativity constructively. It can also help keep you from taking on too many things at one time.

When you choose activities to schedule while feeling hypomanic, keep several things in mind:

■   Schedule only a few activities. Design your schedule so that it is comparable to those times when you don't feel hypomanic.

■   Don't schedule activities that are overstimulating. If you do things that are very stimulating, it could increase the level of hypomania you experience.

- Try to refrain from jumping into additional, unplanned activities. Again, consider what your schedule looks like when you are not feeling hypomanic.

- Schedule activities that are calming, relaxing, nurturing, and enjoyable. Try to choose things that are interesting enough that you won't become bored quickly but that are not too stimulating.

- Schedule activities that involve staying within surroundings that are familiar to you.

- Schedule activities that are not related to red flags or past problems with hypomania. For instance, if you tend to spend excessive amounts of money while hypomanic, you probably don't want to schedule an outing to go shopping. If you tend to have problems with sexual indiscretions, stay away from situations that have made this easy to do in the past.

Avoid Alcohol and Illicit Drugs

Alcohol and illicit drug use is another topic that is useful to revisit in managing hypomania. Recall that in one study of patients diagnosed with bipolar disorder, at least 50 percent had a history of substance abuse (Regier et al. 1990). You may also remember I identified two main reasons people with mood disorders use alcohol or illicit drugs: to self-medicate and to enhance the highs of hypomania. Regardless of the reason, alcohol or drug use has significant consequences for people with bipolar disorder. Substance use often leads to increased problems with mood, difficulties sticking with your daily rhythms, conflicts in relationships, and problems at work or school.

If you feel you need support in managing your alcohol or drug use, you might consider joining a support and recovery program like Alcoholics Anonymous (AA), Narcotics Anonymous (NA), or Self-Management and Recovery Training (SMART). Contact information for these groups is listed in the Resources section.

Regulate Your Sleep

In chapter 2, I talked about how disturbances in your sleep patterns can throw off your circadian rhythm, leading to increased problems with hypomania. Even small changes in your sleep patterns can have noticeable effects on your mood. Of course, both depression and hypomania can disrupt your sleep patterns. This is all the more reason to pay close attention to your sleep patterns as well as things that can prevent you from maintaining your sleep-wake cycle.

You have already done several activities in this workbook that have addressed your sleep patterns. In chapter 2, you used your Sleep Inventory (exercise 2.3) to examine how sleep has affected your mood over time. You also noted things that have interfered with your ability to sleep as well as things you have done to help yourself sleep better at night. In chapter 6, you recorded on your Mood Chart (exercise 6.1) the number of hours of sleep you got each night during a given week. On your Rhythm Chart (exercise 6.3), you recorded the extent to which you were able to adhere to your self-assigned times for going to bed at night and waking up in the morning. Finally, on your Monthly Mood and Rhythm Chart (exercise 6.4), you plotted a visual representation of how your sleep is related to things like mood and stress.

From these charts, you have gathered valuable information about things that influence your sleep patterns as well as about how problems with sleep affect your mood. And, of course, this information can help you identify those red flags or early warning signs that signal problems with your sleep cycle.

Table 8.1   Tips for Managing Your Sleep

In *The Anxiety and Phobia Workbook* (2002), Edmund Bourne provides some nice suggestions to help you get a good night's sleep. Some are summarized below.

- The main goal is to go to bed at the same time each night and get up at the same time each morning, even on the weekends, and even if you are still tired in the morning. Don't fluctuate on these times. Even slight changes in your sleep-wake schedule can make it more difficult to sleep and get good rest. If your schedule is altered by events beyond your control, try as best as you can to get back on your sleep-wake schedule as soon as possible.

- Don't force yourself to sleep. If you find you cannot fall asleep within about thirty minutes, get up and do something relaxing away from your bed. Don't try to go back to bed until you are tired. Trying to force yourself to sleep can make going to bed an unpleasant experience. This can just perpetuate the problem, since lying in bed may become associated with discomfort and frustration.

- Before going to bed at night, give yourself some downtime. For an hour or two before you plan to go to sleep, let yourself relax physically and mentally. Avoid things that are too stimulating, such as exercise, conflicts, or working on projects.

- Create a regular routine before going to bed. Do something that helps you to relax and unwind. A nice hot bubble bath or a shower can help you feel more relaxed and sleepy. You might also do some relaxation exercises to help calm your mind and body. See the next section, "Managing Stress," for relaxation exercises you can do.

- Rather than rely on prescription or over-the-counter medications to help you sleep, speak with your doctor about natural supplements that can serve a similar purpose.

- Get some exercise during the day. Aerobic exercise is preferable, but even long walks are sufficient.

- Stay away from heavy meals, alcohol, caffeine, and nicotine before going to bed.

- Don't let yourself take naps during the day. This can disrupt your ability to fall asleep and stay asleep later on.

- Consider practical matters such as getting a comfortable mattress, adjusting the temperature of your bedroom, eliminating noise or distractions, and managing difficulties with your sleeping partner.

- Sexual activity before going to sleep can help you rest better.

- If you become anxious about being able to sleep well, let yourself accept the fact that you will have some difficulties from time to time. Even if you are only able to get a few hours of sleep, you will still be able to function the next day. The less you fear these difficulties, the more they will diminish. It might be helpful to complete an Automatic Thought Record around fears, irritations, or other concerns about being able to sleep. Sometimes it's the thoughts themselves that keep you wired and awake.

- If sleep problems persist, you should see your physician for a medical evaluation. It may also be useful to see a psychologist or counselor, since problems with sleep can also be caused by emotional difficulties or other mental health problems.

Additional Thoughts about Managing Hypomania

Some people find it useful to enlist the help of others when they start to feel hypomanic. Sometimes, the people closest to you will notice signs of hypomania even before you do. You can ask family or friends to let you know when they notice changes in your behavior and allow them to help you implement management strategies.

When you're feeling hypomanic, avoid making major decisions. Although you can feel very inspired and elated, this is not the time to make life-changing decisions such as getting divorced, getting married, quitting your job, asking for a raise, or moving to a new city. Delay any decisions you want to make until you've had a chance to consider them when you are not feeling so hypomanic.

Avoid spending money excessively. Money becomes much harder to manage during hypomania. Many people with cyclothymia find that they make poor decisions about how they spend their money: purchasing big-ticket items, investing in get-rich-quick schemes, overtipping at restaurants, giving to charities, making impulse purchases using credit cards, or the like. While you feel hypomanic, it might be useful to have someone else hold your credit cards. Also, stay away from your favorite stores, avoid going to the bank, and wait on making investments. Give yourself at least two days before making a desired purchase and discuss the decision with some friends before giving in. This can keep you from spending money in a way that you might regret later on.

Avoid risky sexual encounters. People with cyclothymia are much more likely to engage in sexual indiscretions when they are becoming hypomanic or fully hypomanic. You may find yourself becoming very sexually driven and let yourself get into situations that increase your risk of making decisions about sex that you wouldn't make when you are not feeling hypomanic. If you go out, you might take a good friend who knows about your cyclothymia and who can help steer you away from making poor decisions.

If, during a hypomanic episode, you do something about which you later feel embarrassment, regret, or guilt, you may need to apologize and make amends in order to maintain relationships with people. Also, during this difficult time, don't forget that it is the illness of cyclothymia that led you to do things you wouldn't normally do. Finding ways to forgive yourself will be important as you manage cyclothymia in your life.

If your hypomania becomes worse than you have experienced before, it doesn't seem to abate, you engage in behaviors that cause serious problems, or you begin to have hallucinations or strange perceptual experiences, you should seek professional help from your physician, a psychiatrist, or a psychologist. See chapter 5 for how to find professional help.

MANAGING ANGER

Let me start by dispelling a myth about anger. Anger is not inherently a "negative" or "bad" emotion. It is not an emotion that shouldn't be felt or expressed. It is also not something you should avoid or suppress. Instead, anger is a very normal emotion that can be quite useful. Anger signals that something is wrong, unfair, or needs changing. Used properly, it can be a wonderful motivational force, inspiring you to take action to correct a problem.

The real trouble with anger is not in feeling it but in what you *do* with it. Expressing anger inappropriately can cause serious problems for you and for those you care about. It affects how you interact with your partner, how you parent your children, how you get along with your friends, how you perform in the workplace, and certainly how you feel about yourself.

As a person with cyclothymia, you know that anger, irritability, and frustration are par for the course. These feelings are not foreign to you; neither are the problems that can come with them. Everyone's experience with anger is different. For some, anger comes on suddenly with a volcanic rage, spewing lava onto those who happen to be nearby. For others, anger can be more of an internal experience, boiling beneath the surface. For others still, anger seems like a snarling beast that is uncontrollable and dangerous when unleashed. However you experience anger, it is important to know that you can learn to manage the worst of it.

Remember when I said in chapter 7 that it is our perception of a situation that causes us to have feelings, not the events themselves? Well, the same thing applies here. It is common to believe that other people "make" us angry; or that when we get angry, we are justified in doing so; or that the world should conform to the way we want it to be. These really are mistaken beliefs. The first step in managing anger is to let go of these mistaken beliefs and recognize that we are each responsible for our own anger. We create our own anger and we are responsible for managing it.

■ Marcus

Problems with anger have affected every area of Marcus's life, including his family, his friendships, his relationships with women, and his coworkers. He has lost many relationships, and a few jobs, as a result. Marcus says, "I have discovered that my big trigger for anger is believing that people should be doing something a certain way. When they don't seem to listen to me, or do things too slowly, or do them wrong, I get pissed off. It's as if they're doing it just to make me mad. I've been working on trying to express myself without blowing up, and I'm learning to catch the kinds of thoughts that cause me to get angry with people."

Your Red Flags for Anger

As we did for depression and hypomania, let's start by identifying your red flags. What things do you notice just before you experience angry feelings and behaviors? Oftentimes, people find it takes paying attention during further experiences with anger to become adept at noticing the more subtle signs.

EXERCISE 8.6 RED FLAGS FOR ANGER

As you look at the following list, I recommend you spend a few extra minutes trying to recall physical sensations in your body just before you have an outburst of anger. Many people find that physical signs—such as a clenched fist, feeling warm all over, racing heart—become their best red flags signaling that they need to take action to manage their anger.

Physical and Behavioral

- ☐ clenched fists
- ☐ racing heart
- ☐ vision becomes blurred
- ☐ clenched teeth, jaw
- ☐ stomp, pound fist, kick, punch wall
- ☐ restless, pace the room
- ☐ voice gets louder
- ☐ say mean things you later regret

- ☐ feel warm (face, body, all over)
- ☐ perspiration
- ☐ sudden burst of energy
- ☐ frown, furrowed brow
- ☐ sudden, jerky movements
- ☐ feel rush of adrenaline
- ☐ skin tightens

Emotional

- ☐ irritated, annoyed
- ☐ filled with rage
- ☐ discouraged
- ☐ hopeless
- ☐ remorseful
- ☐ jealous

- ☐ frustrated
- ☐ fearful, anxious
- ☐ helpless
- ☐ inadequate, incompetent
- ☐ insulted, humiliated
- ☐ resentful

Thoughts

- ☐ *It's not fair.*
- ☐ *That's not how I would do it.*
- ☐ *I must get back at him/her.*
- ☐ *They won't do what I want them to do.*
- ☐ *They are disrespecting me.*
- ☐ *He/she is a threat to me.*

- ☐ *He/she shouldn't have done that.*
- ☐ *That shouldn't happen.*
- ☐ *This is the worst that could happen.*
- ☐ *They should change.*
- ☐ *He/she took advantage of me.*
- ☐ *I should always be treated well.*

☐ *I can't tolerate this.*

☐ *He/she did this on purpose.*

☐ *I'm trapped in this job, relationship.*

Angry Thinking Styles (see exercise 7.1)

☐ blaming

☐ "shoulds"/"musts"

☐ jumping to conclusions

☐ fallacy of fairness

☐ _____

☐ _____

☐ all-or-nothing

☐ filtering

☐ being right

☐ reward fallacy

☐ _____

☐ _____

Your Other Red Flags

☐ _____

☐ _____

☐ _____

☐ _____

☐ _____

☐ _____

☐ _____

☐ _____

People who have problems with anger generally have a low tolerance for frustration. That is, they can become irritated or upset more quickly and more easily than other people. Whether this tendency is genetic, biological, or learned may be hard to tell. Whichever the case, anger can come up for the following reasons:

 You *react* with anger when you believe you have been wronged, hurt, treated unfairly, disrespected, or threatened.

 You *use* anger to try to change the behavior of others, to get revenge, to punish others, to get others to conform, to get your way, to force people to interact with you, or to protect yourself.

 You *feel* angry when you would otherwise feel helpless, hopeless, trapped, discouraged, abandoned, anxious, inadequate, remorseful, or jealous.

Interestingly, behaving in angry ways has likely had some payoff for you over time. I know this may sound like a strange idea. You might think to yourself, *I don't want to get angry and hurt my partner's feelings. Why would I do that?* Being a powerful force, anger has likely gotten you some things you have wanted. Other people may back down when you express anger. They want to do whatever is necessary to keep the peace, to calm you down, to avoid embarrassment around others, and so forth. Whether you have thought about it in a conscious way or not, anger has had some benefits. You may not have been encouraged to use methods other than anger to react to and solve problems. Why should you, if anger works for you?

Here is another idea that may seem strange: People who have been in your life for a number of years have let you know that your anger is acceptable. By doing little or nothing about your angry reactions, they have taught you that it is okay with them if you use your anger to cope with problems. They may have complained about your anger in the past or suggested they might leave if you don't change, but in the end, they continue to live with it. It often takes a partner setting an ultimatum within a relationship before a person will really seek help for problems with anger.

Unfortunately, the more you use anger with other people, the more you risk pushing them away from you. Expressing excessive anger has never really solved a problem in such a way that all parties come away satisfied. It just doesn't work. There are better, more effective ways to solve problems. You and others involved are likely to be much more satisfied by dealing with problems in more appropriate ways.

Managing anger more effectively can involve using strategies such as relaxation techniques, cognitive behavioral approaches, communication skills, and problem-solving skills, as well as a few other tips described below.

Strategies for Managing Anger

The goal of anger management is to reduce your physiological arousal (the physical symptoms of anger) and the intensity of your emotions while controlling your angry reactions to situations.

You can reduce your physiological arousal by using progressive muscle relaxation, deep breathing exercises, or imagery exercises. I'll discuss these techniques in the next section, "Managing Stress."

You can reduce the intensity of your emotions with the following cognitive approaches:

Modify your thoughts. Use an Automatic Thought Record (exercise 7.2) and strategies for balanced thinking (table 7.1) to modify automatic thoughts that lead to anger. Notice that with the red flags in exercise 8.6, I have included some specific thinking styles that are most closely related to thoughts that lead to feelings of anger. Try to notice if these apply to situations you have recently experienced.

Consider your anger objectively. Determine whether your anger is helpful or not helpful, not whether it is good or bad. If you judge your anger as bad, it is easy to take the next step of believing *you* are bad, and this self-criticism is just not useful for you. Conversely, if you believe your anger is good, then you come from a stance of believing your anger is justified and you don't need to change. Instead, think about whether your anger is helpful to you or not, whether it enhances your life and the lives of those around you.

Accept what you cannot change. Find ways to accept that there are things you cannot change, that life inherently has difficult challenges, and that ultimately you are able to handle your problems.

Try to adopt the other person's point of view. Put yourself in the shoes of the other person and recognize that the other side of the argument has valid points as well. Take a moment to validate the other person's position as realistic without succumbing to your own pressing desire to be right. Listen to the other person's thoughts and feelings and acknowledge that you can understand this position. You don't have to agree with it, just let the other person know you understand. Taking this moment to step outside yourself and see another's position can have a calming effect for you.

Apologize and forgive. Be ready to apologize for excessive anger, for things you said that you did not mean, and for any other behaviors that you regret. Be willing to forgive the other person's behaviors as well.

Here are some ways you can control your angry reactions.

Become a good problem solver. When conflicts arise, take the tack that you will approach the situation in a logical, problem-solving manner. For instance, you can take out a piece of paper and begin to write advantages and disadvantages of solving the problem in various ways. Refrain from arguing the points as you write them; just sit down and make the list. This can serve two purposes. One, it can naturally help you calm down, since you have to take the time to make the lists. Two, it can help distract you from the emotions you were feeling, since you are coming from a logical rather than emotional perspective.

Improve your communication skills. In the next chapter, you will learn some effective communication skills. I'll focus on how to listen, how to be heard, and how to be assertive.

Temporarily avoid the hot situation. If you feel your anger is overwhelming or you believe you are at risk of hurting someone or damaging property, you may need to remove yourself from the situation until you feel calmer. Don't get in your car and drive away angry, since that puts you and other drivers at risk for an accident. Instead, walk away from the immediate vicinity. You might take a long walk, go to a friend's house, or go to a park.

Give yourself a time-out. Essentially, this is a shortened form of a relaxation exercise. Rather than explode at another person, make yourself spend a few moments taking some long, slow, deep breaths. Counting backward from one hundred by sevens is another way to distract yourself and take some time to calm down.

MANAGING STRESS

In chapter 2, I spoke briefly about the negative impact stress can have on those with cyclothymia. Stressful events, managed poorly, can put you at risk for having increased problems with mood; this can exacerbate the stressful situation, causing even more problems with mood. It can be a vicious cycle. The good news is that you can minimize the effects of stress if you learn and practice stress management strategies. I'll discuss some of those techniques shortly.

Stress is a common topic of conversation. At one time or another, we have all felt stressed out, burned out, overwhelmed, or on the verge of "losing it." While we speak of feeling stressed, we don't often stop to think about what this word really means. "Stress" can be defined as any mental, physical, emotional, or behavioral reactions to a perceived demand or threat. The demand or threat needn't be a life-or-death situation, although it certainly can be. People feel stress in all kinds of situations they perceive as demanding, such as speaking in front of a large group of people, preparing taxes, arranging day care for children, and driving in heavy traffic.

Once again, recall that it is your thoughts about an event that cause you to have feelings, not the event itself. When it comes to stress, you have to perceive a situation as demanding, threatening, or overwhelming before you will feel stressed about it. Inherent in such a perception is either the belief that you won't be able to cope or the belief that the solution is somehow very difficult or inconvenient. It's as if there is an underlying assumption that life should not be difficult, that we should never have to struggle or suffer. M. Scott Peck opens his best-selling book *The Road Less Traveled* by writing, "Life is difficult. This is a great truth, one of the greatest truths. It is a great truth because once we truly see this truth, we transcend it. Once we truly know that life is difficult—once we truly understand and accept it—then life is no longer difficult. Because once it is accepted, the fact that life is difficult no longer matters" (1978, 15).

Indeed, stress is a normal part of life. Experiencing a mild or moderate amount of stress from time to time can protect you and help you adapt. Your response to stress helps you prepare for difficult challenges and react appropriately in times of crisis. In fact, a certain amount of stress is necessary to help you perform at your best. Stress adds flavor, challenge, and opportunity to life. Without stress, life could become quite dull and unexciting.

You might think about stress as the volume knob on a stereo. When the volume is too low, you can't enjoy the music. Things may seem dull and boring, or you may feel unmotivated to accomplish things you want to do. On the other hand, when the volume is too high, you can feel overstimulated by the music and overwhelmed in general. When the volume is somewhere in the middle, the music is more enjoyable. There is a healthy amount of stress that motivates you to address the challenges before you. Your task is to determine what volume level works best for you.

Recall that in chapter 2 you filled out your Stress Chart (exercise 2.4). You identified mood problems, their relation to stressful events, and the outcome of the combination of mood problems and stressful events. Please continue to use that chart.

■ Jerry

Jerry has known for some time that stress is a big trigger for him. When things get tough at work, he starts feeling stressed out rather quickly. According to Jerry, "Stress seems to sneak up on me. I finally realize when I'm stressed out because I yell at someone, usually over something stupid. I finally got fed up with it and started working part-time last year. That has helped a lot. I've gotten better at seeing my stress warning signals, though. My neck and back muscles get tense, I feel light-headed, and I start getting snappy with people and frustrated with myself. I've been able to head off a few arguments with my wife after seeing that I'm getting stressed. When I notice it, I either go take a walk or do some woodworking in the garage. That seems to help calm me down so I can work on what's stressing me out."

Your Red Flags for Stress

People tend to pay a lot of attention to things in the outer world that are related to stress, such as financial difficulties, conflicts in relationships, and overwhelming responsibilities. People generally don't pay enough attention to their inner world, the internal signals and reactions that stress is starting to take a toll. Interestingly, many people are quite good at ignoring those signals and pushing themselves even harder. However, this can put them at risk for developing more severe physical and emotional problems.

EXERCISE 8.7 RED FLAGS FOR STRESS

Below is a list of some, but not all, possible reactions to stress. Check all of the symptoms you experience when you feel stressed. Write in additional ones as necessary. Notice that symptoms of stress can affect you physically, behaviorally, emotionally, and cognitively. You can learn to recognize these symptoms or red flags in yourself before stress gets too far out of hand. When you recognize your unique signals, that's the time to take action.

Physical

- ☐ headaches
- ☐ indigestion, digestive problems
- ☐ stomachaches
- ☐ sweaty palms
- ☐ cold hands or feet
- ☐ dizziness
- ☐ fatigue
- ☐ muscle tension
- ☐ _____
- ☐ _____

- ☐ back pain
- ☐ tight neck and shoulder muscles
- ☐ racing heart
- ☐ shallow breathing
- ☐ restlessness
- ☐ ringing in the ears
- ☐ constipation
- ☐ diarrhea
- ☐ _____
- ☐ _____

Behavioral

- ☐ smoking excessively
- ☐ more controlling, bossy
- ☐ critical attitude toward others
- ☐ short-tempered
- ☐ procrastinating
- ☐ sleeping too little, sleeping too much
- ☐ _____
- ☐ _____

- ☐ driving too fast or recklessly
- ☐ clenching jaw, grinding teeth
- ☐ eating too little, eating too much
- ☐ inability to finish tasks
- ☐ nail biting
- ☐ fidgety
- ☐ _____
- ☐ _____

Emotional

☐	bothered by small things	☐	crying easily
☐	nervousness, anxiety	☐	sense of overwhelming pressure
☐	boredom	☐	anger
☐	edginess	☐	loneliness
☐	irritability	☐	discouragement, frustration
☐	feeling "burned out"	☐	"moodiness"
☐	feeling powerless or helpless	☐	hopelessness
☐	_____	☐	_____
☐	_____	☐	_____

Cognitive

☐	trouble thinking clearly	☐	inability to make decisions
☐	difficulty concentrating or focusing	☐	frequent worry
☐	forgetfulness	☐	loss of humor
☐	lack of creativity	☐	flood of thoughts
☐	_____	☐	_____
☐	_____	☐	_____

Of course, the symptoms or red flags listed above could be associated with causes other than stress. If they persist over time, you should consult with your physician.

Strategies for Managing Stress

So, you are working on identifying your red flags for stress, including situations and perceptions that trigger stress and the internal signals you may experience. Now it's time to look at some practical strategies for managing stress.

Create a support system. Find someone to talk to about your feelings and experiences. Speak to friends, family, a teacher, a minister, or a counselor. Sometimes it helps to just vent or get something off your chest. Expressing your feelings can help you feel a sense of relief, help you feel supported by others, and help you work out your problems.

Change your attitude. Find other ways to think about stressful situations. Talk to yourself positively. Try saying, "I can handle it," "This will be over soon," or "I have handled difficult things before, and I can do it again." Also, practice acceptance. Do your best to learn to accept things you cannot change, without trying to exert more control over them.

Be realistic. Set practical goals for dealing with situations and solving problems. Develop realistic expectations of yourself and others. Setting your expectations or goals high may seem like a useful way to push yourself and get things done, but you may also set yourself up for disappointment and continued stress. Find the courage to recognize your limits.

Get organized and take charge. Disorganization and poor planning often lead to frustration or crisis situations, which in turn lead you to feel stressed. Plan your time, make a schedule, and establish your priorities. Do this regularly until it becomes a productive habit. Take responsibility for your life. Be proactive. Problem-solve and look for solutions rather than worry. Don't hesitate to go to your family and friends for support if you need it.

Take breaks; give yourself "me time." Learn that taking time for yourself for rejuvenation and relaxation is just as important as giving time to other activities. At a minimum, take short breaks during your busy day. You might purposely schedule time in your day planner just for yourself so that you can recharge for all the other things you need to do. Learn your red flags for stress, and be willing to take time to do something about it.

Take good care of yourself. Eat properly, get regular rest, and keep a routine. Allow yourself to do something you enjoy each day. Paradoxically, the time you need to take care of yourself the most—when you are stressed—is the time you do it the least. When you feel overwhelmed, you're more likely to eat poorly, sleep less, stop exercising, and generally push yourself harder. This can tax the immune system and cause you to become ill more easily. If you take good care of yourself to begin with, you will be better prepared to manage stress and accomplish your tasks in the long run.

Learn to say no. Learn to pick and choose which things you will say yes to and which things you will not. Protect yourself by not allowing yourself to take on every request or opportunity that comes your way. It is okay to decline a request for a favor. Saying no does not mean you are bad, self-centered, or uncaring. Learn skills of assertiveness so that you can feel more confident and have effective ways of saying no.

Get regular exercise. Exercising regularly can relieve some symptoms of depression and stress and help you to maintain your health. Exercise can build confidence, self-esteem, and self-image. It is also a great way to take time for yourself, blow off steam, and release physical tension.

Get a hobby; do something different. For a balanced lifestyle, play is as important as work. Leisure activities and hobbies can be very enjoyable and inspiring, and they can offer an added sense of accomplishment to your life. For ideas on new hobbies, browse through a bookstore or a crafts store, surf the Internet, look up local organizations, or see what classes are available in your community or from a nearby college or university. Don't quickly dismiss new opportunities.

Slow down. Know your limits and cut down on the number of things you try to do each day, particularly if you do not have enough time for your ordinary responsibilities or for yourself. Be realistic about what you can accomplish effectively each day. Also, monitor your pace. Rushing through things can lead to mistakes or poor performance. Take the time you need to do a good job. Poorly done tasks can lead to added stress.

Laugh; use humor. Do something fun and enjoyable, such as seeing a funny movie, laughing with friends, reading a humorous book, or going to a comedy show.

Learn to relax. Learn some relaxation exercises such as those discussed in the next section. Develop a regular relaxation routine. Try yoga, meditation, or some simple quiet time. Relaxation techniques are skills that need to be developed with patience and practice so that you can use them effectively during times of stress.

EXERCISE 8.8 OTHER STRESS MANAGEMENT IDEAS

What other things have you done to help manage stress?

_____

_____

_____

_____

_____

_____

_____

What things would you like to start doing to manage stress?

_____

_____

_____

_____

_____

_____

_____

_____

Relaxation Exercises

Learning and practicing relaxation exercises can be a wonderful way to reduce feelings of stress. Relaxation techniques can help reduce emotional and physical sensations of stress, as well as the worry or stressful thoughts that may accompany them. If you can learn to relax your breathing and reduce your muscle tension, your mind will follow. Conversely, if you can learn to ease stressful thoughts and worry, your body will relax as well.

Approach these exercises as skills that need to be practiced and developed over time, rather than as something you can do once in a while. Without practice, these exercises will not be as effective for you at the time you need them most.

Deep Breathing

When you feel stressed, your rate of breathing increases. You are also likely to breathe shallowly and high in your chest, rather than fully throughout your abdomen. A deep breathing exercise allows you to take slower, more full breaths that reflect a truly relaxed state.

EXERCISE 8.9   DEEP BREATHING

Slowly take a long, deep breath. Hold it for a count of four. Then, gently and slowly let it all out to another count of four, releasing tension from your body as you exhale. With each out-breath, let more and more tension leave your body. Because your breathing becomes rapid and shallow as you feel tension, a few deep breaths can help more oxygen enter your system, literally breathing more life into your body. Try doing this exercise for at least two or three minutes several times each day.

Progressive Muscle Relaxation

Stress can lead to increased muscle tension throughout your body. You may have noticed having achy or tight muscles in your neck, shoulder, or back. It is common not to recognize muscle tension as a sign of stress. In fact, you can get so used to holding tension in your body that it seems like a normal state of being. Progressive muscle relaxation allows you to really feel what it is like to fully relax your muscles by comparing a tense state with a relaxed state.

EXERCISE 8.10   PROGRESSIVE MUSCLE RELAXATION

While sitting upright in a chair, let yourself relax for a few moments, taking in several long, deep breaths. You might even close your eyes to help cut down on distractions and promote a relaxed state. Take turns tensing and releasing certain muscle groups (see below), beginning at the top of your head. Tense each muscle group for about eight to ten seconds, but not so tight that you cause cramps or hurt yourself. Really notice what it feels like to hold that tension in your muscles. Then, release each muscle group for another eight to ten seconds before tensing another group. When you release your muscles, do so rapidly, letting them collapse and relax fully. Again, let yourself notice what it really feels like to experience relaxation in your muscle groups. As you go through this exercise, compare the difference between tense muscles and relaxed ones. This will help you become more sensitive to those moments when tension starts to creep into your muscles, increasing your feelings of stress.

Muscle Group	How to Tense Your Muscles
Forehead, eyes, jaw, tongue, lips	Wrinkle forehead, squint eyes, clench jaw, press tongue to roof of mouth, press lips together
Neck, shoulders, upper back	Raise chin while resisting doing so, bring shoulders up to your ears, and press back against your chair
Upper arms, forearms, hands	Clench fists, bring arms up to shoulders, tighten biceps
Chest, abdomen, lower back	Tighten stomach and chest muscles, arch lower back
Buttocks and thighs	Tighten buttocks, lift legs straight out in front of you
Calves, shins, ankles, feet	Pull feet and toes up toward your shins

Imagery

Using *imagery*, or visualization, is a nice way of giving your mind and body a minivacation during a busy day. It involves closing your eyes and letting your mind become fully immersed in a calm, comforting scene. The scene you choose should be something that is calming and peaceful for you. It might be a place you visited one summer, your grandparents' home, snuggling up on the couch by a nice fire, taking a stroll down a beach, resting on a rock by a stream in the forest, or taking a nice, hot bubble bath. It can be anything you like.

EXERCISE 8.11 IMAGERY

Let yourself rest in a comfortable position and close your eyes. For a few moments, take in several long, smooth breaths, letting all the tension in your body melt away. Begin to imagine your chosen scene. Let yourself become immersed in your scene by observing everything that is around you. Notice the smallest details of what you see, the things you smell, the sounds you hear, and the tactile sensations you feel. Study the details of each of these things while you let yourself be fully present in your calming place.

DEVELOPING AN EXERCISE PLAN

Creating and implementing an exercise plan for yourself can strengthen not only your body but your mind and spirit as well. There are so many positive effects to exercise that you would be doing yourself a disservice not to do it!

Regular exercise can

- improve mild to moderate symptoms of depression

- calm hypomania, if the exercise is not too intense

- help manage stress and release tension

- increase your energy level

- help you to sleep better at night

- regulate your appetite

- help you to feel better about yourself, improve your self-confidence, give you a sense of personal accomplishment, and increase your overall feeling of well-being

- help you reduce your reliance on alcohol and illicit drugs

- bring a regular activity into your life by which you can structure your daily rhythm (see chapter 6)

- give you an easy opportunity to interact with friends and be around people, or conversely, it can be a good way to have some "me time."

When you feel depressed, you may find that it is more difficult to motivate yourself for something like regular exercise. During such times, it can be quite helpful if you already have an exercise routine in place. You may be more willing and able to follow an existing plan than you would be to start a new exercise plan for the first time. If you find you need to cut back on your exercise when you are not feeling well, that is fine. Just do as much as you can do toward the plan you develop for yourself.

If you are feeling hypomanic, consider engaging in more mild exercise. Sometimes people find that rigorous exercise exacerbates hypomanic symptoms. Pay attention to this for yourself as you implement your exercise plan. Use your Mood Chart (exercise 6.1) and Rhythm Chart (exercise 6.3) from chapter 6 to record the effects exercise has on your mood.

■ Maria

Maria used to play some sports in high school, but she got busy and didn't continue with them in college. She says, "I used to love working out and going for a long run. It was relaxing, and I could get out all my stress and tension. Just a few weeks ago, I started running again. I had to start off slow, but I've enjoyed it so far. It still seems to be a good way to release stress, and it has been helping my mood already. I'm keeping track of how I feel using my Mood and Rhythm Charts just to see if it works for me. Even if it doesn't help my mood in the long run, I am still enjoying it."

While exercise can help improve your mood, there are certainly many physical benefits as well. According to the American Heart Association (2004) and the Weight-Control Information Network (2003), these benefits include

■ reducing your risk of—or helping to manage—conditions such as heart disease, type 2 diabetes, high blood pressure, elevated cholesterol levels, osteoporosis, arthritis, and some cancers

■ helping you manage your weight

■ increasing your flexibility and balance

■ increasing your muscle strength, allowing you to engage in other physical activities

■ helping to deter illnesses as you age, enhancing quality of life and independence

The Weight-Control Information Network (2003) reports that experts recommend at least thirty minutes of moderate-intensity physical activity on most, if not all, days of the week. Physical activities can include many things. Walking, running, aerobics, basketball, and other sports are good structured activities. Alternatives to the more traditional types of exercise include activities like yoga, tai chi, or Pilates, which can have some of the same benefits. You can also gain some measure of exercise in daily activities such as household chores, walking the dog, working in the yard, and gardening.

Aerobic exercise is an effective moderate-intensity physical activity. This involves engaging in activity at a pace that causes you to breathe harder than you do when you are resting. Doing this will also increase your heart rate. As you breathe harder, you'll find it more difficult to talk, but your pace should be such that you can still carry on a conversation.

When you take on a new exercise plan, you should first consult with your doctor. Find out if the types of exercise you wish to do are suitable for you. If you have been sedentary for some time or had prior health concerns, you may need to have a physical exam before you start exercising.

Here are some ideas for things you can do to get good exercise.

biking	hiking	jogging or running
walking	lifting weights	aerobics classes
going to a gym	tai chi	yoga
Pilates	dancing (swing, salsa)	organized sports
skiing	raking leaves	taking a walk during lunch
shoveling snow	kickboxing	standing up while talking on the phone
kayaking, canoeing	taking the stairs	
roller-skating or Rollerblading	swimming	parking farther from your destination
gardening	mowing the lawn	using home exercise equipment
going to a museum or mall	karate	joining a fitness center
		starting a recreation league at your office

As you implement your exercise plan, keep the following tips in mind:

- Start small. Don't ask too much of yourself at first by jumping in all at once. Gradually work up to being able to exercise for thirty minutes each day. You might try intervals of ten to fifteen minutes at a time.

- Give yourself some variety in the types of exercises you do so you won't get bored.

- Accept that it will take some time before your body gets used to exercising. You will be sore and tired at first. But hang in there so you can experience the positive effects!

- Don't overdo it. Be careful about putting yourself at risk for injury.

- Plan your exercise for a convenient time of day, but don't exercise too late at night, since doing so could make you feel wired and interfere with your ability to fall asleep. Mornings, afternoons, or early evenings are usually best.

- Get an exercise partner or arrange to exercise with a few friends. This can be a fun way to socialize, and you can help motivate each other to stick to your plans.

- Keep track of exactly what your plan is and how well you stick to it. You can use your Mood Chart and Rhythm Chart from chapter 6 to track your progress.

- If you miss exercising a few days now and again, don't berate yourself or let yourself give up. Just pick up where you left off and continue from there.

Summing Up

This has been a chapter full of ways to manage the highs and lows of cyclothymic mood. As promised, I emphasized identifying your red flags, or early warning signals, so that you can become your own expert at knowing when to take action to keep your mood from becoming worse. When a red flag occurs for you, do not hesitate. Look at your lists of strategies, the ones you checked off or wrote in this workbook, and do something as soon as you possibly can. It may be tempting to try to wait it out and see if your mood improves, but you'll likely be much better off in the long run if you go ahead and implement one or more of your strategies.

I'd like to encourage you again to practice the strategies and skills I discussed in this chapter. I talked about using a Daily Activity Record, regulating your sleep, managing your anger and stress, and developing an exercise plan. You might pick just a few strategies among all of these and practice them each day. For instance, you could develop your ability to use a deep breathing relaxation exercise, take a yoga class three or four times each week, and establish a habit of reading one chapter of a book you enjoy each night as you wind down for bed.

Start off slowly, take it easy, and be patient with yourself. You can do it! It will take some time, but before you know it, you will reap the rewards of all your efforts. If you find it helpful, let people around you support you in what you are trying to do for yourself. In the next chapter, we will focus on managing relationships at home and work, learning good communication skills, and developing a support network.

CHAPTER 9

Managing Relationships

In the second half of this workbook, you have been doing a lot of important work to help manage your mood and other symptoms of cyclothymia. This chapter on managing relationships will help you understand and cope with difficulties that occur in your relationships at home and work, help you educate others about how cyclothymia affects your life, give you tools for effective communication, and help you develop your support system.

As you have been struggling with cyclothymia over time, you have likely had a number of difficulties in your relationships. Perhaps that sounds like quite an understatement. The very nature of cyclothymia makes it difficult to have consistent, untroubled interactions with other people. I have discussed how cyclothymia can bring irritability, outbursts of anger, sudden mood changes, and otherwise inconsistent behaviors around others. Long-standing partnerships, marriages, and family relationships are frequently affected. As a person with cyclothymia, you get frustrated, angry, sad, and discouraged in your interactions with other people. During conflicts, you may have said and done things you later regret, but at the time it may have seemed difficult—if not impossible—to control your actions or choose to act differently.

This chapter appears toward the end of the workbook because the work of managing and improving your relationships builds on all of the skills you have learned earlier in the book. In chapter 4, you explored how other people perceive your mood and behaviors (exercise 4.4). You then went through a checklist of descriptions others have used to characterize your behaviors (exercise 4.5). I also encouraged you to interview a trusted family member or friend (exercise 4.6) to help you gain more awareness of how you come across to others. Take a few moments to review the work you did in chapter 4 around others' perceptions of you and your cyclothymia. This should give you an overview of the kinds of interpersonal challenges you might want to address for yourself in this chapter. In chapter 6, you started keeping track of your interactions with other people using your Rhythm Chart (exercise 6.3). In chapter 7, we looked at how your thoughts about interactions with others influence your feelings and subsequent behaviors. You learned how to use an Automatic Thought Record (exercise 7.2) to identify and modify thoughts that cause distressing feelings. Chapter 8 was full of topics that have an impact on your relationships. I discussed red flags and strategies for managing cyclothymic symptoms, sleep, anger, and stress. I will tap into each of these topics from previous chapters as I offer you ways of managing your relationships.

YOUR FAMILY, PARTNER, AND FRIENDS

Cyclothymia doesn't begin and end with the person who has the condition. It affects partners, family members, and friends as well. Like a stone dropped into a calm pond causing ripples to travel to the shore, cyclothymia will have ripple effects in your relationships. As you have reflected throughout this workbook about the difficulties that cyclothymia has caused in your life, more than likely you have recalled a number of problems with people who are or have been close to you.

■ Helen's Husband, Steve

Steve says, "Last week Helen seemed to be getting more and more depressed. She said she had been really stressed out with the kids and her part-time job. Thursday night she went off on me for two hours about how we needed to start saving for our kids to go to college, that we'd never have enough money for them. She has just been more snappy and withdrawn lately. Usually, this means I have to do what I can to keep things calm around here. I told the kids to be sure to keep the noise down around Mommy. They've gotten used to that. I knew Helen wouldn't be able to do much this past weekend, so I called our friends to postpone our dinner plans for Saturday. They seemed disappointed, but this isn't the first time I've had to do that. I just need to give Helen some space for a while. I get irritated at how much this seems to happen, but if I don't keep the peace, then things just seem to get worse."

The very nature of cyclothymia makes it difficult for you to be consistent in your interactions with others. The highs and lows of mood, changes in activity and energy levels, difficulties with sleep, and fluctuations in judgment are characteristics of cyclothymia that are often related to problems in relationships. Unless people around you also experience mood swings or have a bipolar disorder, they probably will not be able to understand what this is like for you. They will have no insight into your internal experiences, your perceptions, and your struggles. What you try to explain to them makes little sense because their experiences are different. They haven't been where you are, and they wouldn't be capable of going there even if they wanted to.

When others meet you for the first time, your hypomania can be an attractive trait to them. They see your energy, your excitement, and your ability to enjoy yourself. After a time, however, the increased energy and the driven quality of this mood state can lose its charm and become a source of frustration for people around you. While you may feel quite good during hypomania and enjoy your charge of energy and sharp focus, people may see you as self-absorbed and lacking in concern for others. While you feel euphoric and compelled to ride your creative wave, others may see your drive as purposeless and excessive. While others feel frustrated, you don't see that there is a problem. Such discrepancies in perceptions of your mood and behaviors are common and can be a very sore point of contention between you and those around you.

A similar gap in perception develops when you feel depressed. While the world can seem bleak, purposeless, and demanding to you, others cannot understand why you have had a sudden change in your outlook and mood. While you want to be left alone or need some quiet time, others want to know what is wrong or why you can't be like yourself. Since they're unable to understand how your mood is affected by cyclothymia, other people may try to come up with "reasonable" explanations. They may attribute your behaviors to personality traits and use words like "dramatic," "selfish," or "attention-seeking."

If you think about it, there is some logic to other people's reactions to you. If people cannot understand your hypomania, depression, irritability, and anxiety, then confusion, dismay, frustration, helplessness, and anger are normal thoughts and feelings for them. If your sudden mood swings lead to angry outbursts, poor judgment, and impulsive behaviors on your part, then fear, discouragement, irritation, guilt, and sadness would also be normal thoughts and feelings for others to have. It is logical that any combination of these things can lead to arguments, frustrations, and resentments for all parties involved.

This is a compelling and necessary reason to educate those around you about your illness. Your willingness to help others understand you, as well as your openness to understanding them, can go a long way toward improving your relationships. Ultimately, everyone wants the same thing: to understand and to be understood. Both things are quite possible if everyone involved is willing to participate and compromise a bit. What you need to first consider, however, is whether you wish people to know about your illness at all.

To Tell or Not to Tell

You might struggle with whether or not to tell others about your diagnosis. This is certainly a personal choice. On the one hand, it can be helpful for others to know why you are sometimes depressed and other times full of life and energy. This way, they can attribute certain behaviors to the illness rather than to you as a person. Letting others know about your illness is also useful toward gaining support from important people around you. On the other hand, you might find that friends and family treat you differently upon learning your diagnosis. They may even leap to certain conclusions that are untrue about your condition, causing them to become fearful and avoid you.

If you decide you want to tell people about your cyclothymia, I suggest you do it a step at a time. Start with telling just a few of your closest family members or friends and gauge their responses. Be willing to answer their questions about your cyclothymia and let them know you are doing what you can to manage it. You might find that people are actually relieved to know that there is a name for what you have been struggling with. If you have some good experiences letting people know about your illness, then consider telling others as you see fit.

EDUCATING OTHERS ABOUT YOUR CYCLOTHYMIA

You can help your partner, family, and friends cope better with their feelings about your illness by educating them about it. This may also help you gain the support you need to manage your illness as well as help others dispel their misconceptions about what you are going through.

While you know quite well how cyclothymia affects your daily life, people who don't have this illness do not. Your partner, family, or friends are likely to have many questions about cyclothymia. Some of these questions you may find ridiculous or even offensive because of how well you know this experience. Common questions include *Why do you have mood swings? Why can't you control your anger/sadness? Why can't you be more consistent/reliable?* and *How did you get this illness?*

Here is some information that may be useful to share with people as you educate them about cyclothymia. You might even make copies of this information and give them to people as needed.

Table 9.1 About Cyclothymic Disorder

The following information is designed to help educate people about cyclothymic disorder, to increase awareness of the potentially devastating effects it can have on a person's life, and to enhance understanding of the challenges those with cyclothymia face daily. For more information, see www.AllAbout Cyclothymia.com or *The Cyclothymia Workbook: Learn How to Manage Your Mood Swings and Lead a Balanced Life* by Prentiss Price.

WHAT IS CYCLOTHYMIC DISORDER?

Cyclothymic disorder or *cyclothymia* (pronounced sigh-klo-THIGH-me-uh) is a condition that medical and mental health professionals categorize as a mood disorder. More specifically, it is a mild form of *bipolar disorder* or manic depression. Cyclothymia causes a person to experience rapid shifts in mood from the lows of feeling down, empty, sad, or fatigued (depressed) to the highs of feeling euphoric, goal-driven, irritable, and impulsive *(hypomanic)*. Outbursts of emotion, including anger, are not uncommon. Intense or unpredictable mood swings can happen over several minutes or several days. Symptoms of cyclothymia frequently interfere with relationships, parenting, work and career, and personal goals and accomplishments.

Cyclothymic disorder tends to be a lifelong condition, typically beginning when a person is a young adult. Cyclothymia is believed to affect up to 1 percent of the population. There is a 15 to 50 percent chance that a person with cyclothymia will go on to develop a more severe bipolar disorder.

WHAT IS IT LIKE TO HAVE CYCLOTHYMIA?

People with cyclothymia may come across as moody, dramatic, unreliable, or inconsistent in their behaviors, feelings, and decisions. Fluctuations in mood color the world. For instance, when the person feels depressed, things seem oppressive, bleak, dangerous, or hopeless. A person with cyclothymia may withdraw, become tearful, give up on things, feel fatigued and unmotivated, have trouble with thinking and making decisions, and become irritable, snappy, argumentative, and pessimistic.

While hypomanic, a person may feel "high," on top of the world, elated, impulsive, energized, and outgoing. Although hypomania can feel very good to the person experiencing it, there can be some devastating drawbacks. Hypomania can cause a person to become overly optimistic to the point of making rash decisions. Judgment can become impaired. For instance, people with cyclothymia may have problems with spending too much money, making poor business decisions, driving too fast, and engaging in other reckless behaviors. Hypomania can also bring increased libido, causing people to commit sexual indiscretions they would not otherwise become involved in.

WHAT CAUSES CYCLOTHYMIA?

Cyclothymia is likely caused by a variety of factors, none of which a person has control over. Researchers believe one of the strongest causes of mood disorders has to do with genetics. Having a close relative with depression, bipolar disorder, or cyclothymia increases a person's likelihood of developing it. There are also biological theories that implicate a person's brain structure, neurotransmitters, endocrine system, and sleep disturbances. Certain medical conditions—including hyper- or hypothyroidism, influenza, mononucleosis, head injuries, multiple sclerosis, and Huntington's disease—can be related to problems with mood. Stress is also believed to exacerbate difficulties with mood. We do not yet know for sure what causes a particular person to develop cyclothymic disorder.

WHAT IS NOT HELPFUL FOR A PERSON WITH CYCLOTHYMIA? WHAT IS HELPFUL?

It is not helpful to criticize, reject, scold, or fear someone who has cyclothymia. A person cannot control the fact that mood swings happen and cannot simply will away distressing mood states or "snap out of it." What may seem like exaggerated or outrageous behaviors can make sense to a person who is in the midst of hypomania. Similarly, depressed mood truly makes things seem dreary and useless. A person's behaviors, thoughts, and feelings will reflect this.

What is helpful for those with cyclothymia is support, encouragement, and understanding. That you are reading this material certainly demonstrates your support and desire to understand the effects of this illness. Open communication, honesty, and working together to get through difficult times is important for everyone involved. It is also helpful to have patience, to listen, to educate yourself about cyclothymia, and to empathize as much as possible. And, of course, it is also helpful simply to ask, "How can I be of help to you as you cope with this illness?"

YOUR WORKPLACE

Researchers have studied the effects of bipolar disorder on the workplace. Olfson and colleagues (1997) found those with bipolar disorder to be seven times as likely to miss work because of their illness. Zwerling and colleagues (2002) found that those who reported having bipolar disorder were 40 percent less likely to be employed than those who did not have this illness. Bipolar disorder is also associated with increased health care costs. Simon and Unutzer (1999) showed healthcare costs of those with bipolar disorder to be approximately two and a half times that of a comparison group. Their overall mental health costs were twenty times higher.

For those who have a bipolar disorder, including cyclothymia, the ability to function in the workplace can be compromised at times. Recall that the depressive and hypomanic symptoms of cyclothymia include reduced energy and motivation, problems with concentration and sleep, agitation, and irritability. These are all things that detract from your ability to perform on your job. It makes sense that you will struggle from time to time in what you can do and how much you can do it.

Your hypomanic symptoms may lead you to react to irritations by lashing out at your coworkers. You may be more prone to conflicts and arguments, sometimes getting yourself into trouble by saying more than you really should. The optimism and goal-directed behaviors of hypomania can lead you to take on more tasks or projects than you can ultimately manage, causing you to berate yourself later. On the other hand, hypomania can sometimes be a time of enhanced productivity if you are able to direct it properly. It may be helpful for you to recognize what you can reasonably do during these times without setting yourself up to become overwhelmed when you are no longer feeling hypomanic.

Your depressive symptoms will likely make it harder to do things that you normally do without difficulty. If depression causes you to feel slowed down, fatigued, and unmotivated, you may find it challenging to do things such as type memos, respond to phone calls or e-mail, do clerical tasks, and operate machinery. Problems with concentration will make it difficult to read and process information, stay on task, and make good decisions. You may also find yourself struggling with feelings of anxiety about your ability to work, worrying about what others are thinking of your performance. This is certainly a time when you should not expect too much from yourself. Instead, allow yourself to be patient and recognize that these distressing feelings will pass. It may be helpful to do an Automatic Thought Record (exercise 7.2) if you find yourself struggling with negative thoughts.

To Tell or Not to Tell in the Workplace

Just like the decision to tell your family and friends about your cyclothymia, disclosing your illness in the workplace is certainly a personal choice. There are a number of options to consider, each with pros and cons. For instance, some people choose not to tell anyone about their illness and simply find ways to cope with the effects of it. Others may tell a few coworkers who they trust and who don't have any authority over them in their job. Still others choose to disclose their illness to everyone, including their boss. There is no one right choice for everyone. I'll offer a few advantages and disadvantages of telling coworkers about your cyclothymia.

■ Marcus

Because he has had problems with jobs in the past, Marcus decided that with his current job, he would start off telling his employer about his cyclothymia and about what would be helpful to him on the job. He says, "My boss took it well. I didn't know what to expect. Based on past experience, I told him it's not good for me to work a lot of late nights or have too many tight deadlines. He said to let him know if I have any problems, that he'd try to help me out. It turns out that his sister has depression, and he understands needing a break once in a while."

Disadvantages of Disclosing Your Cyclothymia in the Workplace

Workplace discrimination. Although it is unlawful for employers to discriminate against people with disabilities, this can still happen in one way or another. People have reported being fired, passed over for promotions, demoted, or denied employment after revealing that they have a mental illness. The Americans with Disabilities Act (U.S. Equal Employment Opportunities Commission 1990; see www.ada.gov) was designed to protect employees against workplace discrimination. Your employer is not allowed to ask you whether you have a mental illness. If you wish to inform your employer of your illness, you can seek reasonable accommodations, which may include altering your work schedule or otherwise providing an atmosphere of low or moderate stress and stimulation.

Stigma. Letting others know about your illness can lead you to feel stigmatized. It may seem that others interpret your actions through a filter of cyclothymia rather than seeing them as within a normal range of behaviors. This feeling of stigma will likely be prevalent both during and immediately following mood problems, conflicts or disagreements with others, or any other difficulties that bring attention to you. People may be quick to attribute your behaviors to your illness rather than recognize that others are having similar reactions. Some coworkers may treat you with more caution or avoidance. Others may also go out of their way to let you know it's okay for you to talk with them about your "problems."

Advantages of Disclosing Your Cyclothymia in the Workplace

Support. Letting one or two trusted people at work know about your illness can help you gain support and encouragement as you manage your cyclothymia on the job. You can use information from this workbook, including the "About Cyclothymic Disorder" section (table 9.1), to help educate people about the effects of cyclothymia. It can be useful for them to know that your irritability, problems with concentration, and changes in mood and energy level can be attributed to the illness. Your coworkers are likely to be more understanding if they know there is a reason for some of your difficulties.

Prevention. If you choose to tell your manager or supervisor about your cyclothymia, giving a heads-up about challenges you may encounter, you pave the way for greater understanding if and when things get tough. This can be a good way to help prevent problems in the workplace and give you more flexibility to take action to help yourself when symptoms arise. If you wait to disclose your illness until a time when you are experiencing symptoms and pressure is high in the workplace, you may not get the same level of consideration you would have had you disclosed the information ahead of time; in fact, your employer may perceive your disclosure as an additional demand and become annoyed.

Discussing your cyclothymia early on can also allow you and your employer to consider what kinds of regular, preventive accommodations will be helpful and what further actions can be taken should you need them. This can feel like an important way to take control of your illness where you can. Making a plan to reduce stress in the workplace can go a long way toward helping you manage stress in general, thereby allowing you to better manage your cyclothymic symptoms overall.

Destigmatization. Revealing your illness in the workplace can help destigmatize mood disorders and allow you to become more accepting of your own illness. It has a way of reducing any shame or embarrassment you may feel, as you demonstrate to others that you have self-respect. You might find that your self-disclosure encourages others to share their own struggles or speak with you about someone close to them who has had similar challenges.

Fortunately, increased awareness of mood disorders and other mental illnesses is beginning to remove the social stigma associated with these conditions. The media regularly cover mental health issues, educating the public about recognizing warning signs and increasing acceptance of these illnesses. Numerous celebrities have also told their stories about personal struggles with mood disorders. Patty Duke, William Styron, Tipper Gore, Mike Wallace, Carrie Fisher, and Rod Steiger, among others, have made their stories public. Kay Jamison and Martha Manning, mental health professionals themselves, have written books about their struggles with bipolar disorder and depression respectively. See the Resources section for books written by some of these people.

Tips for Managing Cyclothymia in the Workplace

Because no research has been done about what kinds of jobs are most suitable for people with cyclothymia, I'll make a few assumptions based upon what we know about the illness. I realize that not all of the following tips are going to be practical ones for you.

- A consistent work schedule can help you maintain regular daily rhythms. Positions that require variable shifts or long work hours may upset your sleep pattern and otherwise exacerbate cyclothymic symptoms.

- Jobs that are low in stress may be better for symptom management than ones that are highly stressful, demanding, or overly stimulating. Similarly, jobs that have some consistency and predictability in schedules and daily activities may be beneficial.

- Flexibility in your schedule and workload can be helpful during difficulties with mood swings, depression, irritability, or stress. This flexibility could include sharing some responsibilities with others, leaving work a little early on occasion, or taking several short breaks rather than one or two long breaks during the workday.

- Bring relaxation and stress management techniques into the workplace. A five- or ten-minute deep breathing exercise, for instance, can help you relax and refocus on your work.

- Do what you can in your workspace to create a soothing, low-stimulation atmosphere. Placing a favorite piece of artwork on your wall or a nice plant on your desk can provide a visually calming workspace.

- If you find music enjoyable and calming, bring a portable CD player and headphones to work and listen to it during your breaks or lunchtime.

- If you have disclosed your cyclothymia to your employer, communicate openly about when you need a break or foresee a difficulty. Be prepared to request accommodations from your employer if you need them. Your employer likely won't offer unless you first ask.

- If you have disclosed your cyclothymia to one or more trusted coworkers, let them support you during times you feel are challenging for you. Sometimes, just letting someone else know you are struggling can be helpful. Be willing to ask for help when you need it.

DEVELOPING GOOD COMMUNICATION SKILLS

Most people are not specifically taught how to be good communicators. It isn't something that is generally taught in school or at home. People just tend to figure it out as they go, sometimes developing some bad habits along the way. While I offer some strategies for developing effective communication skills, it will probably not be as easy as it seems on the surface. However, learning to be a good communicator can pay off enormously by helping you to

- develop more meaningful, intimate relationships

- deliver a message so that you can be heard and taken seriously without others feeling defensive or attacked

- let others know your needs and desires

- really hear and understand the needs and desires of others

- keep conflicts at a minimum

- work with others to solve problems effectively

- feel good about yourself

- earn the respect and appreciation of others

- prevent or mitigate potentially stressful situations in all areas of your life

Like all the other skills presented in this workbook, becoming a good communicator takes practice. Regular practice not only strengthens your communication skills but also prepares you to handle those difficult moments when tensions are high. Becoming a skilled communicator allows you to take control and make active decisions about how you want to interact during a disagreement. You have probably already spent many years communicating in pretty much the same way. If this has worked well for you in all the ways listed above, that's great. If not, you might consider learning and practicing some of the strategies in this chapter. Whether you wish to solve a problem, express an opinion, resolve a conflict, or change something that's happening around you, you'll find it helpful to set the stage for mutual respect and use effective listening skills and verbal skills in your communications.

Setting the Stage

Effectively setting the stage is a critical first step in successful communication and problem solving. The goal is to reach a state of mind in which you are focused on mutual respect and a true desire to understand and empathize with the other person. To empathize is to understand a situation from that person's point of view as well as you are able. While you cannot fully know the experiences of other people, you can actively try your best to understand them. Being empathetic is challenging and requires a true desire to understand. It is like putting yourself in the shoes of another person.

EXERCISE 9.1 SETTING THE STAGE

This exercise lists strategies for effectively setting the stage for good communication. To rate how well you do each one, check the appropriate column.

	I don't do this at all	I need to do this better	I do this very well
I approach the conversation with an attitude of respect for the other person's thoughts and feelings.			
I demonstrate a willingness to understand the other person's message. (When people feel understood and accepted, they are more likely to want to return this attitude.)			
I keep in mind that I do not have to agree with the other person's message in order to have successful communication. I simply have a desire to understand the message.			
Even if I feel annoyed or attacked, I refrain from name-calling, using put-downs, cursing, or anything else that might encourage the other person's feelings to escalate.			
I avoid taking a position that my viewpoint is the only right one. I focus on common themes rather than differences. I have a win-win scenario as my goal.			
I avoid interrupting and take the attitude that I want to learn what the other person feels and thinks about the matter.			
If I need to communicate with someone about a difficult matter, I choose a moment when emotions are calm and we have plenty of time to discuss the issue thoroughly. I choose a quiet place where we won't be distracted or bothered. I let the other person know ahead of time that I wish to discuss the matter, rather than bringing it up without warning.			

Listening Skills

On the surface, listening might hardly sound like a skill that needs to be learned. Perhaps you're thinking to yourself, "I listen to people all the time. I don't need to learn how to do this." I would suggest that most of the time, we really only *hear* people; we don't always *listen* to them. There is an important difference. Hearing a person simply involves hearing the words, the content of what a person is saying. Your brain is aware that something is being vocalized. Really listening to a person involves so much more. It includes not only hearing the content of what is being said but also understanding the meaning, taking in the whole message, catching the subtleties of what is said or not said, and even empathizing with the speaker's point of view. When you truly listen, your intention is purposeful. You want to really know what the other person thinks, feels, and desires. This is not true of simply hearing a person's words.

Think about the times when you have felt that someone has really listened to you. How did it feel? What was it that helped you feel this way? What were the behaviors of the other person? What did the person say, and how was it said? We tend to feel good when another person has really listened to us. It feels like what we have to say is important and useful. We feel good about ourselves and about the relationship with the other person. We may feel encouraged to reveal more about our thoughts and feelings. We also develop more trust in the relationship and feel that we are more valued by the other person. The more we can be good listeners to people in our lives, the more likely this will be returned to us as well.

EXERCISE 9.2 LISTENING SKILLS

This exercise describes some important listening skills. After you read each one, rate yourself on how well you do them in your interactions with others.

	I don't do this at all	I need to do this better	I do this very well
I make eye contact with the person speaking to me. I don't constantly look away or stare off into space. I keep myself from being distracted by things around me. (It's okay to glance away from time to time so the other person doesn't feel like you are staring.)			
I nod my head once in a while to indicate I am attending to what is being said.			
I occasionally encourage the speaker verbally by saying "uh huh," "yeah," or "oh really?" (This gives the message you are interested and respect what the person is saying.)			
I use facial expressions such as smiling, raising my eyebrows, frowning slightly, or furrowing my brow when appropriate. (This gives the message that you are listening closely to the content of what is being said.)			
My body language is welcoming. I face the speaker directly and display a relaxed, comfortable body posture. (Turning away from the speaker or tightly crossing your arms may be interpreted as signaling impatience or irritation).			
If I miss something that was said, I ask the speaker to repeat the message. (People tend to appreciate your desire to make sure you have heard everything they've said.)			
If I am not sure I understand what the other person has said, I ask for clarification. For example, "When you said you didn't like what we did last weekend, what specifically were you thinking of?"			
I check with the speaker to make sure I received the message as it was intended. I paraphrase what I heard the person say and follow up by asking something like, "Did I get that right?"			
I check in with myself to make sure I am truly listening, rather than letting myself get into a mode of waiting for an opening in the conversation to state my own point of view or convince the other person of my side. (When you start looking for that opening, you cease to be a good listener).			

Verbal Skills

Think back for a moment on a few recent or past conflicts you have had with people. Try to recall the messages you heard from others, and think about whether the tone of the conversation was helpful or unhelpful to you in resolving the situation. If someone called you names, scolded you, disrespected you, or made snide or cutting remarks, you probably found it very hard to listen to the message any longer. It is common to react to such messages by shutting down, withdrawing, lashing out, or feeling angry, sad, discouraged, irritated, or annoyed. When these things occur, good communication goes out the window. The interaction remains filled with conflict, and the problem continues.

In addition to thinking about how you might have thought, felt, and behaved during moments of conflict, be honest with yourself and acknowledge whether you have done any of the things mentioned above to other people during arguments. How did they react? What did they say? Did the problem get resolved in a way that was satisfying for everyone involved?

In this discussion of verbal skills, I will focus on two approaches. First, I'll guide you through a three-step method for receiving a message and conveying understanding in a way that allows the other person to feel understood. Second, I'll address how to use I-statements, which allow the other person to listen to you without becoming defensive or feeling attacked. The higher the emotional arousal in a situation, the harder it is to do this well. When you feel angry, it can be very tempting to just lash out, even though that approach tends to be unsuccessful in the end. The techniques I'll teach in this chapter provide a structure that can help you feel more in control of your reactions during emotional situations.

The Three-Step Method of Communication

The three-step method of communication is a wonderful way of structuring conversations between you and another person, especially if either or both of you find it difficult to keep emotions in check. It is often taught in couples counseling to help partners communicate more effectively.

It begins with one person making a statement or otherwise expressing a feeling, opinion, or desire. The speaker keeps the statement to no more than three or four sentences, so the listener can remember and respond to the details of one chunk of information at a time. While the speaker makes a brief statement, the other person listens carefully to the content, meaning, and feelings expressed in the message. Then, the listener responds using the three steps: *paraphrasing, confirming,* and *empathizing.*

Paraphrasing. This involves accurately reflecting back to the speaker the content of what was said. In your own words, you interpret the meaning of the message as you heard it. In doing this, you communicate your willingness to put aside your own views for a time in an attempt to understand the other person's point of view. After you paraphrase the message, the other person has the opportunity to let you know whether your understanding was accurate. If necessary, the speaker repeats or restates the message, and you paraphrase it until you understand the message as it was intended.

You could begin your paraphrasing by saying, "What I understand you to be saying is . . ." or "It sounds like you're saying . . ." or "Let me make sure I understand. You said that . . ."

Confirming. The second step is your message to the other person that what was said makes sense to you. You demonstrate that you can see the other person's point of view. Whether you agree or disagree with the message is not important here. In fact, you don't have to agree at all in order to confirm another person's message. All that is important in this step is that you suspend your viewpoints for a moment and validate that what you heard is logical and real for the other person. The underlying message in this step is that there are multiple ways to interpret any situation. What's "right" or "wrong" is not the issue; the issue is to accept that each of us has our own truth and the right to our own perspectives. In confirming another person's message, you validate that person's reality and build mutual trust and respect. Confirming messages could begin, "I can see how you would think that . . ." or "It makes sense that . . ." or "I understand your view that . . ."

Empathizing. Although I have defined the concept of empathy earlier, it is worth revisiting here. In this three-step method, empathizing involves engaging in a deeper level of understanding. You allow yourself to take the other position to the extent that you can tap into what the other person likely feels about the situation. Empathizing can be a powerful experience for both of you, reflecting a true meeting of the minds.

Empathizing statements may begin with, "When that happens, you must feel..." or "It makes sense that you would feel . . ." or "I imagine you feel . . ."

Let's take a look at an excerpt of conversation between Jerry and his wife, Sue. They have been having disagreements about housework duties, sometimes getting into heated arguments about who does what and when things get done around the house. Sue begins by making her brief statement to Jerry, and he responds using the steps of paraphrasing, confirming, and empathizing.

Sue: When you don't help me around the house, I get really angry and frustrated. I feel like you don't care that I have to work all day and then come home to clean the house. It would really help me if you would take some initiative to vacuum, or fold the laundry, or clean the kitchen in the evening, or anything.

Jerry: It sounds like you have been really irritated that I haven't helped around the house as much as you'd like, particularly since you have to work every day. I hear that if I did a few specific things, it would be of help to you. I can understand that. It makes sense that you would feel frustrated and angry. It must be discouraging to feel that way.

Using the three-step method well takes some practice and patience on the part of both people. I realize that after reading about how to do it, you may find the technique a bit tedious and unnatural. That's understandable. Communication as structured as this certainly does take some time to get used to, but it will pay off if you stick with it.

You may have also noticed that Sue and Jerry's problem was not resolved in this brief scenario. This was a short demonstration of how to begin a dialogue about a tough issue. When both parties use good communication skills and demonstrate a spirit of wanting to reach a mutually satisfying agreement, they provide the necessary ingredients for solving problems.

I-Statements

Using I-statements allows you to communicate your feelings clearly and directly without attacking another person. It is a good technique for structuring what might be a difficult message to give someone, particularly if you feel strongly about it.

There is a subtle yet important difference between messages that have "you" as a focus and ones with "I" as the focus. Read the sentences below as if someone close to you were directing them toward you, and notice how you feel as a result.

"You make me so angry!"

"When you say that, I feel angry."

What differences do you notice about these two sentences if you are on the receiving end of them? You-messages, such as the first example, might elicit defensiveness or anger in you, thereby shutting down further communication. It also appears to blame the speaker's feelings on you. I-messages, as in the second example, express the speaker's feelings—and responsibility for those feelings—and facilitate continued discussion.

There are three steps to creating a successful I-message.

1. Describe the *behavior* in an objective, nonjudgmental way.
    "When you _____ . . ."

2. Describe your *feelings* about the behavior.
    "... I feel _____ . . ."

3. State what you'd like to be different or how the behavior distresses you.
    ". . . because _____ ." or ". . . I would like for you to _____ ."

For example, "When you tease me in front of our friends, I feel embarrassed and anxious. I would like for you to stop doing that."

Another example: "When you stay out late with your friends, I feel taken advantage of because it's hard to get the kids to bed all by myself."

When you start using I-statements to communicate with other people, make sure you also consider the other concepts I have addressed in the communication portion of this chapter. Be careful about letting yourself indulge in name-calling, sending passive-aggressive messages, or otherwise disrespecting the other person in your I-statements.

For example, it is not helpful to say, "When you are such a jerk, I get pissed off!" Aside from calling the other person a name ("jerk") and using a loaded phrase ("I get pissed off"), this statement is likely to encourage the other person to become defensive and perhaps react by taking the argument up a notch. The problem has no chance of getting resolved, and both people walk away more frustrated. The relationship may suffer as a result. It is more helpful to say something like, "When you yell at me, I feel angry and want to yell back." There is virtually nothing in this statement that the other person can grab onto to become angry or defensive. This way of putting things provides much more opportunity for solving the problem.

Additional Tips for Good Communication

Here are a few final thoughts about developing better communication with others.

- Have patience with other people, and encourage them to have patience with you as well, while you learn good communication skills.

- Consider couples counseling or family therapy if you continue to struggle with communication.

- Accept that changing and improving your communication skills takes time, patience, and practice. If you have long-standing problems with others, it may be hard for them to accept your new communication style and behaviors.

- Accept that some people may not be able or willing to communicate better with you.

■   The stress and anger management skills you learned in chapter 8 can help you remain calm and focused as you work on improving your communication skills.

Even if you learn to be the best communicator in the world, it doesn't mean that other people will always be able to return the favor by respecting you, listening to you, and empathizing with you. However, being a good communicator does increase your chances of interpersonal success, and you can feel good that you have done what you can to enhance the relationship.

DEVELOPING A SUPPORT NETWORK

In chapter 2, I briefly mentioned the importance of social support for those who have bipolar disorder. Researchers have found that the level of support people have from partners, family, friends, and community resources can have a significant impact on their illness. Good social support moderates the course of the disorder and speeds recovery from bipolar episodes (Johnson et al. 1999).

When you feel depressed, it can be very difficult to interact with others. In fact, you probably don't really want to. However, having good interactions with other people can help improve or prevent depressive symptoms. This is why it is important to have good relationships already in place so that when you really need the support, it will be there for you. This can be challenging if your close relationships tend to be filled with conflict. If you find it difficult to rely on some relationships for support, seek out other ones that can provide what you need. Here is a list of ideas for possible sources of support.

partner	clergy
siblings	religious community
parents or grandparents	teachers
other relatives	support groups
friends	therapy groups
coworkers	clubs and organizations you belong to
counselors, psychologists, psychiatrists	hotline or crisis workers
family doctor	Alcoholics Anonymous and the like

EXERCISE 9.3 SOURCES OF SUPPORT

In the spaces below, list your sources of support. In the first column, put the name of the person or group, and in the second column, write in at least one phone number for that contact. If things get tough, it will be useful to have your list in one place. You may have trouble thinking clearly and remembering certain information when you are emotionally distressed.

Name of Support   **Phone Number(s)**

_____   _____

_____   _____

_____   _____

_____   _____

_____   _____

_____   _____

_____   _____

_____   _____

_____   _____

_____   _____

_____   _____

■ Maria

After Maria started going to her college counseling center for individual therapy, she found out that they offered psychoeducational workshops on managing depression and anxiety. She started attending and learned a lot about mood disorders: what they are, what causes them, how they are treated, and what you can do on your own to manage them. Maria says, "Not only have I learned a lot about mood disorders, but I like that the other people there can understand what I'm going through. I'm not alone. It feels good knowing I'm not being judged or thought of as crazy or strange."

Several national organizations, such as the Depression and Bipolar Support Alliance and the National Alliance for the Mentally Ill, offer local support groups or chapters in many cities. See the Resource section for more information. One of the main benefits of support groups is being with people who have had experiences, struggles, thoughts, and feelings similar to yours. Members support each other and share knowledge gained through their experiences. They provide hope and encouragement to each other. It can be very satisfying to have support from people who have "been there" themselves.

As you seek to develop social supports for yourself, remember that quality will be more important than quantity. Sometimes, just one or two good supports—like a close friend and a support group—can make all the difference in helping you manage difficult times.

Summing Up

In this chapter, I addressed the ripple effects of cyclothymia—its impact on your relationships with your partner, family, and friends. Your workplace is also affected by challenges you may have on the job as well as your interactions with coworkers. I offered strategies for managing a variety of situations and gave you tools to develop more effective communication skills. I finished up this chapter discussing the importance of social support. If you have difficulty finding support in people close to you, make sure you seek out additional resources. Having good support is very important in helping you manage and prevent symptoms, and it connects you with people who understand what you are going through.

Perhaps this is a good place to acknowledge that it takes at least two people to make up a relationship. The fact that you are the one who has cyclothymia doesn't mean you are the only one responsible for working hard to make your relationships run smoothly. It may be easy to get that impression since you are the one using this workbook. Rather than labeling one person's behaviors as the "problem," each person must take responsibility for what happens in the relationship. Each person must take ownership for mistakes, acknowledge shortcomings, and be willing to make changes to enhance the relationship.

People in your life will likely vary in how willing or able they are to work with you on your relationship. Some people will be very supportive, understanding, and patient; others less so. Certainly, doing what you can to enhance your relationships and develop effective communication skills gives you every opportunity to gain the support you need every day and during tough times.

CHAPTER 10

Leading a Balanced Life

If you've been able to progress through this workbook chapter by chapter, you will certainly have done a lot of good work for yourself! Even if you have been skipping around among the chapters, you have likely found some things here and there that will be useful to add to your life. In this final chapter, I will help you bring all of the pieces together so that you can develop and meet your own personal goals for managing the mood swings of cyclothymia and leading a balanced life.

You have been presented with a lot of information, on a variety of topics, throughout this workbook. It may seem overwhelming to think about making so many changes. You might be wondering how to keep track of it all. If you find yourself feeling that all this information is a lot to handle, keep in mind that you don't have to do it all at one time. Just proceed at your own pace, in a manner that is comfortable to you. Remember that this workbook is meant to be supportive and useful, not stressful or frustrating.

PUTTING IT ALL TOGETHER

Let's start bringing together what you've learned by organizing some of the main topics we have covered. Table 10.1 is a comprehensive list of exercises, chapters and chapter sections, and tables, organized by topic. I hope this table will help you find things you need very easily. It will also give you an idea of issues you may wish to focus on as you develop goals for coping with cyclothymia.

As you can see from the chart, many topics are interrelated. For instance, as you work on managing anger, it will be useful to consider stress, relationships, and how your perceptions of situations influence your feelings and behavior. Few, if any, issues I have discussed throughout this workbook stand in isolation from others. Instead, most issues you have worked on complement others quite nicely. For example, developing your communication skills will likely improve your relationships, subsequently reducing stress and anger. It may also indirectly help you sleep better and curtail alcohol or drug use.

Table 10.1   Elements of This Workbook Organized by Topic

CH = Chapter

EX = Exercise

T = Table

F = Figure

Topic	Relevant Information	Associated Topics
Symptoms of cyclothymia	T 1.1 - Symptoms of Depression and Hypomania T 1.2- Mania vs. Hypomania CH 3 (all)	F 1.1 - Mood Disorders
Your experience with cyclothymia	CH 4 (all) EX 6.1 - Mood Chart EX 6.3 - Rhythm Chart EX 6.4 - Monthly Mood and Rhythm Chart EX 6.5 - Interpreting Your Charts EX 6.6 - Your Patterns, Red Flags, and Daily Rhythms EX 7.2 - Automatic Thought Record EX 7.3 - Depressive Thoughts and Thinking Styles EX 7.4 - Hypomanic Thoughts and Thinking Styles EX 8.1 - Red Flags for Depression EX 8.4 - Red Flags for Hypomania	T 3.1 - Diagnostic Criteria for Cyclothymic Disorder EX 3.1 - Symptoms of Depression EX 3.2 - Symptoms of Hypomania EX 3.3 - Symptoms of Cyclothymia EX 8.6 - Red Flags for Anger EX 8.7 - Red Flags for Stress
Managing symptoms, mood	CH 6 (all) CH 7 (all) CH 8 (all)	EX 2.3 - Sleep Inventory EX 2.4 - Stress Chart CH 9 (all)
Relationships	CH 4 - "How Others May Perceive You" EX 4.4 - Others' Statements EX 4.5 - Others' Descriptions EX 4.6 - Informational Interview EX 4.8 - Your Patterns CH 9 (all)	CH 8 - "Managing Anger" EX 8.6 - Red Flags for Anger CH 8 - "Managing Stress" EX 8.7 - Red Flags for Stress
Communication	T 9.1 - About Cyclothymic Disorder CH 9 - "Developing Good Communication Skills" EX 9.1 - Setting the Stage EX 9.2 - Listening Skills EX 9.3 - Sources of Support	CH 8 - "Managing Anger" EX 8.6 - Red Flags for Anger CH 8 - "Managing Stress" EX 8.7 - Red Flags for Stress

Stress	CH 2 - "The Role of Stress" EX 2.4 - Stress Chart EX 6.1 - Mood Chart EX 6.4 - Monthly Mood and Rhythm Chart CH 8 - "Managing Stress" EX 8.7 - Red Flags for Stress EX 8.8 - Other Stress Management Ideas EX 8.9 - Deep Breathing EX 8.10 - Progressive Muscle Relaxation EX 8.11 - Imagery	EX 2.3 - Sleep Inventory CH 7 (all) CH 8 - "Managing Anger" T 8.1 - Tips for Managing Your Sleep EX 8.6 - Red Flags for Anger CH 9 (all)
Sleep	EX 2.3 - Sleep Inventory EX 6.1 - Mood Chart EX 6.3 - Rhythm Chart EX 6.4 - Monthly Mood and Rhythm Chart T 8.1 - Tips for Managing Your Sleep	CH 8 - "Managing Stress"
Anger	CH 8 - "Managing Anger" EX 8.6 - Red Flags for Anger	CH 7 (all) CH 8 - "Managing Stress" EX 8.7 - Red Flags for Stress EX 8.8 - Other Stress Management Ideas EX 8.9 - Deep Breathing EX 8.10 - Progressive Muscle Relaxation EX 8.11 - Imagery CH 9 (all)
Alcohol and drug use	CH 2 - "Effects of Substances" CH 4 - "Alcohol and Drug Abuse" CH 8 - "Avoid Alcohol and Drugs"	EX 6.1 - Mood Chart CH 8 - "Managing Anger" EX 8.6 - Red Flags for Anger CH 8 - "Managing Stress" EX 8.7 - Red Flags for Stress EX 8.8 - Other Stress Management Ideas EX 8.9 - Deep Breathing EX 8.10 - Progressive Muscle Relaxation EX 8.11 - Imagery CH 9 (all)
Exercise	CH 8 - "Developing an Exercise Plan"	EX 6.1 - Mood Chart EX 6.3 - Rhythm Chart
Cognitive behavioral strategies	CH 7 (all)	EX 4.1 - Common Thoughts EX 4.2 - Common Feelings EX 4.3 - Common Behaviors EX 8.3 - Daily Activity Scheduling

Your red flags	CH 4 - "Spotting Your Red Flags" EX 4.7 - Recognizing Your Patterns EX 6.6 - Your Patterns, Red Flags, and 　　Daily Rhythms EX 8.1 - Red Flags for Depression EX 8.4 - Red Flags for Hypomania EX 8.6 - Red Flags for Anger EX 8.7 - Red Flags for Stress	CH 6 (all) CH 7 (all)
Monitoring your mood	CH 6 (all)	CH 7 (all) CH 8 (all)
Cyclothymia in the workplace	CH 9 - "Your Workplace" CH 9 - "Developing Good 　　Communication Skills" EX 9.1 - Setting the Stage EX 9.2 - Listening Skills EX 9.3 - Sources of Support	CH 4 - "How Others May Perceive You" EX 4.4 - Others' Statements EX 4.5 - Others' Descriptions EX 4.6 - Informational Interview EX 4.8 - Your Patterns EX 6.1 - Mood Chart EX 6.3 - Rhythm Chart EX 6.4 - Monthly Mood and Rhythm Chart CH 8 - "Managing Anger" EX 8.6 - Red Flags for Anger CH 8 - "Managing Stress" EX 8.7 - Red Flags for Stress EX 8.8 - Other Stress Management Ideas EX 8.9 - Deep Breathing EX 8.10 - Progressive Muscle Relaxation EX 8.11 - Imagery T 9.1 - About Cyclothymic Disorder
Educating yourself and others about cyclothymia	CH 1–5 (all) CH 9 (all)	

If you have not done the exercises throughout this workbook, I highly recommend that you go back and do them. It can be tempting to read the concepts and quickly dismiss the deeper work of responding, believing that you have already grasped the information. However, you are likely to gain much more insight into issues and find it easier to see how they relate to each other if you have your recorded information to go by. Admittedly, doing the written activities takes some time. The time you spend will help the concepts really sink in and allow you to understand them as they apply to your unique situation. If you read the material without spending time with the exercises, you bypass a key part of learning and integrating the material in a way that will be most useful for you. It can also be rewarding to come back to what you have written in this workbook later on and see the progress you've made.

■ Helen

Helen's biggest struggle with cyclothymia has been her depressive symptoms and how suddenly they can come on. She says, "When I feel depressed, everything seems to go downhill. I don't want to do anything or be around anyone. I feel more sensitive and personalize things people say to me." Helen has had a few problems over time with hypomania. She says, "I've spent too much money on things we really didn't need, and I got us into a tight spot financially. I also have to watch that I don't get a little too 'wild' when Steve and I are out with friends." However, Helen notes, "My hypomania has had a good side, too. I feel more energized and active, I get more things done that I want to do, and Steve and I enjoy our sexual relationship during those times. Overall, I'm working mostly on managing the depression. I know most of my red flags, and I am doing well on my goal to take quick action to head off problems. I use Automatic Thought Records and monitor my mood pretty closely nowadays."

YOUR PERSONAL GOALS FOR MANAGING CYCLOTHYMIA

So, where to start? I'll discuss some strategies for effective goal setting and provide some exercises along the way. As you work on these activities, you'll be encouraged to make decisions about how you want to prioritize, structure, and work toward the goals you choose for yourself.

What Is Goal Setting?

Simply stated, goal setting is a way of choosing what you want to accomplish in your life. By identifying exactly what it is that you want to accomplish, you know what things to focus on and what things are only distractions. Setting a goal also helps you acquire information you need and structure your resources. Finally, goal setting can give you the short-term motivation you need in order to realize your long-term vision.

Choosing Potential Goals

To identify possible goals, you can go back through the workbook and note which issues have been of interest to you. You can also review the exercises you have been working on, or you can take another look at the chart I provided at the beginning of this chapter. In choosing potential goals, you can use the Potential Goals chart (exercise 10.1). I have offered an example of Helen's chart in figure 10.1. On her chart, you see that she has identified five potential goals. You also see that she has proposed a time frame and prioritized her goals. Although I will describe how to fill out your own chart, you can follow Helen's as a guide.

When you identify a potential goal for yourself, go ahead and write it on a line in the first column of your chart. It doesn't matter how you write it at this point. We will get to that later. For now, just write your goal as it comes to mind.

In the second column, identify the time frame in which you would like to accomplish each potential goal. It can be general or specific. For instance, you might decide you want to reach your goal in three weeks, in three months, or in several years. If you have an idea of a specific date, go ahead and write it in.

My Potential Goals

Name: _____ *Helen* _____   Date: _____ *July 30, 2005* _____

With this worksheet, you can start the process of identifying *potential* goals you want to accomplish. This is just a place to keep track of possibilities, not a list of everything you are going to do all at one time.

1. List any potential goals you have for yourself.

2. Identify the time frame of the goal. If you know a tentative date, month, or year, write it in.

3. Note whether the goal is an *immediate* (I), *short-term* (ST), or *long-term* (LT) goal.

4. Prioritize your potential goals. Rate each using a 1 (most important), 2 (important), or 3 (least important).

Potential Goals	Time Frame	I/ST/LT	Priority
Learn how to change negative thinking (CBT)	*by Dec 31 '05*	*LT*	*2*
Manage stress at work better	*by Aug 31 '05*	*ST*	*1*
Join a support group	*by Spring '06*	*LT*	*3*
Use the Mood, Rhythm, and monthly charts	*months of Aug, Sept, Oct*	*ST*	*2*
Stop embarrassing my husband in public	*party this weekend*	*I*	*1*

Figure 10.1 Helen's Potential Goals

The third column asks for a slightly different kind of time frame. Indicate whether your goal is immediate, short-term, or long-term. How you define these categories is up to you. You might think about it in the following way:

- *Immediate goals* are ones that are pressing or should be accomplished right away. This may be "tomorrow," "next week," " ten days from now," or "by the time we go on vacation next month."

- *Short-term goals* are ones that you might begin very soon and want to have accomplished in the near future. For example, this could be "by the end of the semester," "one month from now," "when my parents visit this summer," or "by the start of the new year."

- *Long-term goals* may be thought of as ones that require several steps, or short-term goals, to accomplish. Progress is gradual. Long-term goals can span the course of a year, several years, or even a decade.

After you have identified all your potential goals, go to the last column on your worksheet and prioritize each one according to how important it is to you. Place a 1 next to goals that are most important, a 2 next to ones that are important, and a 3 next to goals that are least important to you.

Ultimately, it will be useful to have a good mix of short-term and long-term goals, as well as an even spread of priorities. If all of your goals are immediate and prioritized as most important, you will overwhelm yourself with too much to do, and you may not accomplish any of them. If you need to go back and modify your potential goals, time frames, or priority levels for more variety, go ahead and do that.

Setting Appropriate Goals

Now that you've identified some potential goals and prioritized their importance to you, a few of them probably rise to the surface as ones you might choose to work toward first. Before too long, I'll encourage you to select one, two, or even three of these goals to shape further. First, I'll offer some principles to consider for setting appropriate goals.

Goals should be specific. Writing your goal in specific terms helps you know whether you are making progress or not. If you write a goal in vague terms, it will be impossible to measure progress or know when you have truly reached it. For example, a vague way to write a goal would be, "I want to stop drinking so much." What does that really mean? A better, more specific way to write this goal is, "I will limit myself to four beers on Friday and four beers on Saturday for the month of May." In this second example, it will be clear whether you are making progress, whether you need to make changes in your steps along the way, and when you have finally accomplished the goal.

Goals should be measurable. How will you know whether you are making progress or whether you need to make some adjustments as you work toward your goal if there are no markers along the way? Especially for goals that will take some time, it can be helpful to know how you are doing as you proceed. If you have smaller goals or steps to measure your progress, then you can be assured you are on course to meet your larger goal. For instance, suppose you have a goal of completing a Monthly Mood and Rhythm Chart (exercise 6.4). There are a number of smaller goals or steps toward this larger goal. These include making daily recordings in your Mood Charts (exercise 6.1) and Rhythm Charts (exercise 6.3), completing an entire chart of both each

EXERCISE 10.1 MY POTENTIAL GOALS

Name: _____   Date: _____

With this worksheet, you can start the process of identifying *potential* goals you want to accomplish. This is just a place to keep track of possibilities, not a list of everything you are going to do all at one time.

1. List any potential goals you have for yourself.

2. Identify the time frame of the goal. If you know a tentative date, month, or year, write it in.

3. Note whether the goal is an *immediate* (I), *short-term* (ST), or *long-term* (LT) goal.

4. Prioritize your potential goals. Rate each using a 1 (most important), 2 (important), or 3 (least important).

Potential Goals	Time Frame	I/ST/LT	Priority

week. Upon finishing four or more weekly charts, you can complete your Monthly Mood and Rhythm Chart. Each day of the month, you can measure progress toward your larger goal by whether you make entries in your weekly charts or not. If you missed some days during the month, this will be apparent when you fill out your monthly chart.

Goals should be realistic. Goals should be set neither too high nor too low. Setting goals at the right level can take some practice and a bit of trial and error over time. Realistic goals are ones that are just outside your grasp, but not so far that you have no chance of reaching them. If you set your goals unrealistically high, you invite failure and disappointment, not to mention a dislike for setting goals in the future. You may set goals too high for several reasons, including having high expectations of yourself, giving in to pressure from others, or not having enough information about what it takes to reach a particular goal.

On the other hand, you might set your goals too low. This can happen because of a fear of failure or a desire to take things easy. Either way, it depletes your motivation. When you feel challenged about working toward something important, accomplishing it will feel like a valued and deserved reward.

Goals should be based on performance, not outcome. Define your goals based on things over which you have control. You have control over your actions but not necessarily over the outcome of your efforts. For example, if you would like to communicate better with people, you might focus on whether you consistently use good listening skills. You have control over this. If you define your goal as getting your partner to agree with you, you set yourself up for disappointment. There are many factors outside of your control that can keep something like that from happening. At the simplest level, your partner may simply disagree with you no matter how skillfully you listen. With a performance-oriented goal—using good listening skills—you have a greater chance of reaching the goal and feeling good about your accomplishment.

Goals should be written in a positive form. The wording of your goal is important. It should sound positive. It should also be something you move toward rather than something you wish to avoid. For example, an unhelpful way to write a goal would be, "I have to try to manage my depressive symptoms because if I don't, my partner will leave me." To begin, the word "try" implies both a lack of desire and an expectation of failure. There is also a vague goal to "manage my depressive symptoms." As you have seen in this workbook, there are many ways to approach doing this. Specifically, how will this be done? The goal is also written in terms of avoiding an undesired outcome. There is a sense that this goal is forced onto one person by another.

Another way to write this goal is, "I will keep daily Automatic Thought Records, take a walk around the neighborhood each evening, and take a class in woodworking because it feels good to do it!" This goal is positive and specific, it eliminates the word "try," and it sounds like a choice made because it is enjoyable, not because it must be done. It also includes specific strategies for managing depressive symptoms.

■ Marcus

Marcus has been able to make some improvements in managing his anger in the past, but he has decided to rededicate himself to a three-month short-term goal to take specific steps to manage his anger, with the full support of his current girlfriend. He says, "I plan to work on my relaxation exercises every day, continue exercising four days a week, use my Automatic Thought Records and Mood and Rhythm Charts, and learn better communication skills. I started reading a book on anger and communication. It's all doable!" He continues, smiling, "My girlfriend has even offered to practice with me."

Selecting and Writing Specific Goals

Now it's time to select one or two goals that you want to spend some time thinking about in more detail. I'll walk you through using the Goal Worksheet (exercise 10.2). You can retrieve a copy of this worksheet online at www.CyclothymiaWorkbook.com. Figure 10.2 is Helen's Goal Worksheet.

Take another look at your Potential Goals chart (exercise 10.1) and select one goal that you gave a priority of 1 (most important). Be sure to put today's date at the top of your worksheet so you will know when you started your goal. Write out your goal in specific, measurable, realistic, positive, and performance-based terms. It might take a little practice to write out your goal this way. Try writing your goal on a separate sheet of paper, and when you like how it's worded, transfer it to your worksheet. Then set an appropriate date for reaching your goal.

In the bottom section of your worksheet, break down your main goal into smaller goals or steps and give each one a deadline as well. The following questions may help you identify the small goals you need to reach to achieve your main goal:

- What skills must I have?

- What information must I have?

- What help do I need from others?

- What resources are needed?

- What obstacles can impede my progress?

- What assumptions am I making?

- What are the best ways for me to do this?

- What options am I overlooking?

■ Jerry

Because of a variety of problems over the years, Jerry's two oldest children from his first marriage have not kept in contact with him. Jerry states, "We talk briefly on some of the holidays, but I know I made things tough for my kids while they were growing up. I feel bad about that. They don't seem to want to have much to do with me anymore. One of my main goals now is to try to repair my relationship with my kids. If they find it hard, I understand, but I'm going to give it a try. I'm working on communication skills, and I'm thinking about how I can start talking with them. I know I also have to be willing to hear some tough stuff from them about their feelings toward me. It's worth a good try."

My Goal Worksheet

Name: _____ Helen _____   Date: _____ July 30, 2005 _____

At the top, write a statement that describes your goal in specific, measurable, realistic, performance-based, and positive terms. Then set an appropriate date for reaching this goal. Finally, break down your goal into smaller steps and give each one a deadline as well.

My Goal	Deadline
By the end of next month, I will do things to manage stress better at work. I will monitor progress on items 2-4 using my Mood Charts and Rhythm Charts.	August 31, 2005

List specific and measurable steps that will help you reach your goal.

		Deadline
1.	Start keeping Mood Charts and Rhythm Charts	August 1
2.	Go to bed by 11:00 every night	every day
3.	Take the new yoga class that starts this Tuesday and meets two days a week	August 2
4.	Do some relaxation exercises or listen to music during my afternoon break	each workday
5.	Talk with Brian about our overlapping responsibilities and recent argument	August 8
6.	Disclose my cyclothymia to my manager and to Brenda (coworker)	August 15
7.	Speak with my manager about reducing amount of overtime	August 15
8.		
9.		
10.		

Figure 10.2 Helen's Goal Worksheet

EXERCISE 10.2 MY GOAL WORKSHEET

Name: _____   Date: _____

At the top, write a statement that describes your goal in specific, measurable, realistic, performance-based, and positive terms. Then set an appropriate date for reaching this goal. Finally, break down your goal into smaller steps and give each one a deadline as well.

My Goal   Deadline

_____   _____

_____

List *specific* and *measurable* steps that will help you reach your goal.

1. _____   _____

2. _____   _____

3. _____   _____

4. _____   _____

5. _____   _____

6. _____   _____

7. _____   _____

8. _____   _____

9. _____   _____

10. _____   _____

Reaching Your Goals

Now that you've set your main goal, identified the necessary smaller goals, and assigned deadlines for each of them, you are ready to get going! This is the challenging part of goal setting. It's easy to feel quite motivated early on in the process, but many people find that their motivation wanes a bit over time. To help yourself stay on track, consider the following tips:

Review your goals frequently. Keep your worksheet in a place where you will see it each day. Don't let it get lost in a drawer or among papers on your desk. Incorporate your daily review with another regular habit, such as having breakfast in the morning or reading before bedtime.

Be flexible. If you need to modify aspects of your main goal or your smaller goals, that's fine. You can't always foresee situations that might come up or opportunities that could prove to be advantageous.

Use motivational reminders. There are many strategies for reminding yourself of your goal, from posting notes on your refrigerator or mirror to putting motivational quotes in your day planner. You can adopt a favorite image, such as a butterfly or an eagle, as your symbol for success. Purchase a representation of your image in the form of artwork or a small sculpture that you can put on a wall or desk where you will see it frequently. Whenever you see it, reaffirm your dedication to reaching your goal.

Another strategy is *visualization*. As you did in the imagery relaxation exercise you learned for stress management in chapter 8, let yourself visualize or imagine the experience of reaching your goal. Notice how you feel, what you are doing, and how others respond. Replaying that image of success over and over will set the stage for your conscious and subconscious mind to accept and move toward your goal. It will also diminish any negative thoughts about achieving your goal.

A goal bracelet can be another nice motivational reminder. You might start off with just the bracelet, adding charms as you achieve small steps toward your main goal. Wearing your motivational symbol will provide a continuous reminder of what you want to accomplish. Your bracelet will be complete when you finally reach your goal.

Elicit support from others. Let someone in on the goal you set for yourself. Ask this person to be a cheerleader of sorts by inquiring how you are doing, reminding you of a few of your small goals, or providing other support or encouragement you'd find useful.

Learn from your mistakes. Mistakes and setbacks are some of your best teachers. If you make a mistake, miss deadlines on any of your goals, or find it difficult to stick with your plan, spend some time analyzing what went wrong. Were your goals too high or too low? Did you have enough information about your goals before you started? What got in the way of accomplishing what you wanted for yourself? Would it be useful to elicit help from supportive people to rework your goals?

Reward yourself. You might give yourself a little reward each time you reach a small goal. This could be renting a favorite movie, going out for dinner, taking a long bubble bath, or purchasing a desired item. Of course, don't forget to reward yourself somehow once you reach your main goal!

After you accomplish your goal, let yourself really enjoy the satisfaction of a job well done. Acknowledging your work and achievement is an important part of goal setting, and it should never be overlooked. Feeling good about what you have done can increase your self-confidence, your motivation, and your resolve for taking on other meaningful challenges in your life.

■ Maria

Maria has seen the toll bipolar disorder can take on a family. Her mother has struggled with significant problems since Maria was a child. Hospitalizations, substance abuse, and suicide have hit her family hard over time. She wants to do what she can to avoid a similar fate. She says, "My long-term goal is to maintain overall mental and physical health. I plan to take good care of myself by eating right, exercising regularly, staying in therapy for a while, avoiding alcohol and drugs, and learning a lot more about my mood patterns. I have been keeping charts on my mood and daily rhythms, and I plan to continue them for at least six more months. I figure if I can really understand myself, I'll be prepared to manage anything."

A Final Message

This last chapter has been a culmination of all that you have been doing for yourself throughout this workbook. You have educated yourself about cyclothymia, explored in detail how it affects your life, and learned a variety of ways to help manage your symptoms. In doing this, you have demonstrated both the courage to hope for something different in your life and the determination to do something about it. All this has laid the groundwork for setting important goals for yourself and developing plans for achieving them.

At times, the effects of cyclothymia can seem unmanageable. Things can feel hopeless. It will be normal for you to struggle occasionally with hope, motivation, and belief in yourself. During these tough times, let this workbook help you out. Go back to the strategies you learned. Pull out your Mood Charts and Rhythm Charts from chapter 6 or your Automatic Thought Records from chapter 7. Go back and spend time with the topics that are relevant to your struggles. Be compassionate with yourself and take care of your needs. Reach out to people in your support network or seek the assistance of a medical or mental health professional. There are people and resources available to you. Let yourself use them.

I would like to offer my support and encouragement as you move forward with the challenges that lie ahead. I truly believe that your patience, practice, and persistence in using the strategies in this workbook will pay off for you. While scientific research has demonstrated the positive effects of the strategies I've presented, time and again I have witnessed what matters most: I have seen real people conquer real problems. You can do it too!

Resources

NATIONAL ORGANIZATIONS, WEB SITES

Alcoholics Anonymous
http://www.alcoholics-anonymous.org/
Alcoholics Anonymous is a support group for those struggling with alcohol abuse and dependence. Their Web site lists local AA meetings, offers information for those new to AA, and provides information about alcoholism.

All About Cyclothymia
http://www.AllAboutCyclothymia.com
This Web site, created by Prentiss Price, is a resource for cyclothymic disorder and offers updates for this workbook.

All About Depression
http://www.AllAboutDepression.com
This Web site, created by Prentiss Price, is a resource for information about depression and other mood disorders.

American Psychiatric Association
1000 Wilson Boulevard, Suite 1825
Arlington, VA 22209-3901
(703) 907-1085 or (888) 35-PSYCH
http://www.psych.org

American Psychological Association
750 First Street, Northeast
Washington, DC 20002-4242
(202) 336-5510 or (800) 374-2721
TDD/TTY: (202) 336-6123
http://www.apa.org

Anxiety Disorders Association of America
8730 Georgia Avenue, Suite 600
Silver Spring, MD 20910
(240) 485-1001; Fax: (240) 485-1035
http://www.adaa.org

Bipolar Disorder Sanctuary
http://www.mhsanctuary.com/bipolar
    This Web site offers information about bipolar disorder, chats, discussion boards, "Ask the Therapist," personal stories, and support.

Bipolar Significant Other Mailing List
http://www.bpso.org
    This Web site provides a forum for family and friends of those with bipolar disorder to share information and give and receive support.

Bipolar World
http://www.bipolarworld.net
    This Web site offers education and support for people with bipolar disorder as well as for their families and friends.

Center Watch
http://www.centerwatch.com/patient/studies/cat20.html
    This is a patient resource Web site for clinical trials and research on bipolar disorder.

Child and Adolescent Bipolar Foundation
(847) 256-8525
http://www.bpkids.org
    This Web site offers information about bipolar disorder in children.

Cyclothymia–Psycom.net
http://www.psycom.net/depression.central.cyclothymia.html
    This Web site, operating since 1996, is a large resource for Internet links to information about mood disorders and other mental health issues.

The Cyclothymia Workbook
http://www.CyclothymiaWorkbook.com
    This online resource for cyclothymic disorder includes updates for this workbook. By Prentiss Price.

Depression and Bipolar Support Alliance
730 N. Franklin Street, Suite 501
Chicago, IL 60610-7224
(800) 826-3632 or (312) 642-0049
http://www.dbsalliance.org/

Depression and Related Affective Disorders Association
2330 West Joppa Road, Suite 100
Lutherville, MD 21093
(410) 583-2919
http://www.drada.org/

Equal Employment Opportunities Commission
http://www.ada.gov
    This Web site contains the text of the Americans with Disabilities Act of 1990 and offers other work-related information and assistance.

Harbor of Refuge Organization, Inc.
http://www.harbor-of-refuge.org
    This Web site offers peer support for people with bipolar disorder and for their families and friends.

Harvard Medical School, Bipolar Research Program
50 Staniford Street, Suite 580
Boston, MA 02114
(617) 726-6188
http://www.manicdepressive.org
    This Web site provides general information, referrals, news about research, treatment information, charts, and self-help tools.

International Society for Bipolar Disorders
P.O. Box 7168
Pittsburgh, PA 15213-0168
(412) 605-1412
http://www.isbd.org

Internet Mental Health
http://www.mentalhealth.com
    Since 1995, this has been one of the largest online resources for information about specific mental disorders, treatments, medications, and research.

Medline Plus Health Information
http://www.nlm.nih.gov/medlineplus/bipolardisorder.html
    This site offers clinical information about bipolar disorder, diagnosis, research, and treatment, as well as referrals to other organizations.

Narcotics Anonymous
http://www.na.org/
    This Web site offers information about NA as a support group for those struggling with drug abuse and dependence. This site offers general information about substance use and can help you find a local NA meeting.

National Alliance for Research on Schizophrenia and Depression
60 Cutter Mill Road, Suite 404
Great Neck, NY 11021
(516) 829-0091 or (800) 829-8289; Fax: (516) 487-6930
http://www.narsad.org

National Alliance for the Mentally Ill
Colonial Place Three
2107 Wilson Boulevard, Suite 300
Arlington, VA 22201-3042
(703) 524-7600
Helpline: (800) 950-6264; Fax: (703) 524-9094; TDD: (703) 516-7227
http://www.nami.org

National Institute of Mental Health
6001 Executive Boulevard
Bethesda, MD 20892
(800) 421-4211
http://www.nimh.nih.gov or http://www.nimh.nih.gov/publicat/bipolar.cfm
    These Web sites offer information on disorders, treatment, and research. Free brochures can be ordered online.

National Institute on Alcohol Abuse and Alcoholism
5635 Fishers Lane, MSC 9304
Bethesda, MD 20892-9304
http://www.niaaa.nih.gov

National Institute on Drug Abuse
6001 Executive Boulevard, Room 5213
Bethesda, MD 20892-9561
(301) 443-1124
http://www.nida.nih.gov

National Mental Health Association
2001 N. Beauregard Street, 12th Floor
Alexandria, VA 22311
(800) 969-6642 or (703) 684-7722; Fax: (703) 684-5968; TTY: (800) 433-5959
http://www.nmha.org

National Women's Health Resource Center
157 Broad Street, Suite 315
Red Bank, NJ 07701
(877) 986-9472
http://www.healthywomen.org

Pendulum Resources

http://www.pendulum.org

This Web site offers information on diagnostic criteria, treatment, favorite books of consumers, articles on coping with mood disorders, writings and poetry, and the Pendulum e-mail list, an online support group for those with bipolar disorders.

Screening for Mental Health, Inc.

One Washington Street, Suite 304

Wellesley Hills, MA 02481

(781) 239-0071; Fax: (781) 431-7447

http://www.mentalhealthscreening.org/

Self Management and Recovery Training

http://www.smartrecovery.org/

The mission of this organization is "to support individuals who have chosen to abstain, or are considering abstinence from, any type of addictive behaviors (substances or activities), by teaching how to change self-defeating thinking, emotions, and actions; and to work toward long-term satisfaction and quality of life."

Substance Abuse and Mental Health Services

http://www.samhsa.gov

This agency of the U.S. Department of Health and Human Services provides information about addictions, resources, statistics, prevention, and treatment.

Suicide Prevention Action Network USA, Inc.

1025 Vermont Avenue, NW, Suite 1200

Washington, DC 20005

(202) 449-3600; Fax: (202) 449-3601

http://www.spanusa.org

SupportPath.com

http://www.supportpath.com/

This Web site describes itself as "a directory for support-related online communities and message boards, chats, organizations, and information on over 300 health, personal, and relationship topics."

Surgeon General of the United States

http://www.surgeongeneral.gov or http://www.surgeongeneral.gov/library/mentalhealth/home.html

Systematic Treatment Enhancement Program for Bipolar Disorder

(866) 240-3250

http://www.stepbd.org

This organization conducts large-scale research on treatment for bipolar disorder funded by the National Institute of Mental Health.

Treatment Advocacy Center

3300 N. Fairfax Drive, Suite 220

Arlington, VA 22201

(703) 294-6001

http://www.psychlaws.org

This legal advocacy organization works to address problems in the mental health treatment system.

SELF-HELP BOOKS: ANGER

Bilodeau, L. 1992. *The Anger Workbook.* Minneapolis: CompCare.

Ellis, A., and R. C. Tafrate. 1997. *How to Control Your Anger before It Controls You.* Secaucus, N.J.: Birch Lane Press.

Lerner, H. 1997. *The Dance of Anger: A Woman's Guide to Changing the Patterns of Intimate Relationships.* New York: Harper Perennial.

McKay, M., P. Rogers, and J. McKay. 1997. *When Anger Hurts.* Oakland, Calif.: New Harbinger Publications.

Potter-Efron, R. 1994. *Angry All the Time: An Emergency Guide to Anger Control.* Oakland, Calif.: New Harbinger Publications.

Potter-Efron, R., and P. Potter-Efron. 1995. *Letting Go of Anger: The Ten Most Common Anger Styles and What to Do about Them.* Oakland, Calif.: New Harbinger Publications.

Tarvis, C. 1989. *Anger: The Misunderstood Emotion.* New York: Touchstone Books.

SELF-HELP BOOKS: ASSERTIVENESS

Alberti, R., and M. Emmons. 1995. *Your Perfect Right: A Guide to Assertive Living.* San Luis Obispo, Calif.: Impact.

Bower, S. A., and G. H. Bower. 1991. *Asserting Yourself: A Practical Guide for Positive Change.* Reading, Mass.: Addison-Wesley.

Phelps, S., and N. Austin. 1997. *The Assertive Woman.* San Luis Obispo, Calif.: Impact.

Smith, M. 1975. *When I Say No, I Feel Guilty.* New York: Bantam Books.

SELF-HELP BOOKS: BIPOLAR DISORDERS, DEPRESSION

Burns, D. D. 1999. *The Feeling Good Handbook.* New York: Plume.

Copeland, M. 1992. *The Depression Workbook: A Guide for Living with Depression and Manic Depression.* Oakland, Calif.: New Harbinger Publications.

Fawcett, J., B. Golden, and N. Rosenfeld. 2000. *New Hope for People with Bipolar Disorder.* Roseville, Calif.: Prima Publishing.

Greenberger, D., and C. A. Padesky. *Mind Over Mood: Changing How You Feel by Changing the Way You Think.* New York: Guilford Press.

Lewinsohn, P., R. Munoz, M. A. Youngren, and A. Zeiss. 1996. *Control Your Depression.* Englewood Cliffs, N.J.: Prentice-Hall.

Miklowitz, D. J. 2002. *The Bipolar Disorder Survival Guide.* New York: Guilford Press.

Mondimore, F. M. 1999. *Bipolar Disorder: A Guide for Patients and Families.* Baltimore: Johns Hopkins University Press.

Olson, B., and M. Olson. 1999. *Win the Battle: The Three-Step Lifesaving Formula to Conquer Depression and Bipolar Disorder.* Worcester, Mass.: Chandler House Press.

Papolos, D., and J. Papolos. 1997. *Overcoming Depression: The Definitive Resource for Patients and Families Who Live with Depression and Manic-Depression* (3rd ed.). New York: HarperCollins.

Torrey, E. F., and M. B. Knable. 2002. *Surviving Manic-Depression.* New York: Basic Books.

Wider, P. A. 2001. *Overcoming Depression and Manic-Depression: A Whole-Person Approach.* Rutherford, N.J.: Wellness Communications.

Woolis, R. and A. Hatfield. 1992. *When Someone You Love Has Mental Illness: A Handbook for Family, Friends, and Caregivers.* Los Angeles: Tarcher.

SELF-HELP BOOKS: COGNITIVE BEHAVIORAL APPROACHES

Beck, A. 1988. *Love Is Never Enough.* New York: Harper & Row.

Bourne, E. J. 2000. *The Anxiety and Phobia Workbook* (3rd ed.). Oakland, Calif.: New Harbinger Publications.

Burns, D. D. 1999. *The Feeling Good Handbook.* New York: Plume.

Greenberger, D., and C. A. Padesky. *Mind Over Mood: Changing How You Feel by Changing the Way You Think.* New York: Guilford Press.

Lewinsohn, P., R. Munoz, M. A. Youngren, and A. Zeiss. 1996. *Control Your Depression.* Englewood Cliffs, N.J.: Prentice-Hall.

SELF-HELP BOOKS: CREATIVITY AND MOOD DISORDERS

Jamison, K. R. 1993. *Touched With Fire: Manic-Depressive Illness and the Artistic Temperament.* New York: Maxwell Macmillan International.

Ludwig, A. 1995. *The Price of Greatness: Resolving the Creativity and Madness Controversy.* New York: Guilford Press.

Ostwald, P. 1985. *Schumann: the Inner Voices of a Musical Genius.* Boston: Northeastern University Press.

SELF-HELP BOOKS: PERSONAL STORIES

Adamec, C. 1996. *How to Live with a Mentally Ill Person: A Handbook of Day-to-Day Strategies.* New York: John Wiley and Sons.

Behrman, A. 2002. *Electroboy: A Memoir of Mania.* New York: Random House.

Berger, D., and L. Berger. 1992. *We Heard the Angels of Madness: A Family Guide to Coping with Manic-Depression.* New York: Quill–William Morrow.

Duke, P., and G. Hochman. 1997. *A Brilliant Madness: Living with Manic-Depressive Illness.* New York: Bantam Books.

Hinshaw, S. P. 2002. *The Years of Silence Are Past: My Father's Life with Bipolar Disorder.* Cambridge, England: Cambridge University Press.

Jamison, K. R. 1995. *An Unquiet Mind.* New York: Knopf.

Manning, M. 1994. *Undercurrents: A Therapist's Reckoning with Her Own Depression.* New York: HarperCollins.

Simon, L. 2002. *Detour: My Bipolar Road Trip in 4-D.* New York: Washington Square Press.

Solomon, A. 2001. *The Noonday Demon: An Atlas of Depression.* New York: Touchstone.

Steel, D. 2000. *His Bright Light: The Story of Nick Traina.* Des Plaines, Ill.: Dell.

Styron, W. 1992. *Darkness Visible: A Memoir of Madness.* New York: Vintage Books.

SELF-HELP BOOKS: RELATIONSHIPS AND COMMUNICATION

Beck, A. 1988. *Love Is Never Enough.* New York: Harper & Row.

Bolton, R. 1986. *People Skills.* New York: Touchstone.

Bramson, R. 1981. *Coping With Difficult People.* New York: Dell.

Burns, D. 1985. *Intimate Connections: The New Clinically Tested Program for Overcoming Loneliness.* New York: Morrow.

Gottman, J. 1994. *Why Marriages Succeed or Fail.* New York: Simon & Schuster.

McKay, M., M. Davis, and P. Fanning. 1997. *How to Communicate: The Ultimate Guide to Improving Your Personal and Professional Relationships.* Oakland, Calif.: New Harbinger Publications.

Tannen, D. 1986. *That's Not What I Meant! How Conversational Style Makes or Breaks Relationships.* New York: Ballantine.

Viscott, D. 1987. *I Love You, Let's Work It Out.* New York: Simon & Schuster.

SELF-HELP BOOKS: STRESS MANAGEMENT

Benson, H. 1984. *Beyond the Relaxation Response.* New York: Times Books.

Davis, M., E. R. Eshelman, and M. McKay. 1995. *The Relaxation and Stress Reduction Workbook* (4th ed.). Oakland, Calif.: New Harbinger Publications.

Kabat-Zinn, J. 1994. *Wherever You Go, There You Are.* New York: Hyperion.

Madders, J. 1997. *The Stress and Relaxation Handbook: A Practical Guide to Self-Help Techniques.* London, England: Vermilion.

Sapolsky, R. M. 1994. *Why Zebras Don't Get Ulcers: A Guide to Stress-Related Diseases and Coping.* New York: Freeman.

References

Akiskal, H. S. 1996. The prevalent clinical spectrum of bipolar disorders: Beyond DSM-IV. *Journal of Clinical Pscyhopharmacology* 16 (2 Suppl. 1): 4–14.

Akiskal, H. S. 1981. Subaffective disorders: Dysthymic, cyclothymic, and bipolar II disorders in the "borderline" realm. *Psychiatric Clinics of North America* 4:25–46.

Akiskal, H. S., A. H. Djenderedjian, R. H. Rosenthal, and M. K. Khani. 1977. Cyclothymic disorder: Validity criteria for inclusion in the bipolar affective group. *American Journal of Psychiatry* 134:1227–33.

Akiskal, H. S., M. K. Khani, and A. Scott-Strauss. 1979. Cyclothymic temperamental disorders. *Journal of Affective Disorders* 2 (3): 527–54.

Alda, M. 1997. Bipolar disorder: From families to genes. *Canadian Journal of Psychiatry* 42:378–87.

American Heart Association. 2004. The benefits of daily physical activity.
http://www.americanheart.org/presenter.jhtml?identifier=764 (accessed March 1, 2004).

American Psychiatric Association. 1980. *Diagnostic and Statistical Manual of Mental Disorders*. 3rd ed. Washington, D.C.: American Psychiatric Association.

American Psychiatric Association. 2000. *Diagnostic and Statistical Manual of Mental Disorders*. 4th ed., text revision. Washington, D.C.: American Psychiatric Association.

Basco, M. R. and A. J. Rush. 1996. *Cognitive-Behavioral Therapy for Bipolar Disorder*. New York: Guilford Press.

Beck, A. T., A. J. Rush, B. F. Shaw, and G. Emery. 1979. *Cognitive Therapy of Depression*. New York: Guilford Press.

Bourne, E. J. 2000. *The Anxiety and Phobia Workbook*. 3rd ed. Oakland, Calif.: New Harbinger Publications.

Brieger, P. and A. Marneros. 1997. Dysthymia and cyclothymia: Historical origins and contemporary development. *Journal of Affective Disorders* 45:117–26.

Colom, F., E. Vieta, A. Martinez-Aran, M. Reinares, J. M. Goikolea, A. Benabarre, C. Torrent, M. Comes, B. Corbella, G. Parramon, and J. Corominas. 2003. A randomized trial on the efficacy of group psychoeducation in the prophylaxis of recurrences in bipolar patients whose disease is in remission. *Archives of General Psychiatry* 60:402–7.

Depue, R. A., R. M. Kleiman, P. David, M. Hutchinson, and S. P. Krauss. 1985. The behavioral high-risk paradigm and bipolar affective disorder. VII: Serum free cortisol in nonpatient cyclothymic subjects selected by the general behavior inventory. *American Journal of Psychiatry* 142:175–81.

Elkis, H., L. Friedman, A. Wise and H. Y. Meltzer. 1995. Meta-analysis of studies of ventricular enlargement and cortical sulcal prominence in mood disorders: Comparisons with controls or patients with schizophrenia. *Archives of General Psychiatry* 52:735–46.

Frank, E., D. J. Kupfer, C. L. Ehlers, T. H. Monk, C. Cornes, S. Carter, and D. Frankel. 1994. Interpersonal and social rhythm therapy for bipolar disorder: Integrating interpersonal and behavioral approaches. *The Behavior Therapist* 17:143–49.

Frank, E., H. A. Swartz, and D. J. Kupfer. 2000. Interpersonal and social rhythm therapy: Managing the chaos of bipolar disorder. *Biological Psychiatry* 48:593–604.

Gershon, E. S. 1990. Genetics. In *Manic-Depressive Illness*, ed. F. K. Goodwin and K. R. Jamison, 376–86. New York: Oxford University Press.

Goodwin, F. K., and K. R. Jamison, eds. 1990. *Manic-Depressive Illness.* New York: Oxford University Press.

Hirschfeld, R. M. A., J. R. Calabrese, and M. Weissman. 2002. Lifetime prevalence of bipolar I and II disorders in the United States (abstract). Presented at the 155th Annual Meeting of the American Psychiatric Association: May 18–23, Philadelphia, Pa.

Howland, R., and M. Thase. 1993. A comprehensive review of cyclothymic disorder. *Journal of Nervous and Mental Disease* 181:485–93.

Hunt, N., W. Bruce-Jones, and T. Silverstone. 1992. Life events and relapse in bipolar affective disorder. *Journal of Affective Disorders* 25:13–20.

Jamison, K. R. 1995. Sliding past Saturn. *Time*, September 11, 83.

Johnson, S. L., and I. Miller. 1997. Negative life events and time to recovery from episodes of bipolar disorder. *Journal of Abnormal Psychology* 106:449–57.

Johnson, S. L., C. A. Winett, B. Meyer, W. J. Greenhouse, and I. Miller. 1999. Social support and the course of bipolar disorder. *Journal of Abnormal Psychology* 108:558–66.

Kraepelin, E. 1921. *Manic-Depressive Insanity and Paranoia.* Edinburgh: Livingston.

Kretschmer, E. 1936. *Physique and Character.* 2nd ed. New York: Harcourt, Brace and Co.

Miklowitz, D. J., and M. J. Goldstein. 1997. *Bipolar Disorder: A Family-Focused Treatment Approach.* New York: Guilford Press.

Monk, T. H., D. J. Kupfer, E. Frank, and A. M. Ritenour. 1991. The social rhythm metric: Measuring daily social rhythms over 12 weeks. *Psychiatry Research* 36:195–207.

National Institute of Health. 2002. *Medications.* NIH Publication no. 02-3929.

National Institute of Mental Health. 2001. *Bipolar Disorder.* NIH publication no. 02-3679.

Nurnberger, J. I., Jr., and E. S. Gershon. 1992. Genetics. In *Handbook of Affective Disorders* (2nd ed.), ed. E. S. Paykel. New York: Guilford Press.

Olfson, M., B. Fireman, M. Weissman, A. Leon, D. Sheehan, R. Kathol, C. Hoven, and L. Farber. 1997. Mental disorders and disability among patients in a primary care group practice. *American Journal of Psychiatry* 154:1734–40.

Ooman, H. A., A. J . Schipperijn, and H. A. Drexhage. 1996. The prevalence of affective disorders and in particular of a rapid cycling of bipolar disorder in patients with abnormal thyroid function tests. *Clinical Endocrinology* 45:215–23.

Peck, M. S. 1978. *The Road Less Traveled: A New Psychology of Love, Traditional Values and Spiritual Growth.* New York: Simon & Schuster.

Perry, A., N. Tarrier, R. Morriss, E., McCarthy, and K. Limb. 1999. Randomised controlled trial of efficacy of teaching patients with bipolar disorder to identify early symptoms of relapse and obtain treatment. *British Medical Journal* 318:149–53.

Regier, D. A., M. E. Farmer, D. S. Rae, B. Z . Locke, S. J. Keith, L. L. Judd, and F. K. Goodwin. 1990. Comorbidity of mental disorders with alcohol and other drug abuse: Results from the Epidemiologic Catchment Area (ECA) Study. *Journal of the American Medical Association* 264:2511–18.

Rivas-Vazquez, R. A., S. L. Johnson, G. J. Rey, M. A. Blais, and A. Rivas-Vazquez. 2002. Current treatments for bipolar disorder: A review and update for psychologists. *Professional Psychology: Research and Practice* 33:212–23.

Rush, J. 2003. Toward an understanding of bipolar disorder and its origin. *Journal of Clinical Psychiatry* 64 (Suppl. 6): 4–8.

Schneider, K. 1958. *Psychopathic Personalities.* London: Cassell.

Simon, G. E., and J. Unutzer. 1999. Health care utilization and costs among patients treated for bipolar disorder in an insured population. *Psychiatric Services* 50:1303–08.

Strakowski, S. M., S. L. McElroy, P. W. Keck, and S. A. West. 1994. The co-occurrence of mania with medical and other psychiatric disorders. *International Journal of Psychiatry in Medicine* 24:305–28.

Torrey, E. F., and M. B. Knable. 2002. *Surviving Manic-Depression.* New York: Basic Books.

Weight-Control Information Network. 2003. Physical activity and weight control. http://www.niddk.nih.gov (accessed March 1, 2004).

Zwerling, C., P. Whitten, N. Sprince, C. Davis, R. Wallace, P. Blanck, and S. Heringa. 2002. Workforce participation by persons with disabilities: The National Health Interview Survey Disability Supplement, 1994 to 1995. *Journal of Occupational Environmental Medicine* 44:358–64.

Prentiss Price, Ph.D., is a counseling psychologist at the Counseling and Career Development Center of Georgia Southern University. She is the creator of the Web site **www.allaboutdepression.com**, a popular informational resource about depression and other mood disorders since 1999. She is an advocate for mental health self-help. She enjoys writing articles, developing Web sites, creating self-guided tools and exercises, and conducting Internet research to help people help themselves understand and manage mental health issues. Price is also the founder of All About Mental Health, LLC **(www.allaboutmentalhealth.com)**, a company specializing in providing online self-help strategies for managing depression and anxiety and promoting good mental health. She lives in Statesboro, GA.

Some Other
New Harbinger Titles

Surviving Your Borderline Parent, Item 3287 $14.95

When Anger Hurts, second edition, Item 3449 $16.95

Calming Your Anxious Mind, Item 3384 $12.95

Ending the Depression Cycle, Item 3333 $17.95

Your Surviving Spirit, Item 3570 $18.95

Coping with Anxiety, Item 3201 $10.95

The Agoraphobia Workbook, Item 3236 $19.95

Loving the Self-Absorbed, Item 3546 $14.95

Transforming Anger, Item 352X $10.95

Don't Let Your Emotions Run Your Life, Item 3090 $17.95

Why Can't I Ever Be Good Enough, Item 3147 $13.95

Your Depression Map, Item 3007 $19.95

Successful Problem Solving, Item 3023 $17.95

Working with the Self-Absorbed, Item 2922 $14.95

The Procrastination Workbook, Item 2957 $17.95

Coping with Uncertainty, Item 2965 $11.95

The BDD Workbook, Item 2930 $18.95

You, Your Relationship, and Your ADD, Item 299X $17.95

The Stop Walking on Eggshells Workbook, Item 2760 $18.95

Conquer Your Critical Inner Voice, Item 2876 $15.95

The PTSD Workbook, Item 2825 $17.95

Hypnotize Yourself Out of Pain Now!, Item 2809 $14.95

The Depression Workbook, 2nd edition, Item 268X $19.95

Beating the Senior Blues, Item 2728 $17.95

Shared Confinement, Item 2663 $15.95

Handbook of Clinical Psychopharmacology for Therpists, 3rd edition, Item 2698 $55.95

Getting Your Life Back Together When You Have Schizophrenia, Item 2736 $14.95

Do-It-Yourself Eye Movement Technique for Emotional Healing, Item 2566 $13.95

Call **toll free, 1-800-748-6273,** or log on to our online bookstore at **www.newharbinger.com** to order. Have your Visa or Mastercard number ready. Or send a check for the titles you want to New Harbinger Publications, Inc., 5674 Shattuck Ave., Oakland, CA 94609. Include $4.50 for the first book and 75¢ for each additional book, to cover shipping and handling. (California residents please include appropriate sales tax.) Allow two to five weeks for delivery.

Prices subject to change without notice.